# Jeff Anderson

# 10 Things

# EVERY WRITER

## Needs to Know

Stenhouse Publishers
Portland, Maine

Stenhouse Publishers
www.stenhouse.com

*Credits*
Pages 11 and 246: Power-Writing Chart from Fearn, L. (1980). *Teaching for Thinking*. San Diego: Kabyn Books, p. 124.
Page 17: Figure 1.6 printed by permission. Dr. Elizabeth Harper Neeld, www.elizabethharperneeld.com, *Writing* © 1987.
Pages 94–96 and 250: "Offramp to Fame Pitted with Potholes" by Leonard Pitts, Jr. *Miami Herald*, January 16, 2011. Used by permission.
Page 148: Figure 7.2: This Wikipedia and Wikimedia Commons image is from the user SilentC and is freely available at http://commons.wikimedia.org/wiki/File:Joinery-throughdovetail.svg under the Creative Commons Attribution-Share Alike 3.0 Unported license.
Pages 206–209: The "Enhance Your Writing with Accurate, Specific, and Concrete Words" lesson has been adapted from "Naming Names: A Concrete Way to Help Students Write" by Jeff Anderson. *Voices from the Middle* 11 (2), December 2003. Copyright © 2003 by the National Council of Teachers of English. Reprinted with permission.

*Library of Congress Cataloging-in-Publication Data*
Anderson, Jeff, 1966–
    10 things every writer needs to know / Jeff Anderson.
        p. cm.
    Includes bibliographical references and index.
    ISBN 978-1-57110-810-4 (alk. paper) — ISBN 978-1-57110-928-6 (e-book)
1. English language—Composition and exercises—Study and teaching. 2. Written communication—Study and teaching. I. Title. II. Title: Ten things every writer needs to know.
    LB1576.A54 2011
    372.62'3044—dc23
                                                                                2011017177

Cover, interior design, and typesetting by Martha Drury
Manufactured in the United States of America

PRINTED ON 30% PCW
RECYCLED PAPER

17 16 15 14 13 12      9 8 7 6 5 4 3

For Peanut

# Contents

# Acknowledgments

So many people have left their mark on my thinking, forever affecting me. Sometimes this occurred as I read their works, such as those of Katie Wood Ray, Nancie Atwell, and all authors of young adult nonfiction and fiction from whom I've learned so much.

Others have also left their mark on me, both as I read their work and learned at their feet. I've learned a great deal from the words and actions of my friend and colleague Vicki Spandel. Her practicality and naming of what makes writing work and how this opens up instruction to young writers echo in my work.

Joyce Armstrong Carroll, Eddie Wilson, and the professors of language and literacy in the master's program at the University of Texas at Austin have all sparked my passions and made my thinking go deeper and deeper. Your words and acts ripple through me.

My editor and friend, Bill Varner, and the wonderful people at Stenhouse Publishers, such as Nate, Chandra, Jay, Philippa, Holly, Dan, Chris, Jill, Rebecca, and Martha, make it all come together. For those Stenhouse authors who keep me on my toes—Charles, Terry, Mark, Aimee, and Kelly—you are amazing.

My gratitude overflows for Unity Church of San Antonio for reminding me of the truth of who I am and continuing to nudge me to do what is mine to do with zeal and enthusiasm.

A big round of applause to those who remind me that life is supposed to be fun: Brandy, Lisa, Marsha, Lola, Edie, Candace, Linda, Amy, Donalyn, and Wiley.

And, of course, Terry and Paisley, I am so glad you are in my life—the best reading, writing, and walking partners a guy could have. You make living and learning fun. See you on the deck!

# *Prologue*

## What Writing Instruction Is and Isn't

*As a single footstep will not make a path on the earth,*

*so a single thought will not make a pathway in the mind.*

*To make a deep physical path, we walk again and again.*

—Henry David Thoreau

What is writing?

Seriously. What is it?

And how do you do it well? And, as a teacher, just how do you teach writing effectively? If we thought we once knew, perhaps now we are told to teach writing differently. What's true? What's everlasting? What actually has changed? What do I need to adjust? And, in making adjustments, what stays? What will always make writing successful?

And what about those students in the back row—arms crossed, no pencil or paper, hair spilling down over their defiant "make me" looks? How do we move them from reluctant to independent writers? Then, how do we move the other students in our classroom, the ones who already want to write, to greater heights? Where do we meet them? How do we light the spark?

Many attempt to define writing, put it in a box, develop a checklist or worksheet, a rubric or analytic, a list of rules or elements of style. They toggle between organizing writing or freeing it. Some have even taken the thicket of theories and experiences and distilled them down to one-way-to-do-it solutions, violating the very research they cite. A good place to start is to define what writing is, and isn't.

# Writing Isn't in a Kit

We may buy into an oversimplified dream of success. However, when we are faced with a class of thirty-two faces, hour after hour, day after day, anyone who really pays attention knows that all these quick-fix, teach-from-a-kit, premade, one-size-fits-all scripted lessons don't convert reluctant writers into independent ones. Textbooks don't make students care about writing, much less revise and polish it. Colorful kits, blossoming with worksheets and activity books passed off as mini-lessons, won't make our students uncover the power of writing. A writer's work*sheet* won't set them on fire with meaning. Correcting sentences won't free the voice within that so desperately needs to be let out. None of these "solutions" will help you assess and give meaningful feedback on 150 papers.

But still, the administration warns of newer, ever-higher expectations and standards. The palpable fear of upcoming writing tests permeates the air like cigarette smoke in an old Las Vegas casino. Students must pass, excel, or adequately progress—or else. Well-meaning administrators distribute the latest mandatory quick fix. After all, it worked for another school down the road or across the state.

Often, it is decided that more must be better. We are volun-told to tutor students before, during, and after school, even on Saturdays. In panic and desperation, we don't always make sound decisions. Instruction is lost. Writing time diminishes in favor of remediation and data mining. Disaggregate data. Data fog. Remediate. Repeat.

# Writing Isn't Test Preparation

I want writing instruction that endures, that gives students steady, irrefutable skills that will be important no matter what they write or will need to write. No matter the purpose or audience. No matter what new way is invented to write in the twenty-first century.

Students lose trust in themselves, in their abilities, in their futures, all because outside test preparation resources, originally designed to help students, pigeon-hole them for remediation, target weaknesses, and remind them, with pages of evidence, of their flaws, their inabilities, and their shortcomings. With the focus on tests, pretests, benchmarks, results, and scores, it appears to students that we care only about raising scores at any cost. Most children have come to believe that the purpose of writing, of school, for that matter, is to pass tests. Getting by until the next test is the goal.

Is this what makes writing successful? Or does it cause more problems in a writer's development? A *New York Times* article (Dillon 2010) reported on explicit findings on test preparation and its effects on test scores.

> *One notable early finding . . . is that teachers who incessantly drill their students to prepare for standardized tests tend to have lower value-added learning gains than those who simply work their way methodically through the key concepts of literacy and mathematics.*
>
> *Teachers whose students agreed with the statement, "We spend a lot of time in this class practicing for the state test," tended to make smaller gains on those exams than other teachers.*
>
> *"Teaching to the test makes your students do worse on the tests . . . It turns out all that 'drill and kill' isn't helpful."*

This study is validated by an earlier study (Langer 2000). Everyone touts embracing research-based best practice. As Paulo Freire (2000) laments in *Pedagogy of the Oppressed*, oftentimes the poor and the underrepresented are subjugated by practices that keep students down. Students who struggle the most academically and economically get more of what we know doesn't work.

Are we listening?

From early on, I resisted doing test preparation. I didn't need research to prove its ineffectiveness. I knew from my experience that test preparation only extinguished my students' spark and joy and curiosity. Test preparation would only instill in my students that tests are what's important, product is the end-all, and process is just unimportant fluff. When, in fact, process is most important.

We can prepare our students for tests, but the best way to prepare students for tests is *not* to prepare them for tests. We'd be better off igniting the truth about what makes writing—any writing—work, so they know what to do when a blank page or screen awaits.

Writing, like life, is an inside-out phenomenon. If our students aren't trusted to use their own knowledge, their own ability to discover, to find and trace ideas, then they will have difficulty taking a test on their own—for academic or work purposes. Even worse, when writing is seen as an outside-in process of telling and memorizing rules, it robs students of the very beauty of writing as a tool for thinking and discovery. They are denied experiencing the power of writing to capture a time, a place, a face, a feeling, a thought.

What things stay true about writing no matter what? What helps all communication sing?

# Writing Is a Transaction

Writing is a transaction between writers and readers. As writers of text—as humans—we desperately want to be heard, to receive a response, or to connect.

We want to elicit certain reactions from our audience when they read our work. An essential power of humanness is communicating with others, thinking about *how* we say *what* we say, and supposing how readers will react in their transaction with our text.

Every adolescent longs to be understood, groping about for power. We have it here for them, in the ability to conquer written expression, as they would tackle a video game, challenged at every turn to move to the next level. Writing makes possible whatever we want to do in our lives, helping us with some aspect of anything we can dream of doing, for example, as a scientist, recording and reporting observations. Increasingly, in any career, we may be assigned multiple roles, such as producing newsletters, incident reports, training materials, PowerPoint presentations, Web sites, and brochures. And then there are "fun," nonacademic strains of writing: blogs, instant messages, texts, tweets, e-mails, and social network posts.

Communication is king.

# Writing Is a Skill That Can Be Learned

While writing is deceptively complex, at the same time, it is deceptively simple. As I have taught, read, pondered, and written over the past twenty-two years, I've come to know some essential, enduring truths about writing. Giving students experience with and an awareness of these building blocks of writing sets them free.

Sure, we can easily photocopy and distribute a prefabricated rubric to students. I've done it. We can even tell them to work on voice or sentence fluency or that their ideas are strong but their organization is weak, but is that teaching writing? Or is it just throwing new and perhaps more abstract terms at them? Terms originating from some far-off place outside our classroom?

I aim to show you simple ways to draw out your students' knowledge and to increase the value of their text interactions. You will be able to show students ways to revise, to draft, and to integrate craft and skill lessons, so that no matter where they are in their learning, they can benefit as writers and readers.

# Writing Ignites Passion

We have to ignite students' passion and let their souls, thoughts, fears, truths, experiences, and arguments shine on the page. We can't motivate them by deluging them with more terminology or someone else's bulleted lists. We can't motivate them to revise their writing by stapling a rubric or checklist to their paper. We can't motivate them by simply hanging some posters on the wall. We must *facilitate* writing behaviors.

Students become part of the process as a result of the writing community you co-construct, an environment that brims with possibility, inspiring literature, their voices, and opinions. You will orchestrate the transaction. They will do the work.

As you guide their discoveries through a carefully executed series of experiences and exposures, your facilitation will lead them to an owned language that looks better than any you could have photocopied and distributed. To do this, students must participate in discovering the neural pathways that connect to the concrete and tangible. The meaning-making interaction is the key to this information sticking.

The knowing comes through the flow of student–teacher transactions, through students' observation and analysis of models, through students' talking, collecting, imitating, writing, experimenting, revising, editing, and reflecting.

# Writing Is Freedom and Power

Free your students to demonstrate their hidden potential, often drowned out by cries for help:

"I can't write!"

"I hate writing!"

"I can't think of anything to write!"

Students don't say, "I can't think of anything to text to my friends," or "I can't think of anything to put in this e-mail, instant message, or note." They don't scrounge for topics to talk to their tablemates about when they are supposed to be listening or doing another task.

Let's plunge into that flow of thinking and passion waiting to be tapped. Writing should be a joyous act, not drudgery, and frankly so should the teaching of it. *10 Things Every Writer Needs to Know* is my answer to how we can show students what writing is, and more important, what it can be.

Writers need to be heard: let's model and inspire. With ten things every writer needs to know, let's show them ways to communicate their passions to real audiences and to know writing's freedom and power.

Writing is waiting for a place to happen. Let's create that space.

# *Overview*

## What *Does* Every Writer Need to Know?

It's no surprise that what every writer needs to know doesn't change much over time. I am not talking about dangling modifiers or split infinitives; I mean the basic art of expressing ourselves so we are understood and validated. Expressing ourselves is an innate human desire. The more we write, read, and talk, the more we have to say. That's what writers do. We orchestrate our classrooms to support writing behaviors.

We know what kills the creative impulse: focusing on test preparation, offering harsh feedback, and assigning rather than teaching concepts. Now it's time to talk about what works. It goes back to what the writing process is based on—what writers do.

What every writer should know are the elements that help writers think deep and wide. Depending on the context, purpose, and audience, we find an appropriate mix and measure of any of them to find writing success. (See the following table.)

## Ten Things Every Writer Needs to Know

| | |
|---|---|
| **Motion** | Writing is not magic. It's work. Splashing the words on the page or across the screen is much easier than fretting about whether what we have to say is good enough. Start writing, and the rest comes. Most of what students hate (and writers for that matter) is the struggle, the procrastination, the pain of being stuck. In the movie *Field of Dreams*, a whisper echoes, "If you build it, they will come." If you write it, more ideas will come.<br><br>When the pen hits the page or the fingers tap the keys, words flow. Indeed, they won't all be perfect. But knowing that is freedom. |
| **Models** | Models are our mentors—supporting and inspiring. Mentor texts offer a vision of what writing is and can be, acting as anchors for writers to learn any of the ten things. Like scientists, writers observe. Through active analysis of texts and experimentation, you integrate what you learn from the study of models into your own writing. Reading like writers, every encounter with text is a writing lesson. |
| **Focus** | Clear and steady writing is built upon an appropriate scope for the topic or form. The breadth of the writing is neither too large nor too small. The writing is a just-right slice, which allows room for appropriate depth. Whether called a main idea, a controlling idea, a central idea, or a thesis, it all comes down to this: What's your focus? |
| **Detail** | Detail should be plentiful without being flowery or overdone. Writers find well-selected details— evidence, sensory images, or support. Powerful detail illuminates without overwhelming, explains without boring to death. Somewhere between enough and too much is a necessary and concrete place. This element clearly relates to all of the other ten things. Because without the right detail, your writing falls flat as the air hisses out of it. |
| **Form** | Any form should be easy to follow and should reflect the purpose and the audience the writer wants to address. This can be done singularly or, more likely, in a mix of patterns, arranged and rearranged until the perfect structure is found. Form not only shapes the message in orderly, sensible, and sometimes surprising ways but also enhances the message. |
| **Frames** | An introduction and a conclusion frame our message. The frame limits the edges of how far our writing can go, keeping our focus within its borders. The lead invites the reader on a journey, promising what is to come. The conclusion is the finishing touch that, in the end, leaves the reader satisfied or hopeful or not. |
| **Cohesion** | Cohesion holds writing together. Cohesion is unity and transition, moving clearly from point to point, scene to scene, or paragraph to paragraph. Cohesive writing appears to have effortless connection. A connection and a progression that, while not obvious, is evident and clear. |
| **Energy** | Writing that sizzles or gets straight to the point embodies energy. Writing can be emotional or removed. Energy moves in rhythms appropriate for the audience or form, but it is always alive. The up and down, the lilt, the rhythm of writing that makes meaning; the flow, the personality that creates mood and brings variety to the eye and ear. Directions on how to play a game may have a different energy than a novel, but every text still needs a modicum of life—if it is ever to be read. |

| **Ten Things Every Writer Needs to Know** *(continued)* | |
|---|---|
| **Words** | The words we choose. The words we combine. Not just any old words, but deft diction. Crisp language brings our thoughts to the page. Without obscuring meaning with needless jargon, we use only enough specific nouns and lively verbs to carry the message clearly and cleanly to the reader. Fresh metaphors and comparisons are creative—not tiresome—and help the reader visualize or understand. |
| **Clutter** | Clutter is removed from writing so the message shines through. A careful second or third revision removes words, phrases, or passages that needlessly repeat or don't move the writing forward. Delete any words or phrases that don't clarify the overall message or story. Rephrase, combine sentences, take away anything that isn't doing new work. |

To one degree or another, all ten things are essential to writing. *10 Things Every Writer Needs to Know* discerns, in digestible chunks, what makes writing work, whether it's fiction or nonfiction, a brochure or a literary analysis, or any task a writer tackles.

We can, for a time, put the ten things every writer needs to know into discrete categories, which will help students access concepts and patterns of success. However, the lines between the ten things every writer needs to know will always be blurred.

These things writers need to know come alive through models found in literature and discussions grounded in inquiry. We don't get lost in abstract labels. Powerful literature starts the conversation. In one piece of good writing, many of the ten things may surface. For example, in this opening passage from *The Lightning Thief* by Rick Riordan, many attributes could be discussed:

> *Look, I didn't want to be a half-blood.*
>
> *If you're reading this because you think you might be one, my advice is: close this book right now. Believe whatever lie your mom or dad told you about your birth, and try to lead a normal life.*
>
> *Being a half-blood is dangerous. It's scary. Most of the time, it gets you killed in painful, nasty ways.*
>
> *If you're a normal kid, reading this because you think it's fiction, great. Read on. I envy you for being able to believe that none of this ever happened.*
>
> *But if you recognize yourself on these pages—if you feel something stirring inside—stop reading immediately. You might be one of us. And once you know that, it's only a matter of time before they sense it too, and they'll come for you.*
>
> *Don't say I didn't warn you.*

The first thing I see is how Riordan toggles between the first-person point of view—"*I*-voice"—and directly addresses the audience with *you*—the second-person point of view. This sets a casual tone—a conversation between writer and reader. It would be an entirely different story if he had chosen the third-person point of view instead: *Look, one doesn't want to be a half-blood.*

What a difference words—and a point of view—make. And the narrator, Percy Jackson, uses short sentence patterns, continuing this conversational tone, creating a fast-paced directness and energy. Since this passage is the lead to *The Lightning Thief*, we can't help but notice how the passage frames the beginning of the novel, making promises. In a strong text, many aspects of successful writing can be addressed—the things every writer needs to know.

However, our purpose is to help students develop and own concepts. We can't instruct, spewing layer after layer of information and expect it to stick. The brain overloads, shuts down, and nothing is learned. The information is merely presented, not taught. Without interaction, no analysis or active processing occurs. No meaning is made. As writing teachers, we find a focus, just like writers do. Sometimes we simplify, breaking concepts down, distilling key points, and delineating different strategies a writer uses to successfully communicate an idea or tone.

Several principles will come in handy as we explore all ten things throughout this book, but the most consistent principle across chapters is the use of literature as models. These models give writers a vision of what writers can do. Writers slow down and notice, spurring meaningful talk and collaboration, while embedding it all in the writing process.

# Embedding the Ten Things in the Writing Process

There is *a* writing process, but there isn't *the* writing process. When Donald Graves (1984) warned "the enemy is orthodoxy" early on in the writing-process movement, he was ensuring that, even though he was attempting to define the process in words and order, he noted that process, by definition, cannot be statically defined.

You already know this as a writer. Your process isn't mine. You might learn from hearing mine. I might learn from hearing yours. But in the end, with every piece, my writing process may be a little different. When the research report *Writing Next* (Graham and Perin 2007) says that writing process works, most teachers say, "Yeah, I do that." But when I look around at what some people call process writing, I wonder whether we need to remain in a constant state of doubt, so we never get too sure. The minute we think we know the writing process in an exact way is the moment we have lost contact with the writing process.

That's what writing process is—a collaborative exploration that grapples with and constructs meaning. We don't have to reinvent the wheel. A basic writing process path exists; we may dip into it and roll around. When we read a model text and freewrite, we're drafting. We may take what we learned from reading and drafting and revise or edit some of our other writing. Of course, we know the basics of a writing process—generating ideas, drafting, revising, editing, and publishing. Although it looks predictable, it's not. We don't teach writing process as if it is a process. It's recursive, messy, ever changing, and flexibly used as needed.

# Part and Process: The Ten Things

Structuring each lesson to move through the entire writing process is beyond the scope of this book. Instead, I will share some ways students experience the essential elements of writing: how I motivate students to write, and what model texts I use to demonstrate writing's power and inspire imitation. What motivates them to look again, revise, edit, and write more? What first steps do I take in any concept-building lessons of the ten things every writer needs to know? It's all part of the writing process.

# Looking Forward

This book is meant to supplement an already-humming writing workshop classroom as a source of mentor texts and mini-lessons, tips, information, and launching points for larger works and process pieces. These are the works that inspired my students to care about writing, motivating them to review, to edit, to write, to clarify, to explore, to refine, and to know.

What follow are ten chapters built around the ten things every writer needs to know. Each chapter helps students form and own concepts, getting to know them deeply through mentor texts, discussions, and writing. I want students to be able to articulate and apply what they know about writing outside the mini-lesson. We'll dwell on the ten things, one at a time, moving in and out, constantly revising, editing, and redrafting our instruction along the way. Writing instruction is meant to be systematic, yet alive, responsive, and evolving.

I suggest that you read Chapters 1 ("Motion") and 2 ("Models") first, because much of the other ten things are built around these essential principles of what worked in my writing classroom and what supports writing behaviors. The rest of the ten things every writer needs to know may be read in any order you wish. I did, however, order them in a way that makes sense to me because one logically flows into the next.

Let's begin.

# Motion

## Getting and Keeping Writers Motivated

*If you hear a voice within you say, "You are not a painter," then by all means paint . . . and that voice will be silenced.*

—Vincent Van Gogh

When my alarm rang this morning, I wanted to hit the snooze button and skip working out. You know the drill: stay in bed a few minutes longer so you'll finally feel rested. But I've learned over time, if I get up and exercise, I'm always glad I did. I feel better. Guaranteed. I know this is true because I have experienced it, time and again. Still, almost every day, resistance pulls the sheets back over my head. But because I've been rewarded with the good feelings that result from exercise—stamina, endorphins, strength, stress reduction—I act. I get up.

Writing is like that for students. Resistance constantly rears its head, telling them writing is too hard or boring. They don't have anything to say. If they do write, they'll be wrong. To put it simply, students suffer from page fright.

Although the cliché "going through the motions" means doing something half-heartedly, sometimes that's what it takes to get moving. Once I start writing, I write more. Once I scribble that first word, more come. I am in the flow.

> Get it down. Write. You have to write badly to write well. Inspiration comes from the chair and that part of the anatomy that belongs there.
>
> —Anonymous

> Time never passes so quickly and unaccountably as when I am engaged in composition, i.e., in writing down my thoughts. The clock seems to have been put forward.
>
> —Henry David Thoreau

To get past page fright, writers need to experience the power of motion. Like Isaac Newton's law of motion, unless some force moves an object at rest—such as a keyboard—it stays at rest. Likewise, an object in motion stays in motion until some force stops it. The same is true for writers. Before we start a piece of writing, the page is blank. To get the ballpoint rolling, we must simply begin.

The best metaphor for motion I found is in Kim Stafford's book, *The Muses Among Us*. Stafford (2003) recounts the story of a physicist who also plays the violin. One day he takes his violin to his lab and uses an electron microscope to measure how long the instrument vibrates after it's been played. He found the violin strings continued to vibrate for twelve hours.

> Work itself, after awhile, takes on a rhythm. The mechanical begins to fall away. The body begins to take over. The guard goes down.
>
> —Ray Bradbury

*Musicians know this without a microscope. An instrument dies if it is not played daily. A guitar, a violin, a lute chills the air for the first fifteen minutes of fresh play. It will need to be quickened from scratch. But the fiddle played every day hangs resonant on the wall, quietly boisterous when it is lifted down, already trembling, anxious to speak, to cry out, to sing at the bow's first stroke. Not to rasp, but to sing. The instrument is in tune before the strings are tuned.*

*Pablo Casals used to put it so: "If I don't practice for even one day, I can tell the difference when I next cradle the cello in my arms. If I fail to practice for two days, my close friends can also tell the difference. If I don't practice three days, the whole world knows." (Stafford 2003, 1)*

> Language will not be a tool for thinking unless our students are able to allow language to run free and stumble and fall.
>
> —Don Murray

Students need to know the truth: writing is cumulative. Everything we write today prepares us for the writing task of tomorrow. We must have the courage to write those first words, stringing them together and perhaps stumbling, but staying in motion. Only then can our writing be revised or made better. Only then can it be edited and refined. Only then will our writing be heard.

Once writing stops being a chore and students are heard for the first time, truly heard, something changes within them. Humans are imprinted with an innate desire to communicate, to express. Writing is a valve that lets us release pent-up stores of experiences, thoughts, knowledge, and feelings. But unlike talking, writing gives us the choice to go back, rework, revise, and rewrite until our creation is the way we want it. Even if our attempts are unsuccessful, they build our writing muscles for the next time we write.

There is no wasted motion.

To get in motion, writers can use several strategies (see Figure 1.1).

### Making MOTION Work

- Spill your words on the page.
- Speak up and be heard.
- Set time limits.
- Generate momentum by talking.
- Capture inspiration and information.

*Figure 1.1*

# Spill Your Words on the Page

The late Steven J. Cannell, prolific writer of novels and television scripts, said, "All writer's block boils down to perfectionism." Fear of imperfection keeps us perched on the edge, afraid to dive in and start writing. If we sit and wait for the perfect words, they don't come. Inertia sets in. Our mind halts. The clock slows. Much like hesitating at the edge of the ocean, afraid of the shock of cold, we wait. And in waiting, our anxiety spins.

If we start spilling words on the page or computer screen, magically, writing gets completed. We only have to move our thoughts from our mind to the page.

How many times have you avoided writing something as a student or a professional? How many times did you fret, suffer, wait, avoid? Then, when you finally began writing, something akin to hitting the first domino happened—the rest of the dominos toppled. Sweet freedom. Whenever the dominos stop falling, we simply have to tip the next domino to begin again.

How do we get students to know this truth? How do we facilitate them knowing it, so they can rescue themselves from the intimidating blank page? How do we show them the power of leaping over the naysayer within to simply begin?

We orchestrate a lesson in which they spill words on the page—carelessly and quickly—so they can feel thoughts moving to their hands and to the page. We have opened the floodgates.

## Power Writing

I don't want my students to suffer alone with page fright. Every year, the first lesson I teach about motion is how to leap over the voice that says "you can't" with power writing (Fearn and Farnan 2001).

"Writing is like a sport," I say. "In sports, we practice. We build our speed and agility. Writers do this too."

I write the words *avoid* and *pickle* on the whiteboard.

"Choose one of these words and write it at the top of your page."

Students select their word.

"Now, when I say 'go,'" I say, "write for one minute using the word at least once. You will write as much as you can, as fast as you can, as well as you can." I explain that the point of power writing is to get as many sentences down on the paper as they can. "Whatever comes to your mind, write."

Since they only have one minute, their hands should move the whole time. "Whatever you think, you can write. Just write as much as you can, as fast as you can, as well as you can—in one minute." (See Figure 1.2 for a step-by-step process.)

> Don't fear mistakes—there are none.
>
> —Miles Davis

> The story builds and expands while you are writing it. All the best stuff comes at the desk.
>
> —Roald Dahl

> So go ahead and make big scrawls and mistakes. Use up lots of paper. Perfectionism is a mean, frozen form of idealism, while messes are the artist's true friend . . . we need to make messes in order to find out who we are and why we are here, and by extension, what we're supposed to be writing.
>
> —Anne Lamott

*Figure 1.2*

## Power-Writing Rounds

- Teacher displays two words.
- Students select one.
- Teacher says, "Write as much as you can, as fast as you can, as well as you can in one minute. Go!"
- Students write for one minute.
- Teacher calls time: "Stop writing. Lift your pencil up in the air. Draw a line underneath what you just wrote. Count the number of words you wrote."
- Students record word count under the line.
- Teacher records results for each round on chart.
- Repeat for a total of three rounds.

> You can't wait for inspiration, you have to go after it with a club.
> —Jack London

The words act as triggers (Carroll and Wilson 2008). Emphasize that the writing won't be perfect. It's a first draft. Students may write about their selected word, their experiences or connections to the word, or merely use the word once within the minute. The writing can be factual or fictional. It doesn't matter. What matters is that students write for the entire minute. Hands are in motion. Thoughts are in motion. The word is in motion, spilling over the "I can't" dam of resistance. Although students shouldn't fret about their grammar and punctuation, they should use what they know.

As kids write for one minute, some freeze. Reinforce and support this message: It can't be wrong as long as they write something. Ask such questions as, "What are some things you avoid? Just write and see where your thoughts take you."

I point to the chart. "If you wrote, 0–10 words, raise your hand."

I count and record the total on the power-writing chart in the "Round 1" column. I continue recording word counts until I include all students' counts for Round 1 (see Figure 1.3 and the appendix).

> Quantity gives experience. From experience alone can quality come.
> —Ray Bradbury

Between rounds, clarify any misunderstandings: students shouldn't write lists of sentences or brainstorm instead of writing connected sentences in prose form.

For the second round, display two new words. Choose a noun, a verb, or an adjective. For a change of pace, let students choose one or both words, like *soccer* and *Pop-tart*. Then, repeat the process.

> Write as much as you can, as fast as you can, as well as you can.
> —Leif Fearn

As we continue recording the word counts after each round, students notice that the number of words often increases from round to round and day to day. Ask them to think about why that occurs.

*Figure 1.3*

## Power-Writing Chart

| Number of Words | Round 1 | Round 2 | Round 3 |
| --- | --- | --- | --- |
| 121+ | | | |
| 111–120 | | | |
| 101–110 | | | |
| 91–100 | | | |
| 81–90 | | | |
| 71–80 | | | |
| 61–70 | | | |
| 51–60 | | 1 | |
| 41–50 | | 4 | |
| 31–40 | 2 | 7 | |
| 21–30 | 6 | 5 | |
| 11–20 | 9 | 4 | |
| 0–10 | 6 | | |

*Source: Fearn and Farnan (2001)*
No one is excluded from the count. Recording the number is a personal challenge to increase the number of words written in each successive round. It actually happens without effort on anyone's part. As students dip into the writing zone, it gets easier to write more fluently. A blank power-writing chart can be found in the appendix.

Students enjoy sharing their power-writes, which reinforces that writing is for expression and communication. Students:

- have an audience,
- hear various ways they could have responded to the prompt, through various genres,
- notice there is no right answer, just a path that follows their thinking, and
- hear their writing voice and how it is like or different from their speaking voice.

The fullness of power writing is realized over time. By doing this activity a few times a week, students' writing muscles are enhanced, as well as their ability to get into the flow of writing quickly. (See Figure 1.4 for variations.)

> The idea that excellence at performing a complex task requires a critical minimum level of practice surfaces again and again in studies of expertise. In fact, researchers have settled on what they believe is the magic number for true expertise: ten thousand hours.
>
> —Malcolm Gladwell

| Power-Writing Variations | |
| --- | --- |
| Extend to three minutes | Do all three rounds at once (write for three minutes continuously). Do this three days in a row and see how students grow—or don't—and talk about why or why not. |
| Use as content review | Power writing works well as a review for specific words or concepts in any content area. For example, students write for two minutes about photosynthesis. In composing and listening to what others share, the concept is deepened. Power writing, a writing-across-the-curriculum strategy, deepens students' content knowledge, as described in *Writing Next*: "Writing has been shown to be an effective tool for enhancing students' learning of content material" (Graham and Perin 2007, 20). |

*Figure 1.4*

# Speak Up and Be Heard

> **Progress grows out of motion.**
>
> —Richard E. Byrd

Writing is looking for a place to happen. Let's provide our students that place. Let's ignite their motivation to express their thoughts in writing. In a speech given at the Texas Council of Teachers of English, Andrea Lunsford (2011) reported on students' beliefs and attitudes about writing. One student's response represented many: "Writing has to stand up and do something. Good writing makes something happen in the world." If we care about something, we have more gumption to get to it. Humans feel. We have passions, beliefs, and opinions. Knowing our writing will have an audience (and be heard) influences our motivation to write. Interactive social media is evidence of this trend.

## Writing as a Civil Right

To begin the conversation about what writing can do in the world, I read aloud the nonfiction picture book *Elizabeth Leads the Way: Elizabeth Cady Stanton and the Right to Vote* by Tanya Lee Stone. The story of Elizabeth's standing up against society's unacceptable norms encourages students to reflect on how speaking up and being heard in writing affects the world. The book ends with the image of a pebble in a pond, rippling outward, affecting the world.

> **The pen is mightier than the sword, but they both can ruin a good shirt.**
>
> —Dr. Cuthbert Soup

*Word of the meeting spread like wildfire. Newspapers across the country scolded Elizabeth for her boldness. But other women joined her battle. The idea of women having the right to vote began to buzz in the ears of people from Maine to California. Elizabeth had tossed a stone in the water and the ripples grew wider and wider and wider. Many said*

*Elizabeth must be stopped. But she was unstoppable. She changed America forever.*

> **Fill your paper with the breathings of your heart.**
> —William Wordsworth

Our words can bring forth change, and our words can ripple on long after we are gone.

Even when writing is assigned or tested, we can find a way to turn it toward something we care about, some aspect of interest to us.

# Set Time Limits

It may seem counterintuitive to set a time limit to spur more writing. We tend to think that more time equals more writing. Anyone who's ever tried timed writing exercises knows that sometimes students write better quality prose in five minutes than in five days.

As with power writing, writers use a time-limit strategy to get motivated to write:

- Brainstorm the pros and cons about a subject for three minutes.
- Write everything you have to say about your subject in five minutes.
- Revise a paragraph by covering up the original and trying to rewrite it in three minutes on another sheet of paper.

We can orchestrate timed-writing discoveries for students with a series of experiences.

## The Timer Method to Freewriting on Your Own

The kitchen timer method has gotten me writing for more than twenty years. I learned about the strategy in Meredith Sue Willis's *Blazing Pencils* (1991). As Elbow (1998) and Rief (2003) have recommended, timed writings, or quick-writes, are a fruitful practice. Write for a set period of time, say, fifteen minutes. We can stop writing when the timer sounds, or we can keep writing. Once we're writing, we usually keep working. But even if we don't, we have a beginning. Maybe we realize a need to do more research. Maybe we know what we're not going to write about. The timer strategy has helped me get many unfinishable, or "I-don't-want-to," writing projects started.

This same principle can be used in class. Longer than power writing, a freewrite may or not be prompted. A stimulus can be anything:

- A word (worry, field trips, gym, conflict)
- A line from a short story, novel, or article (especially leads or a conclusion to write from or toward)

> **The true self is always in motion—like music, a river of life, changing, moving, failing, suffering, learning, shining. That is why you must freely and recklessly make new mistakes—in writing or life—and do not dwell on them but move on and write more.**
> —Brenda Ueland

- A question
- A reading
- A prompt (written or picture)

Giving students a choice between the stimulus and their own idea works best.

Then, considering your students' stamina, students can write for five, ten, or twenty minutes. They should start small and build, word after word, sentence after sentence, to put their thoughts down on the page. Students go where the writing takes them, shifting gears if they want to. This reinforces that everything they write is just like the thoughts floating through their heads. Like Gracie in *Write Before Your Eyes* by Lisa Williams Kline, students follow their thoughts in freewriting:

> *Now Gracie clicked her pen. She thought about writing a story about Dad's new apartment, and then decided to write instead about her dream of the houseboat on the crest of the huge wave.*
> *. . . And she put her pen to paper.*

Not everything we write will be great. That's natural. Elbow (1998) says we have to write a lot of garbage to find a gem. We are building fluency. We are building momentum.

> **Growth, in some curious way, I suspect, depends on being always in motion just a little bit, one way or another.**
> —Norman Mailer

# Generate Momentum by Talking

> **Reading and writing float on a sea of talk.**
> —James Britton

Talking drives our writing forward. When I am stuck or need a new perspective, I talk. When I am getting ready to draft or revise, I talk. I may read my words aloud to hear them. I may listen to someone else's writing. Ideas connect and flow and grow through talk.

Every part of the writing process is enhanced by talk, and I want students to experience how talk generates ideas, passions, connections, revisions, and words. Students experience how talk builds momentum at any stage of the writing process.

> **Collaborative writing involves developing instructional arrangements whereby adolescents work together to plan, draft, revise, and edit their compositions. It shows a strong impact on improving the quality of students' writing.**
> —Steve Graham and Dolores Perin

## 5–7–10

Another freewriting variation that illustrates the value of talking throughout the writing process is a 5–7–10. I learned this nifty strategy from Dr. Joan Shiring at the University of Texas. This strategy alternates between freewriting and talking with peers. Freewriting plus talk gets even more motion out of adolescent writers. Remember we're getting them to dip down into that writing zone so they know how easily words can come.

Make a list of hot topics on the board, such as music, skateboarding, dancing, sports, makeup, or any topics of the day tailored to your students' interests. You can use a prompt or stimulus if you like. Then, invite students to freewrite for five minutes.

After five minutes of writing, students turn to a partner and read what they have written. They have seven minutes to read their writing aloud to one another and discuss their writing. If there is time, a few students can share their writing with the larger group. During this activity in one class, I ask, "What happens when you hear other people's writing?"

"It reminded me of some things I didn't think of," says Sasha.

"Yeah," Ramon says. "When she said all this stuff about skateboards in her writing, it made me think of another way to write about mine."

When students pay attention, they get more ideas. I remind them to jot down these new ideas that, in turn, spark more of their own writing. "That's why writers talk to each other," I say. "Your ideas help mine grow."

Next, students write for ten more minutes. We are modeling how writers get their ideas flowing by interacting with other writers. We are supporting writing behaviors. As they experience it, they begin to integrate this into their own writing processes.

> The way a subject becomes clear is by collecting concrete specifics about it, and you collect the specifics by observing and asking why, who, what, when, where, and how. The most ordinary things . . . can be subjects.
>
> —Donald Murray

# Capture Inspiration and Information

The most important thing is to write. I stand by that. Get your hand moving: typing, scrawling—whatever, get in motion. However, a paradox exists. A writer needs time for temporary detours to gather information and inspiration.

But how do you capture the information that falls around you like sporadic snowflakes between writing sessions? Writers use many strategies to capture inspiration (see Figure 1.5). Find one that works for you and your resources. What do you usually carry with you most of the time? What could you easily have with you? Because, trust me, if you don't write down the inspiration and information as it comes, it melts away.

Gathering ideas is an important part of the writing process, but writers shouldn't use it as an excuse to avoid writing. Research is a seductive form of procrastination: you feel as though you're doing something, but when research is done in excess, your writing does not move forward.

> If you are seized by inspiration, grab the nearest thing at hand. You can scribble on the margins of a newspaper, write on the back of your science homework, use an envelope (one of my favorites), or commandeer a napkin. When I was a teen, I wrote on my jeans. (Don't do this if you wear the hundred-dollar kind.)
>
> —Ellen Potter and Anne Mazer

## Write What's in Front of Your Nose

Writing is not about impressing; it is about expressing. Writing is about what's important to you and your world. Collect ideas and inspiration from books, articles, television shows, Internet sites, conversations, and current events you encounter every day.

*Figure 1.5*

> ## Capturing Inspiration and Information Between Writing Sessions
>
> - **Carry an index card.** Anne Lamott folds one in half and stuffs it in her pocket with a golf pencil as she goes out the door.
> - **Create a file or document on your desktop or thumb drive.** Use the name of the project or simply call it "Ideas."
> - **Keep a writer's notebook.** Record connections and observations.
> - **Use your cell phone.** It is a technological substitute for lugging around a writer's notebook to capture ideas. Use your cell phone's notes feature. Record voice memos. Text yourself. It's compact, hassle free, and always with you.
> - **Call yourself and leave a voice mail.** Write the idea down when you check your messages later.
> - **Place a notepad and pen by your bed.** As you wake or before falling asleep, when the judgment faculty is weak, our best ideas may surface. The ability to jot down these fleeting ideas keeps them from escaping into the ether.
> - **E-mail your ideas.** Find your idea in your in-box when you're ready. Use the project name in the subject line.

> Take some time to notice patterns, sounds, and objects in your everyday life. Look at the floor of your closet. Notice the paper bag flapping on the parking meter near your office. Listen to the phrases that occur to you before you drift off to sleep. Touch the rough concrete post by a neighbor's meadow. You'll find an abundance of images and ideas in the things you've taken for granted. This receptive approach to the familiar is the beginning of the discovery of voice.
>
> —Thaisa Frank and Dorothy Wall

Poet William Carlos Williams discovered he didn't have to write about fancy things he'd never seen—just about the things that were right "in front of his nose." In *A River of Words: The Story of William Carlos Williams*, biographer Jen Bryant shares some of the things that William Carlos Williams learned about writing:

> *I want to write about ordinary things—plums, wheelbarrows, and weeds, fire engines, children, and trees—things I see when I walk down my street or look out my window.*

There is no one place or time to write. Williams, a family physician, wrote many of his poems on prescription pads, scribbling a few lines between patient visits.

Where do real ideas come from? From your life: the people, places, events, and things you see every day. In his memoir, *Knucklehead*, Jon Scieszka put it this way:

> *The more I think about it, the more I realize that I get a lot of my ideas from all the strange things that happened to me growing up with five brothers.*

Ideas are all around us. We're constantly thinking, ideas flowing through our heads like a river of words. Writers just need to pay attention. Students must notice what they see, think, and wonder, and when they do, ideas flow, momentum builds, and motion begins.

## Classical Invention Defined

When I write nonfiction, sometimes it is hard to begin. Classical invention gets my ideas flowing. In ancient Greece, Aristotle advised his oration students to approach a subject from various angles in order to speak convincingly. Forcing his protégés to look again at their topics from many perspectives ensured students' thorough knowledge of their subjects. In *Writing*, Dr. Elizabeth Cowan Neeld (1987) shares how classical invention, a variation on Aristotle's method, jump-starts student writing.

For a preview of how classical invention helps writers look at their subject from various angles, see the adaption of Neeld's questions in Figure 1.6.

> We are cups, constantly and quietly being filled. The trick is, knowing how to tip ourselves over and let the beautiful stuff out.
>
> —Ray Bradbury

*Figure 1.6*

### Classical Invention

**Definition**
1. How does the dictionary define _____?
2. What earlier words did _____ come from?
3. What parts can _____ be divided into?
4. What other words mean approximately the same thing as _____?
5. What are some examples of _____?

**Comparison**
1. What is _____ similar to? In what ways?
2. What is _____ different from? In what ways?
3. _____ is superior to what? In what ways?
4. _____ is inferior to what? In what ways?
5. _____ is most unlike what? In what ways?

**Relationship**
1. What is the purpose of _____?
2. Why does _____ happen?
3. What is a consequence of _____?
4. What comes before _____?
5. What comes after _____?

**Circumstance**
1. Is _____ desirable? Why?
2. Who has done or experienced _____?
3. If _____ starts, what makes it end?
4. What would it take for _____ to happen now?
5. What would prevent _____ from happening?

**Testimony**
1. What have you heard people say about _____?
2. Do you know any facts or statistics about _____? If so, what?
3. Do I know any famous or well-known sayings about _____?
4. Have I heard any poems or songs about _____? Any books or articles? TV or movies?
5. What could I research on _____?

*Adapted from classical invention questions found in Neeld (1987).*

Next, we will explore how to use these inventions in the classroom. Students may need to use the classical invention process two or three times for different purposes to see its value. I have used it multiple times, and swear by it when I can't find a way into a piece of writing—or simply need a concrete way to get in motion.

## Bringing Classical Invention into the Classroom

"Sometimes we write before we write," I tell students as class begins. "Since ancient times, scholars have used classical invention to explore ideas. We can explore our ideas just as great thinkers always have."

On the board, I list basic directions for classical invention, which I adapted from Neeld (1987):

- Read and answer the questions one at a time, thoughtfully.
- Jot down brief notes for answers.
- If you get stuck or have nothing to say, move on.
- Reread your answers, and put a star beside or highlight useful or thought-provoking words or ideas.

To begin, students need a potential subject. One word is enough. After reading *The Giver* by Lois Lowry, my eighth graders pick one theme word or repeated idea they had seen throughout the text.

We brainstorm a shared list of possible theme words. They call out *love, youth, authority, utopia,* and *choices.* After brainstorming, students select a word from the list or choose one of their own.

I model the first category of classical invention—definition—so students can answer the questions independently. For modeling purposes, I use another dystopian fantasy, *The Hunger Games* by Suzanne Collins. I choose the word *fate* for the theme.

In the modeling classical invention chart (see Figure 1.7), I write down the response to each question under the middle column ("What I Write Down"). In the "What I Say" column, I script my think-aloud.

To help students answer definition questions, provide resources such as dictionaries, thesauri, and word origin sources. Borrow references from the library or from colleagues so that you'll have an ample supply. Computers are excellent resources as well.

Once I model definition, I bounce around like a pinball while students grapple with the same questions: nudging, redirecting, and clarifying. I don't worry about repetition in answers because the recurrence of an idea reveals something.

> Vygotsky observed that the very process of writing one's thoughts leads individuals to refine those thoughts and discover new ways of thinking.
>
> —Maryanne Wolf

> The act of composition is a series of discoveries.
>
> —E. L. Doctorow

## Modeling Classical Invention

| Question | What I Write Down | What I Say |
|---|---|---|
| *Definition*<br>1. How does the dictionary define <u>fate</u>? | • Force predetermining events, outcome, destiny<br>• Disastrous consequence | *First, I look up my word in the dictionary. Now that I've found it, I am going to read all the definitions and jot down a few notes that apply.* |
| 2. What earlier words did <u>fate</u> come from? | Fatum—prediction, sentence of the Gods | *Okay, so word origin information is usually at the end of the definition—or I can look in a word origin book or the Internet.* |
| 3. What parts can <u>fate</u> be divided into? | Fatal<br>Fateful—meaning of momentous consequences | *It can't be divided but it can be lengthened. I could skip this part, but I am going to jot a few longer words.* |
| 4. What other words mean approximately the same thing as <u>fate</u>? | Destiny, fortune, chance, providence, luck, doom | *I can look these up in a thesaurus, but sometimes dictionaries have synonyms. I can also add words I think of.* |
| 5. What are some examples of <u>fate</u>? | When someone is told they are dying of a disease. When you fall in love and feel as though it was supposed to be that way. You meet the right person at the right time, or you are in the right place. | *There is no place to look this up, so I've got to think hard about the words and things I have so far. I think about the ways this can happen in my life, including the experiences of people around me or in current events—or even things I've seen on TV or read about.* |

*Figure 1.7*

# Keeping Classical Invention in Motion

Students need a considerable amount of assistance during independent work. Our conversations are crucial to keep students moving. It's work. It takes thinking. When I see that most students are almost finished with the definition questions, I explain the comparison questions: "The answers to these questions won't be in a dictionary or thesaurus. Our experiences and thinking will serve as resources for the next few sections."

I don't model the comparison category. I read through the questions to make sure they are understandable. I inject a few sample answers: "Fate is similar to destiny, as in it's been decided. You can't do anything about it. Fate is different from choice or free will, which says you can do something about your future. It's not decided yet."

I read through the remaining questions, and then students dive back into recording their answers. I continue circulating around the classroom throughout the process. For the testimony section, students refer to books of quotations or computer searches for quotations or current events.

Classical invention questions can happen over two days. As students finish reading and answering one set of questions, introduce the next section by reading through the questions, giving a few examples, and clarifying anything the students don't understand. Making sense of the questions is part of the generative benefit of classical invention for writers.

After guiding my students through classical invention a few times, I set up a center in my writing resources corner. At anytime, if writers need to think through an idea, they can go to the center to explore classical invention questions. A set of cards included in the appendix can be used for this activity. Working through one or two of the question categories can be enough to get students into motion.

## Teacher Feedback on Student Writing Affects Motion

> **The child is more important than the writing.**
> —Donald Graves

According to Donald Graves, a successful conferring session is one in which the writer leaves wanting to write. Reflect on the feedback you give students: Does it make them want to write more? I don't want to be the force that gets writers in motion only to halt them with my feedback.

Second only to the constricting straitjacket of an overly prescriptive writing formula, the most damaging barrier to students' staying in motion is halting feedback. It stops writers in their tracks, creating a chorus of "I can't write" and "I hate writing."

Granted, feedback is intended to be supportive. Some teachers, parents, and principals criticize students' every mistake, with good intentions. Feedback is given in love. However, I've seen Lifetime TV and I know love can become twisted. Just because someone thinks something is love doesn't make it so.

> **People will forget what you said, people will forget what you did, but people will never forget how you made them feel.**
> —Maya Angelou

Frankly, student writers can get overwhelmed with too much feedback—especially if it's mostly negative. They react by shutting down altogether. Just like that we've created a struggling writer. Although it's unintentional, we have to consider a student's perception of our handwritten comments. Most perceive feedback like seventh-grader Holling Hoodhood in *The Wednesday Wars* by Gary Schmidt:

> *She turned back to the pile of essays on her desk, spreading a red plague over them with her pen.*

We can at least temper our feedback, balancing negative comments or marks with good things the writer is doing. Many adolescents think that teachers exist to be instruments of torture, to keep them down, to keep them from doing what they really want. It may not be true, but it's part of adolescent development, angst, and separation. If we overly correct students' writing, they think, "She hates me!"

How students perceive our feedback is key to students staying in motion. Even as an adult writer, when an editor says one too many things are wrong with my writing, doubt clamps my mind shut for days.

Words have extreme power to ignite or to extinguish.

My filter for feedback is this: Will this make students want to write and revise? Will it frustrate or crush? Think hard before you mark. Your good intentions might not pave the road to where you intend.

I have written extensively in my other books about how the words we say to students about writing in general and about *their* writing in particular can have far-reaching effects. Is writing about being right and wrong, or is it

> Students will float to the mark you set.
>
> —Mike Rose

*Figure 1.8*

## 7 Tips to Consider When Providing Feedback and Assessment to Writers

1. **Read through the entire piece of writing before marking.** Don't be tempted to comment on the first three things your eyes spot—unless it's positive.

2. **As you read student writing, scour for what is right and effective.** Not seeing it? You're not looking hard enough.

3. **Inform—don't overwhelm.** When you comment, be choosey. Say what this writer most needs to know right now. Focus.

4. **Positive comments should outweigh negative comments by a minimum of 2 to 1**, especially with struggling writers. What's going well? What needs work?

5. **Inform parents and students early about how you'll provide feedback.** On back-to-school night or in a letter home to parents, share your philosophies. Emphasize you are still teaching the skills but in ways that work to encourage rather than discourage writing improvement.

6. **Use the information you gather as you read students' writing to plan mini-lessons and small-group work.** Model what you want them to do as writers, rather than correcting what you don't. For learning, positive trumps negative. Period.

7. **Students need to be part of the assessment.** They ask:
   - Did I say what I set out to say?
   - What challenged me?
   - What can I do better?
   - What was the best part of working on this piece?

   Self-reflection is an important part of motion. It may seem the opposite of motion, but reflection could be the one thing a writer needs to move to the next level. Like anything, reflection has to be modeled and developed. Motion doesn't only mean spilling words on the page: reflection is just slow motion.

about discovering the multiple options we have for expressing ourselves? Is writing about deciding for ourselves whether we communicate the messages we want?

Your feedback stays with your students long after they leave your classroom. There is no quicker way to stall a writer in motion than to give harsh or poorly timed feedback, whether the feedback comes from you or others. With this in mind, it's imperative that, early in the writing workshop, we establish feedback guidelines in our writing community (see Figure 1.8).

# You Can't Stop the Motion of the Ocean

There isn't any secret. You sit down and you start and that's it.

—Elmore Leonard

Motion ebbs and flows in writing too. It's our job to show students how to dip into their own deep wells of knowing, spilling words freely, learning they really do have a lot to say, and they can access it simply by moving their hand across the page—getting into motion. Sometimes words even come in waves. And sometimes all we have to do is begin and the words keep coming.

# Models

## Using Mentor Texts

*Never hesitate to imitate another writer. Imitation is part of the creative process for anyone learning an art or craft. Bach and Picasso didn't spring full-blown as Bach and Picasso; they needed models. This is especially true of writing.*

—William Zinsser

Are you really good at something? Stop for a minute and think of something you're good at or at least something with which you have some level of fluency. Or think of one thing you do regularly or wish you did more often. Is it singing? Reading? Teaching? Bicycling? Sewing? Cooking? Running? Camping? Gardening? Archery? Stop and consider how you became good at it. I'll bet, at some point, you had a model.

To learn, we don't always need a curriculum or a test. Sometimes we just watch and learn. I remember standing beside my mother, leaning on the harvest gold Formica countertop, watching her brown hamburger meat. Breaking it up with the spatula, pushing it around, squeezing it down, and hearing it sizzle. After I watched her for a while, Mom let me be in charge of the hamburger meat while she made the salad. I moved the meat around a bit, like she did. Harder tasks like pouring off the grease took more direction. "Watch how I make sure the can is in the sink in case it tumps over." All the

> If you stuff yourself full of poems, essays, plays, stories, novels, films, comic strips, magazines, music, you automatically explode every morning like Old Faithful.
>
> —Ray Bradbury

while, Mom modeled how to do the task, and I picked up little clues, not only from what Mom said, but from watching how she did it again and again.

We know the power of models. And we know they are particularly effective with language instruction. All language endeavors—from speaking to reading to writing—are built upon a process of exposure to and the study of models over time. These experiences are followed by imitation, experimentation, and feedback, a natural, repeatable language acquisition process that teachers can use to build successful writers.

Texts are teachers. If you want to write an article, read articles. If you want to write a research report, look at research writing. Open up to the possibilities. Use a stack of books like a menu. Every time you browse in the library, every time you read a book or an article, ask yourself, how could I use this as a writer?

One sure-fire method on the road to writing success is paying attention to models. Really paying attention. Our best writers read the most. The concept of using mentor texts is not new (C. Anderson 2000; J. Anderson 2005, 2007; Dorfman and Cappelli 2007, 2009; Ray 1999). I wrote two books built around using mentor texts. Simply put, mentor texts are model pieces of writing. Students note what works with the models, take them apart, and identify aspects of the writer's style they'd like to try.

But it doesn't stop there. Mentor texts offer examples of every type of imaginable writing—at any level of sophistication. Whether we choose words to create mood, punctuate to emphasize an idea, or uncover how writers share detail, we are reading like writers. The scaffolds other writers provide are boundless. Research tells us that reading, analyzing, and emulating model texts increase students' writing abilities. The research report *Writing Next* (Graham and Perin 2007) recommends the study of models as one gateway to writing success.

> *The study of models provides adolescents with good models for each type of writing that is the focus of instruction. Students are encouraged to emulate the critical elements, patterns, and forms embodied in the models in their own writing.* (20)

The report recommends the specific sequence of experiences with models that improved student writing:

- Read
- Analyze
- Emulate

If writers want to author a great persuasive essay, they can look at a few well-written persuasive essays (read). What makes them work? Is it the statistics, counterarguments, or quotations? Is it the authority of the writer? How did the writer achieve these things? How did the writer weave in these elements (analyze)? As William Zinsser (2006) says, writers use their eyes and ears to try on what others writers do; they find their own voice and energy as they follow the path to successful writing (emulate).

Just reading a mentor text doesn't do the trick, though. If you want the research-proven results of *Writing Next*, interaction and analysis must occur. Active processing of the model includes taking the writing apart and putting it back together, naming its elements, and supposing why authors made the choices they did.

For example, when a student notes that nonfiction writer James Swanson begins his true-crime book *Chasing Lincoln's Killer* by summarizing the civil war in two pages, the noticing is only the beginning of the process. How did Swanson explain a four-year war in two pages? Once we form a question or questions, we have a purpose to reread, to interact with the text, and to look for answers.

> *From 1861 through 1865, the United States endured a bloody civil war between Northern and Southern states. The conflict had begun long before over the right to own slaves and states' right to secede, that is, to leave the union if they disagreed with the government.*

After reading the first paragraph again, the student realizes Swanson actually summarized the entire war in the opening paragraph. In less than fifty words, Swanson summarized the length of the civil war, the rivals, and the causes. He wastes no time describing who, what, when, where, and why. We learn that, in nonfiction writing, as in newspaper writing, we answer the W questions right up front. Then, the question becomes, "Why did the author choose to summarize the whole war in the first paragraph?"

To read like a writer, we reread like a writer, zeroing in on the *why* and the *how*. What did the author do to compress this information? First, he used a prepositional phrase ("From 1861 through 1865") to give us a context of the time period (*when*). He was direct with his words, using only words that do work: "between Northern and Southern states" (*who*), "endured a bloody civil war" (*what*), and "over the right to own slaves and states' right to secede" (*why*).

I can hear you now: "But my kids don't do that!" Well, of course they don't; we haven't shown them how yet. And showing them one time won't do it either. If we want students to follow this research-based model, we will have to demonstrate it first, guide them through several experiences using varying texts, and then slowly release them to apply the process on their own.

We make it possible for students to use this process on their own by demonstrating what writers do—they read to write. They get inspired. We

> Imitation, conscious imitation, is one of the great methods, perhaps *the* method of learning to write. The ancients, the Elizabethans, knew this, profited by it, and were not disturbed.
>
> —Theodore Roethke

> Art begins in imitation and ends in innovation.
>
> —Mason Cooley

have to take them through the process, so they can experience its value. Then, when the need arises, and they know their options and have some fluency with them, they will look to powerful articles and books to figure out what critical attributes will make the genre or form work, what will make writing come alive, or what will make a good ending.

Once they are inspired by and understand the process, they examine texts on their own, taking what they need from a piece of writing. However, the true value is that—eventually—students will look at every reading encounter as a lesson in writing.

To begin, we show them how writers make models work for them (see Figure 2.1).

*Figure 2.1*

### Making MODELS Work

- Use the scientific method to study models.
    - Notice (*Observe*)
    - Interact (*Question*)
    - Name (*Hypothesize*)
    - Experiment (*Test*)
    - Reflect (*Conclude*)
- Discover where models can take you as a writer.
- Refine and revise your theories to respond to new models.
- Collect models.
- Get to know other writers' processes.

# Use the Scientific Method to Study Models

To kick off the study of models as a path to successful writing, I share an excerpt from Bill Nye the Science Guy's book, *Big Blast of Science*. Nye's definition of the scientific method reminds us that through inquiry we can figure out how anything works, including writing. Although the scientific method is usually discussed in science class, this application allows writers to act like scientists, unlocking the secrets of good writing.

*In a way, science is how we handle every question in our lives. It's not just how to do things. Science is the way we figure out how to do these things. Scientists, maybe a scientist like you, call this way of doing things "the Scientific Method." Science means "knowledge," and "method" means "road" in Greek. So the Scientific Method is the "Road to Knowledge."*

Nye describes how the scientific method is a "process, a path, a road to learning," which starts with observation and hypothesis. Scientists observe how clouds behave in the sky, while writing scientists observe how other writers write. As the scientist hypothesizes that dark clouds often lead to rain, a writing scientist sees patterns in a text that elicit a certain response in readers.

Science starts with a question. Here are some underlying questions writers might ask as they look at model texts:

- What do writers do?
- How do writers use the ten things every writer needs to know (motion, models, focus, detail, form, frames, cohesion, energy, words, or clutter) to make their writing strong?
- What patterns of success do we see across texts?
- What's working well? What's not working?
- How is this like or different from other texts we've read?
- What techniques can we try in our own writing?

After the observing and questioning, scientists build hypotheses, and then test them or experiment with them to see whether what they predict is true. With writers, the experiment is emulating another writer and observing its effect on readers.

The scientific method (observe, question, hypothesize, test, and conclude) relates to the *Writing Next* research as well as the scientific method for studying models I use throughout this book (see Figure 2.2).

> Writing is only reading turned inside out.
> —John Updike

*Figure 2.2*

| The Scientific Method of Learning to Write from Models | | |
| --- | --- | --- |
| *Writing Next:* Study of Models | The Scientific Method | The Scientific Method for Studying Models |
| Read | Observe | Notice |
| Analyze | Question | Interact |
| | Hypothesize | Name |
| Emulate | Test | Experiment |
| | Conclude | Reflect |

It's important to use a close-up lens on exactly how we can interact with mentor texts or models, so in this chapter, we look at more discrete actions to guide our students to unlock meaning and create strong writers. In this section, I address the often-repeated first three steps of the process: notice, interact, and name.

## Notice

If we approach writing like scientists, gazing at the road laid out before us, the first step is to notice what a writer does in the text we are reading. When a passage or sentence resonates with us, we pause and consider what the writer did to get that reaction. For example, when I read Pat Murphy's setting description in *The Wild Girls*, I not only enjoyed it, but I also observed how she writes about the character's surroundings as she roams away from her brand-new house for the first time.

The next day, I read the excerpt aloud to my students. A discussion about what they noticed followed.

> *Through the trees and brush, I caught a glimpse of something orange—a brilliant, unnatural, Day-Glo color. I followed the path toward the color and found a small clearing where the weeds had been cut down. A large easy chair, upholstered in fabric that was a riot of orange daisies on green and turquoise paisley patterns, sat under a twisted walnut tree. In front of the chair was a flat-topped boulder, and on the boulder was a teapot with a broken spout. Boards had been wedged among the branches of the tree to make shelves of a sort. Haphazard and not quite level, they supported an odd assortment of items: a jar of peanut butter, a battered metal box, a china cup with a broken handle, two chipped plates, a dingy teddy bear, a metal box of Band-Aids.*
>
> *I stopped where I was. This looked like someplace out of a book— like a troll's living room, like a wizard's retreat in the woods, like a place waiting for something to happen.*
>
> *"What the hell are you doing here?" a kid's voice asked.*
>
> *I looked up, startled.*

After an initial discussion of what students notice—the words or phrases or anything that captured their attention or caused a reaction—I model how I read like a writer.

"When I read a section of text that could teach me something about writing," I say, "I reread it." Just as scientists observe their subjects or phenomenon more than once, we look closer at what we read. "Like a scientist, I let the text tell me what it has to teach. Since this section from *The Wild Girls* describes setting," I say, "I wonder what I can learn about using detail to create a setting. I'm going to look closer at how this author describes."

As we reread the excerpt, we observe more and interact with the text and one another, discussing and analyzing how the writer achieves what we notice. This collaboration among students, this active processing, is key to scaffolding the use of models to improve writing.

## Interact

We know that the twenty-first-century student needs to process information actively, so we give them ample opportunities to be involved: testing what they think, bumping their ideas against others, clarifying, questioning, growing, and owning. If we go too long at anything without an opportunity to react in writing or with talk, then the students' attention drifts.

It doesn't have to be long. Thirty seconds. One minute. Always less than they need. It is worth your time to allow interaction and processing time. It helps them learn. Getting on to the next objective may mean you've covered more, but have you taught? Do your students own the concepts? Do they use them independently as needed?

"The first thing I notice is how the author describes what the narrator sees," I say.

"Like through something," Juanita thinks aloud.

"Show me where you are, Juanita."

"Here," she points. "When she writes 'through the trees and brush, I caught a glimpse of something orange.'"

We discuss how Murphy gives the reader the sense the narrator is in an overgrown area without telling us that. Instead, she helps us visualize it. Another student notices how Murphy writes *clearing* but also gives additional information about what a clearing is, or further details to help a reader visualize the clearing.

> *I followed the path toward the color and found a small clearing where the weeds had been cut down.*

"That's interesting," I say, "Murphy doesn't describe every possible thing. She selects. And, judging by the time she spends describing this clearing, we know it's going to be important."

Jonathan notices how the author lists specific items that really made him wonder and make predictions about the space. He shows us where he is in the text, zeroing in and rereading the passage so that the craft or strategy becomes more apparent.

> *Haphazard and not quite level, they supported an odd assortment of items: a jar of peanut butter, a battered metal box, a china cup with a broken handle, two chipped plates, a dingy teddy bear, a metal box of Band-Aids.*

**Children need models rather than critics.**
—Joseph Joubert

**Unless students interact creatively with information to construct meaning, there is little or no change.**
—Betty Garner

It's natural for this analysis to flow into naming the strategy. I don't worry if we move to the next step. I want the discussion to unfold. The method is a pattern and a path to follow: sometimes we'll skip steps, sometimes it will be better to go left and other times right. Listen to your students and nudge them to the next right place.

If something else that's a key craft lesson is not mentioned before I move on, I ask more direct questions. It's important that I wait to hear what the students notice and that the students are the ones rereading sections of text. If I always jump in, they learn to wait, and I want them to be the processors of the models. I nudge, support, scaffold, question, and model, but I won't rob them of the opportunity to uncover what they can on their own.

"Although Murphy describes for several sentences, she eventually inserts action." I reread the text to show what I mean, modeling that we always return to the text when we are discussing it.

> *I stopped where I was. This looked like someplace out of a book— like a troll's living room, like a wizard's retreat in the woods, like a place waiting for something to happen.*

"It's good to help a reader see the setting, but readers get bored if there is no action moving the narrative along. That's something that Murphy is teaching me. And look here."

> *"What the hell are you doing here?" a kid's voice asked.*
> *I looked up, startled.*

"The shocking dialogue breaks us out of the description," I say.

When we read like scientists, we discover that engaging writing is about blending layers, changing direction from time to time, so the writing never becomes monotonous or completely expected. The text must remain vibrant and alive, and we can learn from published authors about how to do that. "As we read in the future, let's pay more attention to how authors keep us engaged—or not."

## Name

I want my students to observe writing, to note what works, what they can try in their own writing, such as describing a setting. In the scientific method, according to Nye, once we observe or note a pattern, we form a hypotheses to explain our observations—"the idea underneath it all."

Students need to name what they see, what they can take away from this text. A strategy is something they can recognize in their reading and use in their writing. These are the ideas students observed from reading the passages in *The Wild Girls*:

- Use how you see *through* things to show something about your setting.
- Use lists to name an array of specific items that will help your readers visualize the setting.
- Don't describe everything. Spend time describing only those things that will be important to your readers' understanding.
- Move in and out of description. Too much description without action or dialogue becomes boring.

When you look at models, examine them more than once. The power of models comes from seeing principles applied across various texts, which brings the patterns of success to the surface. As writing scientists, we need to observe and dissect several models. Then, we are ready to experiment and apply our observations and hypotheses to our prose.

At this point I have to make a decision. Is it time to write or experiment and tinker?

Maybe.

If I think one model is enough, I send kids off to experiment and write. However, the experience with models is enriched when I add a second or third reading selection. This kind of pattern building is what models offer. Don't rush this phase. Noticing, interacting, and naming is part of the scientific method that is often repeated several times before students progress to application.

In *Vocabulary Unplugged*, Alana Morris (2005) reminds us of why we often need to repeat parts of cycles.

> *The human mind truly doesn't function like a computer system. The human mind loses important details, fails to file information that others may deem vital, and miscodes data, causing it to reappear when least expected—or not at all. The bottom line is that we, as educators, cannot download files into eagerly waiting hard drives and assume that it can be retrieved when needed. What we must do is learn as much as possible about how the human brain processes, stores, and retrieves information.* (1)

Before students write, I model, thinking aloud, how I use a model to start writing (noticing other authors' patterns), especially the first few times we attempt to write. In the next section, we begin again by noticing, but we will also elaborate on the rest of the scientific method for writing from models to see where the models can take us.

> The "best advice" I think is in reading good writers, not seeking advice from them, for we learn the best by emulating the best.
>
> —Gay Talese

# Discover Where Models Can Take You as a Writer

Good poetry can penetrate
your writing like smoke gets
in your clothes.

—John Poch

As we look deeply at models, we discover their power to inspire us to try things in our own writing. It may be the way authors use powerful verbs or sentence patterns. Whatever it is, we can experiment with those techniques in our own prose. First, I demonstrate how to move from the model to my writing. I take students through the entire scientific process of writing from models.

Later, as they start to take on these actions, I take down the scaffolds. As writers, we need to know how to move from models to writing—how to choose one thing and try it, play with it, and see whether it works for us. As students, this is not obvious: it must be modeled.

Here, we will move through the entire method in more depth, as I comment on other options for teachers. As writing teachers, we need methods and options for moving from models to writing to ensure we capitalize on our models.

## Notice Powerful Text

As writing scientists, when we observe and read the world around us, we will stumble upon passages that are worthy of further observation, passages that show something writers need to know: a paragraph, a sentence, a chapter, a picture book. This is all we need. The smaller, the better. When we go for something too big, student focus suffers.

Once we find a powerful passage or sentence, we continue observing by rereading it. We may reread it two or three times, sometimes aloud, sometimes silently, taking in the letters on the page, the phrases or clauses, the verbs, the nouns, the punctuation, the transitions. Everything. Rereading prepares us to truly interact and analyze. In fact, interactions with the text or with other readers occur while you're rereading. The scientific method of studying models is more than discrete steps; it's also a meandering, collaborative, thoughtful path to good writing.

To demonstrate this in my classroom, I share an excerpt from the classic *The Wonderful Wizard of Oz* by L. Frank Baum.

> When Dorothy stood in the doorway and looked around, she could see nothing but the great gray prairie on every side. Not a tree nor a house broke the broad sweep of flat country that reached to the edge of the sky in all directions. The sun had baked the plowed land into a gray mass, with little cracks running through it. Even the grass was not green, for the sun had burned the tops of the long blades until they were the same gray color to be seen everywhere. Once the house had been painted,

*but the sun blistered the paint and the rains washed it away, and now the*
*house was as dull and gray as everything else.*

We reread and start thinking about the things that we react to with our eyes, ears, and minds. We think about the effect this writing has on us and how and why that occurs.

> I learned how to write from writers. I didn't know any personally, but I read.
>
> —Cynthia Rylant

## Interact with the Text and Other Writers

As we reread, we interact with the text—questioning it, zeroing in on certain lines and words we react to, analyzing it. We break it down and talk to our partners, and highlight or jot notes in the margin. It's important to do both. Talking about the writing and reactions in small groups encourages deeper thinking. We ask questions of one another and the text.

- What do you notice that is like something else you've read?
- What's different?
- Does anything this writer did affect you? How? Why?
- What did the author specifically do to get the reaction from the reader?

Interactions can mean discussing with a partner or in a small group, highlighting or scratching down observations in the margins of the book. Here, we analyze, go deeper, and see what the author is doing, focusing on effect.

Sometimes in my classroom I have to kick off the conversation, but soon, after I've modeled, students take over. "Doesn't it just feel like the black and white beginning of the movie *The Wizard of Oz*?" I ask.

"Yeah, it's all gray too," Jacob says. "Is that how you had to write back when they only had black-and-white TV?"

"No," I say, "but the writer made us feel that way. How'd he do it?"

"Well, he tells you all that's not there," Kristen says.

"Like what? Let's zero in on the words or phrases in the text. We need our text evidence to back us up."

"It says the word *nothing*." Javier jumps in.

"And no trees or houses," Kristen says, "and it's all flat and stuff."

"Yeah, and it says gray, gray, gray. Even the grass is gray."

## Name Concrete Actions or Strategies

My students demonstrate that they understand how to observe, but I explain that the trick is getting to know what the author did and translating that into a strategy, which we can repeat in our own writing. We have to consider what we noticed, questioned, and thought through and name the strategy.

When you find something that thrills you, take it apart paragraph by paragraph, line by line, word by word, to see what made it so wonderful. Then use those tricks the next time you write.

—W. P. Kinsella

"So Kristen noticed one strategy: the author listed what wasn't there to make us feel how empty it was," I say. "That's something we can try in our writing. I notice writers tell us a lot of times what *isn't* so we know what *is*." I write the strategy on a piece of chart paper: *Tell the reader what's not there.*

In a way, when we observe this excerpt and list the actions, we are hypothesizing how writers achieve rhetorical effect. We also make sure to name the strategy or action for each observation. That's part of the interaction and analysis of the text that moves us toward experimentation with it.

- Dorothy stood at her door, looking out at what's in front of her.
- Color or lack of color matters.
- Describe the condition of things. New or falling apart?
- Select a few things that tell a bigger story.

## Experiment with What You've Noticed

When we experiment as writers, we try something we've observed in our reading. When I show my students how to write quick imitations of sentence structure or musical elements of writing, such as onomatopoeia or alliteration, they reach a point where they no longer need my guidance. They shake off my scaffolding like an unwanted blanket. That's what we want, isn't it? Once we've gone through it several times, they start to own the process and try it, even without my nudging. But first, we model.

"Let's experiment with what Frank Baum did," I say. "Tonight, we'll go home and stand at our front or back doors and describe what we see in front of us. Write a paragraph or so in which you describe what you see."

Panic ensues. When students panic, it means they're unsure of how to proceed. In early stages, with any concept of higher levels of difficulty, model the processes for your students. Modeling shows them how we move from mentor texts to writing by revealing our thinking as we experiment.

## Model as Verb

So far we've mostly discussed *model* as a noun—a mentor text. However, any chapter on writing models has to address *model* as a verb. The least used and most beneficial example is to write in front of our students, modeling any stage or part of the process. For example, if I want my students to write a description, I need to model what that could look like to ensure student success.

How do you go from observing to hypothesizing to writing? I start writing and thinking aloud (see Figure 2.3).

## Modeling How to Write Using a Model

| What I Say | What I Write |
|---|---|
| *First, I need to look out the window and just see what I see. I could really look out a door or window anywhere and just observe what's in front of me. Write what I see. (I walk over to the window.) Where should I start? Well, that picnic table in the center seems like a good place to start. I mean it's so lonely sitting out there in the courtyard that has no plants or flowers. That's where I want to start—with the table.* | In the center of what could be a courtyard is a disappointment of a picnic table. |
| *In my next sentence, I want to show a little more about the picnic table. I don't just want to tell what I see, I want to describe it so someone who wasn't here could visualize it.* | Weathered wood, visible splinters, sitting on a weedy patch where the mowers can't get close enough. |
| *Look at the way the sun hits the top of the table. It looks almost white, the sun is so bright. I want to fit how the sun looks. Weather played a role in Frank Baum's piece; that's another thing I can borrow from what he did.* | The sun beats down on the table because there are no trees to shade it. |
| *(I look over at the list then back outside.) Another thing Frank Baum did was talk about what wasn't there, like Kristen noticed. I'm going to try that.*<br><br>*(At this point, I just quickly finish jotting down my ideas. If I model more than five or six minutes, students drift. Modeling is not repeating the whole process, it's letting them listen in on what writers do as they compose, something many of them have little awareness of.)*<br><br>*So I just looked out and reported what I saw. What else did I do? How is mine different from the two descriptions we've already read? What might I have done differently? How is it the same? How will you begin this assignment? Is there a right or wrong way to do it really?* | Weeds sway in the wind. There is nothing intentionally planted here. Just what can survive with a mowing every few weeks and the natural rainfall. The picnic table sits on defiantly, pretending this space is something that it's not. The brown brick walls and windows frame it in on three sides. An old white grocery sack blows across the weeds and wraps itself around the picnic table. |

*Figure 2.3*

So with a plan and a few strategies, they take the model home and look out a window or doorway and tell us what they see. Students feel better when they have a plan for success, and are more likely to try what I've asked.

## Reflect on What You've Tried

When students return the next day, we share our descriptions. A surprising number of students bring this assignment back. When students know they'll be successful, their willingness skyrockets. We think about anything else we discover as we look at the list we started when we read from *The Wild Girls* and *The Wonderful Wizard of Oz* the day before.

"Let's look back at the list we've been keeping and see whether there is anything else we may want to think about when we experiment with the ideas we've been studying in our model texts," I say.

After the kids offer some answers, we record them on the board and tinker with our descriptions.

## Can Fiction Be a Model for Nonfiction?

Some in our profession think there are two kinds of writing—fiction and nonfiction. While that is true (nonfiction), I think the oversimplification is the root of a lot of false or made-up teaching (fiction). For example, you may wonder, why would I look at a fiction paragraph from *The Wonderful Wizard of Oz* if my students are writing a persuasive essay?

True. A persuasive essay would be a good model, but that doesn't preclude us from learning and applying elements we see in fiction across forms. For example, if our persuasive piece was persuading readers to change the outdoor student lounge, then we'd better be able to describe its current state, as well as the suggested changes, if we expect readers to take action.

First, we have to help them see the problem, and see the solution. We can do that through description. It doesn't matter whether we learned about description in a different genre or form. And though "setting" in literature may seem foreign in an essay, if we want to create a feeling or persuade a reader about changing a certain space—or not changing a space, for that matter—the elements of fiction will make my nonfiction stronger.

Fiction and nonfiction can serve as models for any writing task. It's an oversimplification to say it doesn't matter at all, but the truth is, well-received nonfiction, for the most part, uses the elements of fiction to make it compelling: real settings, actual characters, factual conflicts.

# Refine and Revise Your Theories to Respond to New Models

With all parts of the writing process, we are on a never-ending refinement cycle. If we get an idea or a theory about how description works from looking at model texts, we might later refine—broaden or narrow—that theory after exposure to additional texts. As we experiment with applying description in our own writing, we may discover some other truth about it, such as interspersing action within description.

Many times we will come across sentences or passages that remind us of a model we've studied. This is when we get a chance to refine or add to what we have already learned. For example, in the following excerpt from *Animal, Vegetable, Miracle*, Barbara Kingsolver's writing echoes the descriptions we saw in *The Wild Girls* and *The Wonderful Wizard of Oz*. We work through the questions: How is this text like what you've read before? What is different? What do you want to try?

> *This story about good food begins in a quick-stop convenience market. It was our family's last day in Arizona, where I'd lived half my life. . . . Now we were moving away forever, taking our nostalgic inventory of the things we would never see again: the bush where the roadrunner built a nest and fed a lizard to her weird-looking babies; the tree Camille crashed into learning to ride a bike; the exact spot where Lily touched a dead snake. Our driveway was just the first tributary on a memory river sweeping us out.*
>
> *One person's picture postcard is someone else's normal. This was the landscape whose every face we knew: giant saguaro cacti, coyotes, mountains, the wicked sun reflecting off bare gravel. We were leaving now in one of its uglier moments, which made good-bye easier, but also seemed like a cheap shot—like ending a romance right when your partner had really bad bed hair. The desert that day looked like a nasty case of prickly heat caught in a long, naked wince.*

This excerpt adds a level of reflection, spurring us to think about what we'd miss or mourn the loss of in a particular setting. We also note how Kingsolver uses description to show rather than tell her feelings. This excerpt connects to students too. The conversation starts. Have you ever moved quickly? If you had to move today, what would you miss?

It's time to write.

> I read in order to write.
>
> —Cynthia Ozick

# Collect Models

If we need models to show our writers the vision of what successful writing looks like, then we need to collect texts, especially short excerpts. You can keep a file or document on your computer. You can keep a writer's notebook, note cards, binders, or blogs. Find some way to keep track of writing you encounter. Find some way to categorize it. I've been categorizing my books around the ten things every writer should know. Of course, well-written books that are strong in one area are usually strong in many areas, but some are striking in certain ways. Categorize those books. However you collect and categorize texts, make sure they're accessible to your students.

Where do we find effective models? The first place to look is in the books, articles, and texts in our classrooms. We don't need new model texts. Good writing is good writing. We also look for articles by columnists such as Leonard Pitts and Rick Reilly, which are available free online or in collections by the authors. I print out appropriate articles and save them for when I need them. Nothing works like a topical article to get kids talking. For instance, Leonard Pitts writes commentary on a variety of topics, from families and game night to questioning what it takes to be a celebrity in the world today. Questioning, arguing, and speaking on current events always stirs kids up. When they are stirred up, they are ready to write.

I look for writing models that

- teach one of the ten things I want writers to know,
- are of high interest to my students,
- model a correct or effective way to do something my students need to improve on, and
- show a curriculum goal in action.

I also look to award-winning books. A selection committee has said, "This is what good writing is," and I think it's important to use these books in our classrooms when they fit. I follow the Caldecott and Newbery winners and honors, the National Book Award, and the Michael L. Printz Award for adolescent fiction. I also look to the nonfiction winners and recommendations from the Orbis Pictus Award sponsored by the National Council of Teachers of English as well as the Robert F. Sibert Medal. For diversity I always look to the Coretta Scott King Award winners and the Pura Belpré Award. I have discovered many authors when I explore these titles, some of which are listed in the bibliography. An Internet search for any of these awards will direct you to many lists. These award-winning books are usually available in libraries at no cost.

# Get to Know Other Writers' Processes

We are curious about how things work. My students love to watch *MythBusters* because the hosts explore myths about everything, from rumors about whether the president was born in the United States to whether a tire will explode if you put too much air in it. They are testing these myths as hypotheses to see whether they are real or not.

While explosions are more attention grabbing, it's still valuable to watch writers at work. You can easily search for and find interviews with favorite authors online, and even on online booksellers' sites. Authors share their processes, and there are numerous books that do this as well.

I have shown my students a clip from the movie *Finding Forrester* to illustrate the power of imitating and the risks of modeling. I've read an excerpt from Cynthia Rylant's memoir, in which she addresses what it's like to be a writer. Web sites change quickly; however, if you search "children's book writers" on the Web, you will find sufficient information.

## You Are a Model Too

Don't forget you are a writer too, and you need to model at various stages of the writing process, especially moving from mentor texts to writing. You can model at the sentence level as well as composition, for revision or idea generation.

Whether through a mini-lesson, a mid-workshop point, or at the end of the workshop, share your process as a writer. Demonstrate to students how you move from what a writer does to applying it to your own work.

"You know I was reading this picture book by April Pulley Sayre yesterday," I say. "May I share it with you?"

I share the simple and beautiful book, *Vulture View*. I model how writers zoom in on a sentence to solve a writing problem. "I am looking for a new sentence pattern to see if I can add some variety to my writing. I saw this sentence, and realized I don't write sentences with this pattern very often: "The vultures gather in vulture trees, *settle and sleep*, like families." (Italics added.)

"I like the way the author places two of the verbs in a surprising place," I say, pointing to the sentence as I write it on the board. First, they *gather* in the trees, then they *settle and sleep*. She could've just written a list. *They gather, settle, and sleep.*" I rewrite it to show what that looks like. "Yet she tried something different."

When modeling, I have to pay particular attention to this step—the intermediate step between noticing and imitating. Sometimes students don't take enough time to figure out what the author actually did in the model. We have to scour, reread, question, and test our understanding. We have to identify something within the text that a writer can do.

"Okay, the author didn't use the regular method of a serial comma to fit in all three verbs. She used the first verb up front," I say pointing to the verb *gather*. "In what looks like a whole sentence: 'The vultures gather in vulture trees.'" I point to the *settle and sleep*. "She shifts the other two verbs, *settle and sleep*, behind the sentence and before the comparison 'like families'."

> Once we realize that language is acquired by imitation—it becomes obvious that language comes from without, not from within . . . Our most original compositions are composed exclusively of expressions derived from others.
>
> —Alexander Graham Bell

I explain how I might apply this pattern as a writer. "Suppose I am writing an editorial about my neighbor, who stapled Christmas lights to my fence in December. It's now three months later and they are still up. I'm trying to show readers why I don't want to bring it up to him, even though it's really bugging me. Here is what I have," I say, and write this sentence on the board:

> He smokes cigarettes and yells at his wife for parking the car in the wrong place. He makes his son move things around the yard.

I rewrite my sentence a few times to see what I like the best.

> Johnny directs his family, yelling and smoking, like a failed drill sergeant.

> Johnny roams around his yard, smoking and yelling and directing, like a boss in a shipyard.

If I try it a few different ways, I am showing my students they can recast their sentences too, letting them listen in on my process. When they find a sentence or section that really sparks good writing, they share it with me. Later, we look at the sentence as a class and do a formal imitation and experimentation lesson together.

## Models Teach

Models are our teachers. Using the scientific method of writing from models, we can do just about anything. The trick is to zero in on what works in a piece of writing and to find what we can use in our own compositions. When we stumble across writing that strikes us, we pause, reading it slowly and closely, analyzing and soaking in what strong writers do.

# Focus

## Narrowing the Scope

*Writing is a dance—sometimes not all that pretty—between the big and the small.*

—Mark Tredinnick

Focus comes early in my list of ten things writers need to know because without it, writing becomes an overwhelming task. Jack Hart sums up the paramount importance of focus: "A running gag among most writing coaches is that the three biggest writing problems are focus, focus, and focus" (2006, 20).

We tell students their writing must have a focus or controlling idea and that they should maintain that focus for the whole writing task. They ask, "But what does that mean?" "How do you do that anyway?"

I like to use author Robert Newton Peck's strategy. Only write about what we can see through a paper towel tube. We don't write about an *entire* school or *all* students; we write about the eighth-grade boy sitting alone at the lunch table, playing with his cornbread. I explain this concrete definition, and students cup their hands as they look around the room. What can we see through our self-made telescopes? Of course, we move them from this concrete definition to its metaphoric intent: Zero in on what's significant or important. Zoom in tight on what matters. Select. For example, instead of writing an argumentation essay about *video games*, students select an aspect:

> The most important thing in a work of art is that it should have a kind of focus . . . There should be some place where all the rays meet or from which they issue.
>
> —Leo Tolstoy

**41**

*Figure 3.1*

**Making FOCUS Work**

- Narrow your topic.
- Maintain your focus.
- Use audience and purpose to shape your focus.
- Find a unifying thread or pattern when writing about more than one topic.
- Discover your focus by writing.
- Capture focus with leads.
- Summarize to hone your focus.

Grand Theft Auto should/should not be allowed for teens. Think of focus like this: If readers were to forget everything else we write, what's the one thing we would want them to remember?

The rest of the chapter will look at actions writers can take to achieve focus (see Figure 3.1).

# Narrow Your Topic

In first grade, students make "All About" books, like *All About Fish*. The wide focus works well for early writing attempts, but after a few years, this format becomes too broad, allowing only surface-level detail. Often students never move beyond this rudimentary focus. I overheard a college professor lamenting that her students still write *All About Shakespeare* or *All About Hamlet*, rather than choosing an aspect of Shakespeare's work or a thread that runs through a play or many of his plays.

*All About* is not a narrow enough focus for most writing tasks. When we attempt to write about everything, the task becomes an endless, fuzzy mess that swerves out of control. When our focus is too wide from the start, it's difficult to narrow later. For novice writers, the concept of focus works against their assumptions. The young writer's thought processes go something like this: "What? I have to fill two pages? Then I better write about something big—like the *ocean* or *water* even!"

In *Bird by Bird*, Anne Lamott (1995) reminds us all writers struggle with finding focus:

> *Often when you sit down to write, what you have in mind is an auto-biographical novel about your childhood, or a play about the immigrant*

**Often he who does too much does too little.**
—Italian proverb

*experience, or the history of—oh, say—women. But this is like trying to scale a glacier. It's hard to get your footing, and your fingertips get all red and frozen and torn up.* (16)

When writers don't take a few minutes to narrow their topic, writing is a painful struggle. Narrow: Do well.

## Narrowing Focus with a Slice

Lucy Calkins tells us to write about small moments. Whitney Houston sang that we should write about "One Moment in Time." Okay, Whitney wasn't singing about writing, but it's good advice. Both remind us to write about a moment, not a lifetime. Metaphors to teach focus are nothing new: Calkins talks of watermelon seeds and Barry Lane talks about using your binoculars, but my favorite go-to metaphor for teaching focus is one I found more than ten years ago when I read the first edition of *Craft Lessons* (1998) by Ralph Fletcher and JoAnn Portalupi. They suggest using a pizza as a metaphor to teach students to narrow their focus.

Holding my writer's notebook, I look at my students. "One thing writers often struggle with is getting started. Where do I begin?"

Students nod.

"Part of the problem is selecting a focus that's too big. We've been talking about and reading some memoirs. How do we decide where to start our own?" I ask.

"You think about things you care about," Albert says.

"Sure," I say. "Let's do that now. Think of someone or something you care about—family members, friends, and places, events that really matter to you."

While students list, I circulate, nudging with a few clarifying questions, just loud enough that anyone else who is stuck can hear too.

We list a few of the students' topics on chart paper.

My Tia
My dog, kitten, snake (pet)
My birthday
Little/big brothers/sisters
My neighborhood
Best friend
Pop Warner football
Skateboarding
Extend-A-Care

"Our topics are coming into focus. Do you know what writers do next—after brainstorming or generating ideas?" I ask.

Several answers flow out: "write," "cluster," "outline." I acknowledge their thinking.

"One thing many writers skip actually makes writing easier. It only takes a minute but can save you hours later. You just have to pause and do this before you write."

I draw a big circle on the board (Figure 3.2). "Writing is like a pizza."

"My dog Paisley is a whole pizza." I write "My dog Paisley" above the circle. "If I start here, I have a whole pizza focus. That means I will tell my readers everything about Paisley."

Students draw their topics above their circles.

"But writers take one more step: They only write about one slice. A slice might be about the day I adopted her at the Animal Defense League. I can write about the time I was there, and what she did that made me want to take her home. That's a slice."

*Figure 3.2*
Focus on a Slice

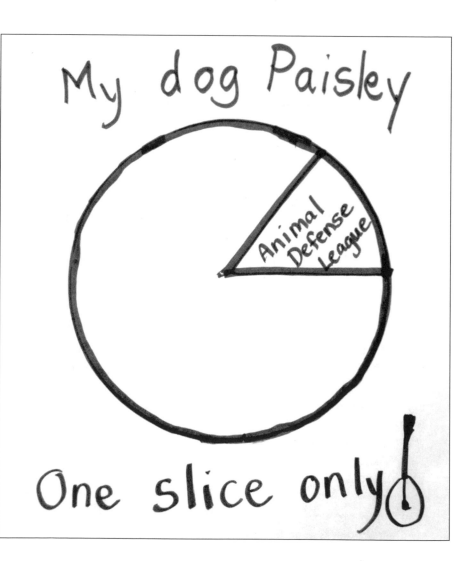

Students share their topics with partners. Together, they find possible slices. After we share, we help Gabriel, who got stuck. He wants to write about his grandma. He says, "I like going to her house after school."

"What do you like to do?" Jonquil asks.

"Play Yahtzee, make tamales, or watch *The Price Is Right*. She DVRs it." Gabriel says, smiling.

"His slice could be things he does after school with his grandma," Jonathan says.

Gabriel nods.

"Or just one of the things or a few of the things he does," I remind them. "Writers select what matters the most."

"But I wrote about my eleventh birthday. That's already a slice," Ramon says. "*Birthdays* is the whole pizza, and my eleventh one is a slice."

"You know, you're right. Your eleventh birthday is a slice, but it's dangerous to write about a whole day," I say. "It's so easy to forget what's important. Suddenly, we are writing about brushing our teeth. While this may be good for your teeth, it doesn't have anything to do with what's important about your birthday. Think about a part of the day you want to write about."

"We went to Chuck E. Cheese's and . . ."

"There's your slice, Ramon, or could there be even a slice of that?"

I play Whitney Houston in the background, commenting on the "one moment in time" lyric as we continue narrowing our focus, finding our slice.

Later, in reading workshop, we use the whole-pizza versus pizza-slice metaphor to discuss our reading. We note how the length of a piece of writing is about narrowing. Books narrow. Each Harry Potter book is about a certain time at Hogwarts, and then each chapter narrows to an aspect of that time. Articles narrow another way: Subheadings narrow. Asking well-placed questions, I facilitate this discovery as we read. We note when a writer takes on the whole pizza when a slice could've been a better solution. Students keep using the metaphor: "That's the whole pizza" or "This is just a slice." The metaphor sticks and works throughout the year.

When writing argumentative essays, controversies and issues they care about are narrowed before writing. Using this narrowed, controlling idea helps students revise their writing. What stays in; what goes? For example, one student wanted to write about kids wearing whatever they wanted to school, and then narrowed it to one slice—tattoos—which he later expanded to tattoos and piercing.

A word of caution: Sometimes we start writing or researching and realize our focus may still be too wide and we narrow it more. It's important to keep the scope narrow, but it is possible to be too narrow. Sometimes we have to widen the scope again. Sometimes we have to change our focus completely; sometimes we alter it a bit. Writing is a process, without one-size-fits-all answers, evolving and changing as we write.

## Taking a Nonfiction Topic Down a Few Rungs

When students write nonfiction, I expand the idea of narrowing focus. How do we take a big fat idea and slenderize it? We take our big ideas down the ladder of abstraction (Hayakawa 1990), a process of step-by step or rung-by-rung narrowing: each descending rung becomes more concrete and less abstract; more specific, less vague; more focused, less broad. In fact, giving kids broad topics that they narrow is a great prereading activity.

When my students study inventions in social studies, I write "inventions" on the top rung of a ladder I'd drawn on the board (see Figure 3.3). "*Invention* could be narrowed to *American inventions* because *American inventions* narrows which inventions we'll talk about." I write "American Inventions" on the rung beneath "Inventions." "How can we narrow American Inventions even further?"

"Time periods?" asks Jacob.

"Yeah. American inventions like we are studying. In the industrial age," says Sean.

*Figure 3.3*

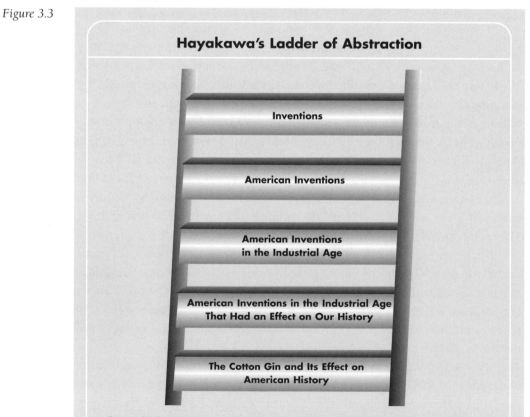

**Hayakawa's Ladder of Abstraction**

- Inventions
- American Inventions
- American Inventions in the Industrial Age
- American Inventions in the Industrial Age That Had an Effect on Our History
- The Cotton Gin and Its Effect on American History

Students take broad topics at the top of the ladder of abstraction, and bring them to more concrete topics by narrowing the categories, rung-by-rung, down the ladder.

I continue modeling how to descend the ladder. Moving from "American Inventions in the Industrial Age," we narrow again to "American Inventions in the Industrial Age That Had an Effect on Our History." We continue narrowing the focus until we get to the bottom and a *specific invention*. They may pick other inventions to research, but the process of narrowing topics has begun.

## To the Ladders

The next day I display the words *transportation* or *unfair* to groups of students, and they pick one and shrink the focus. The processing and discussing is key. Students hear their ideas bump against one another, giving them options for narrowing any topic. This thought process is important to develop and can save writers untold time. Narrowing is something students should do regularly as writers. Since the ladder activity is quick, it can be repeated throughout the year, especially before research reports.

In the student examples shown in Figure 3.4, I helped students generate the last sentence. The ladder brings writers closer to a one-sentence focus, the one dominant thought you want your reader to obtain. Everything we write should elaborate on, connect to, support, or reinforce the dominant thought.

After this activity, Ramon said, "This will help with Google searches." I knew the process was getting through. If students take an idea down the ladder several times, they build a pathway in the brain that helps them narrow topics and focus with fluency and ease.

# Maintain Your Focus

Once we narrow our topic or scope, we make a promise to our reader: Whatever we say we'll write about, we write about. We don't trick a reader. Our lead, our thesis, our theme, our title, our position statement, our words, our tone, our mood all make a promise of what we intend to say.

Have you ever wondered why your high school English teachers were so hell-bent on seeing your thesis or position statements *before* you wrote your essay? They wanted you to focus. They wanted you to make a promise. They wanted assurance that you knew where the boundaries were, that you knew where the edges were of what you planned to say.

If readers grab a book and scan the title, subtitle, and illustrations, they expect a certain content, tone, and scope to follow. For example, if they pick up Rita Williams-Garcia's *One Crazy Summer*, they'll be disappointed if it's really *The Chicago Manual of Style* on the inside. The title is a different promise—a different focus—a different content, a different scope. The author

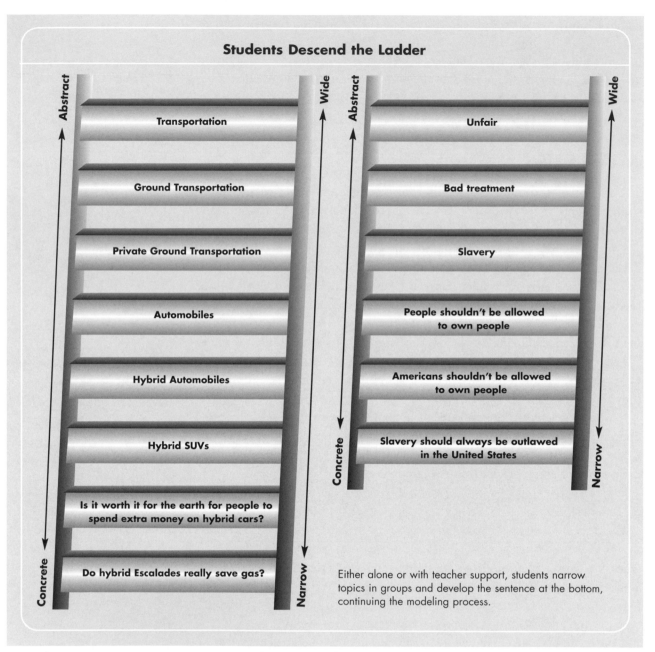

**Students Descend the Ladder**

Abstract → Concrete | Transportation / Ground Transportation / Private Ground Transportation / Automobiles / Hybrid Automobiles / Hybrid SUVs / Is it worth it for the earth for people to spend extra money on hybrid cars? / Do hybrid Escalades really save gas? | Wide → Narrow

Abstract → Concrete | Unfair / Bad treatment / Slavery / People shouldn't be allowed to own people / Americans shouldn't be allowed to own people / Slavery should always be outlawed in the United States | Wide → Narrow

Either alone or with teacher support, students narrow topics in groups and develop the sentence at the bottom, continuing the modeling process.

*Figure 3.4*

and editors of *One Crazy Summer* promised readers this book would be about one crazy summer. When readers open the book and see the first chapter is titled "Cassius Clay Clouds," that sounds crazy. Check.

Focus works on another level too—maintaining what you promise, staying on track, no detours; everything comes back to the central idea, theme, or focus.

> *Good thing the plane had seatbelts and we'd been strapped in tight before takeoff. Without them, the last jolt would have been enough to throw Vonetta into orbit and Fern across the aisle. Still, I anchored myself and my sisters best as I could to brace us for whatever came next. Those clouds weren't through with us yet and dealt another Cassius Clay-left-and-a-right jab to the body of our Boeing 727.*
>
> *Vonetta shrieked, then stuck her thumb in her mouth. Fern bit down on Miss Patty Cake's pink plastic arm. I kept my whimper to myself. It was bad enough that my insides squeezed in and stretched out like a monkey grinder's accordion—no need to let anyone know how frightened I was.*

In this chapter, Williams-Garcia maintains her focus. Three sisters are on a trip to visit their mom for the summer. The bumpy ride through the angry clouds recurs throughout the chapter, adding to the drama of how out of the ordinary this is for the girls, and how alone they are. In the rest of the chapter, readers learn that the girls' father and grandmother, Big Ma, who have been raising them, finally decided the girls should see their mother, Cecile. Even a small element like the clouds being Cassius Clay clouds is extended to communicate a part of the story. The clouds contribute to the weather's craziness, punching the plane, while the name Cassius Clay acts as a vehicle to reveal to readers how Big Ma feels about change in general and about the girls seeing Cecile in particular.

> *Big Ma—that's Pa's mother—still says Cassius Clay. Pa says Muhammad Ali or just Ali. I slide back and forth from Cassius Clay to Muhammad Ali. Whatever picture comes to mind. With Cassius Clay you hear the clash of fists, like the plane getting jabbed and punched. With Muhammad Ali you see a mighty mountain, greater than Everest, and can't no one knock down a mountain.*

At this point, you may ask, so what? Does this matter? Is this part of the focus? (Good focus questions, by the way!) And then Williams-Garcia neatly threads in that "however things are stamped in Big Ma's mind is how they will be, now and forever. Idlewild will never be JFK, Cassius Clay will never be Muhammad Ali. Cecile will never be anything other than Cecile." This links back to the idea that the narrator doesn't really know who Cecile, her mom, will be to her. It's possible she will be Mom, but will she just be Cecile? This tension hints at a crazy summer.

Description and detail work to maintain and enhance focus when they point back to or support the central idea or focus. As we draft, revise, and give our writing its final edit, we consider whether each description or detail will sharpen or blur the focus. Although writers consider focus as we plan, we continue to question ourselves throughout the writing process:

- What have we promised?
- Are we fulfilling it?
- What stays?
- What needs clarification or transition to show the relationship to our focus?
- What goes?

Successful writers stay true to their promise. If they write about the reasons people should recycle plastic, they don't write about composting. Composting may be great, but it's outside the promised focus.

# Use Audience and Purpose to Shape Your Focus

Clarifying our audience and purpose is one way to help your writing come into focus. Audience affects what we write, how much, and the examples and details we emphasize, as well as the words and tone we choose. The Common Core State Standards Initiative says writers "appreciate nuances, such as how the composition of an audience should affect tone . . ." (2010, 7). Who is this writing for and how should I adjust what I include, considering my audience? My purpose also shapes what I say, what angle(s) or aspects I choose. What will I include? What will I leave out? What important commonalities or threads do I see? In other words, what's my point?

Students come to us aware of audience and purpose; we just have to apply their knowledge to their own writing. Students already talk one way to friends, one way to teachers, one way to principals, and another way to parents. If they want to persuade one of these audiences, they already adjust. We must use what is familiar to understand what is unfamiliar. We need to tap into students' innate ability to adjust for different audiences. Writers do the same thing when writing.

- What message do we want to send (purpose)?
- Who is this message directed to (audience)?
- How will this audience ideally be able to receive this message?

Who is the intended audience? A five-year-old? A store manager? Your Mom? Your purpose for writing even affects the genre you use. Am I writing a letter, list, short answer, essay, or novel? Is it fiction or nonfiction? Purpose and audience affect our kickoff, our initiating moment, our lead. Writers ask:

- What will appeal to this reader?
- What am I trying to achieve?

*Figure 3.5*

**Focus Finder Card**

1.  What's one thing that surprised you?
2.  What's one thing that will surprise your reader?
3.  If your reader could take away only one thing, what would that be?
4.  What kinds of questions will your reader have?
5.  What image sticks in your mind?
6.  What's the most important quote you heard or read?
7.  What's one sentence that says what you want to say?

*Based on questions by Don Murray* (1993).
See appendix for a Focus Finder Card template for photocopying.

- What's the best genre to achieve my purpose?
- How do I set the appropriate tone?

## All Leads Point to Focus: That's Their Purpose

When writing a lead we may:

- Describe a character's face or the setting
- Use a quote
- Narrate a conflict or action

We may uncover a lead in the collecting phase of reading, interviewing, and observing. It's a writer's job to watch for those events, quotes, and images that crystallize focus. After collecting, we stand back and process, finding those images or quotes that sharpen our particular angle or focus or show us a common thread. For some ideas on the kinds of questions we might ask to find focus before, during, and after collecting ideas, I give students a list like the Focus Finder card (see Figure 3.5).

See Chapter 6, "Frames," for more on leads.

## Purpose-Audience Lottery

When we start a letter to a friend, we do it one way. Check out the Purpose-Audience Lottery described in Figure 3.6 for one way to get kids thinking about purpose and audience.

---

**Purpose-Audience Lottery**

- Photocopy and cut *Purpose-Audience Lottery* sheet, found in the appendix, so each student will have his or her own audience and purpose slip.

- Label one jar *audience* and the other *purpose*. Put slips in respective jars.

- Let students pull one strip from each jar when they enter class. Direct them not to share them with anyone.

- Students write for about five minutes, using the **purpose** and **audience** on the sheets of paper they chose.

- Students share their writing randomly, and others guess the purpose and audience.

- The class discusses how they determine the audience and purpose, as well as the adjustments we make every day to fit our message and audience.

*Figure 3.6*

# Find a Unifying Thread or Pattern

Once students have grasped the idea of narrowing broad topics, I extend this idea by showing them higher levels of focus that require students to see patterns and synthesize. We may not always want to narrow a topic to a solitary issue. A focus can be about multiple things as long as one common thread or relationship is found among them.

Relationships between seemingly separate ideas can start to make their own whole when we stand at a distance, searching for patterns.

## Give Us Our Daily Thread

In *700 Sundays*, Billy Crystal writes about his father through the thread of his father's one day off—Sunday. Since his father worked six days a week as a plumber, he was only home on Sundays. Crystal calculated he spent about 700 Sundays with his father. Crystal selected Sundays as a narrow lens or thread to reflect on his relationship with his father.

Inspired by Crystal, students and I begin keeping a day journal. Every Monday we write in our writer's notebook about Sunday or another day of the week. We select which day will be our lens, but once we choose it, we stick with it. After several months, students reread and look for patterns and threads beyond the day of the week.

## Taking Just One Bite

I show students how to find a common thread with Lola Schaefer's picture book *Just One Bite*. Schaefer describes the actual size of a bite for eleven animals, from a worm to a whale.

After reading it aloud, I ask, "What's the focus of *Just One Bite*?"

Students turn and talk with a partner. Some argue the book isn't focused because it's about several different animals; others argue it's about how big a bite each animal takes. We eventually arrive at the fact that *Just One Bite* may include eleven different animals, but it has a tight focus. The size of each bite the eleven animals takes is the thread woven throughout the book.

As a writing teacher, I love the double meaning of the title *Just One Bite*. Not only is the book about the size of one bite for various animals, it is also a metaphor to not bite off more than you can chew—or write. Take the right-sized bite for the writing task. For Billy Crystal, the chapter-book-sized bite is 700 Sundays. In an essay, we might tackle a few Sundays or one representative Sunday. Like the bite of the whale, this would often be considerably larger in scope than what most students will tackle. Schaefer's picture-book bite is smaller, but both Schaefer and Crystal took an angle—a common thread—to convey their story or information. And these threads shape and maintain each author's focus.

Expository texts like *Just One Bite* inspire students to make sense of all the information and data that swirl about them in their day-to-day lives.

- What threads or patterns surface in their writing?
- What's another way to see this series of events or information?

These are the kinds of questions I want young writers to ask themselves—igniting thought—which leads to focused writing.

> Each thought has a size, and most are about three feet tall, with the level of complexity of a lawnmower engine . . . or one of those tubes of toothpaste that, by mingling several hidden pastes and gels, create a pleasantly striped product.
> —Nicholson Baker

# Discover Your Focus by Writing

What do writers do when they don't know what to focus on? We've examined ways to narrow a topic, but sometimes writing—simply writing—kicks off a legitimate path to discover what you need to say.

Some people say you don't know what you have till it's gone. Writers often say, I don't know what I have to say until I start writing. Once we start writing, almost like magic, ideas begin to flow, and in that flow, we often uncover our focus. Students started the freewriting journey in Chapter 1, on motion—writing without stopping for a set period of time. This is the crux of another strategy Peter Elbow (1998) calls *looping*, which adds a fresh twist to freewriting and can help writers discover a focus.

## Looping to Find Focus

Eliseo, a former student of mine and current eighth grader, stops by my room for help with an American history assignment. The teacher assigned an essay

> You are learning what you aren't writing, and this is helping you find out what you are writing.
> —Anne Lamott

or short research paper about the Civil War. Eliseo is stumped. This is a common issue: Students are given a broad assignment, which gives them a lot of choices, and students freeze.

I remind Eliseo freewriting is one way to find what you need to say. Write for a set period of time without stopping.

"But this is social studies!" Eliseo protests.

"Writing is writing," I say. "Just start writing about the Civil War for five minutes." I set the timer and point at a desk. Here is what Eliseo jotted in five minutes, while I prepared for my next class.

> The civil war was a long time ago when people in the same country started fighting over what each other was doing. In the south people wanted slaves to work in their fields of cotton so they could be rich, so they wanted to keep slaves. But some people in the north, they started thinking it wasn't human to own other humans, so they wanted the south to stop but the south didn't stop, so the South tried to be its own country, but then the North made them come back and get rid of slavery, which I was reading caused a lot of people in the south to be really mad because they couldn't have someone work their fields for cheap anymore, which I heard on the History Channel is what caused the KKK to come into . . .

When the timer rings, I ask Eliseo to reread what he's written, scouring for a word, phrase, or a sentence that "tugs at you" and circle it.

"Now, skip a line, write that phrase, and start writing again, seeing where that takes you." Since Eliseo watches the History Channel a lot, he saw some other parallels he wanted to explore.

### Mad Because of Losing

> After people lose a war they are mad and they want to find a way to get even. The Germans were mad after the Great War, well it's called War War I now, but before WW II it was called the great war. Anyway, the Germans lost WW I and were really pissed off and had to pay all this money and then they wanted to get even, so that's how the Nazi party got going. And it was the same after the Civil War, they were mad. My Dad says that when the first Iraq war happened it made the Iraqis mad so they wanted to do harm to us. I wonder what . . .

The lunch bell rang, and Eliseo had to go. He closed his binder. "I think I know what I'm going to do now."

I remind him as he runs out the door that he can repeat looping another time or two to see what focus emerges. The next day in the hall I tell Eliseo

Figure 3.7

**Finding Focus with Peter Elbow's (1998) Looping**

1. Select a general topic, word, or phrase.
2. Write for a set period of time, 5–10 minutes.
3. Reread what you have written.
4. Find a word, phrase, or sentence that tugs at you.
5. Skip a line and write that word, phrase, or sentence.
6. Write about that word, phrase, or sentence for a set period of time.
7. Repeat one to two more times.
8. Note what surfaces. Have you found a focus—or found what your focus isn't?

how his writing made me think about an ee cummings quote, "Hate bounces." He made me write it on a sticky note and ran off. He was exploring thinking, looking for patterns, and trying to make sense of war.

Looping can be done before or after you research, but it's one way to discover what needs to be said or, more important, what you want to say (see Figure 3.7).

# Capture Focus with Leads

Every time we model and read leads, we're also building schema for focus. In *All About Sleep: From A to Zzzz*, Elaine Scott kicks off her book with three spectacular narrative events of high interest, approaching the mystery of sleep and, in doing so, sets the tone: factual but not overly serious and perhaps a bit quirky. We even catch her tone from her humorous subtitle: *From A to Zzzz*. The subject is sleep, but this book will focus on interesting facts that aren't widely known. This writer has made a promise of the tone and scope of her book.

Since Elaine Scott had more than sixty pages to write her book, it makes sense that her scope is from A to Z, or all about sleep. I pose this to the class and then ask, "What if we were writing an essay? If we're not planning on writing a book, how could we narrow this to a more manageable report- or essay-sized piece of writing? If you're looking for essay length, where could we look in nonfiction books to see that size of chunk?"

Students stare at me blankly.

"Okay, let's look at the first chapter." I open the book and read the title of the first chapter, "'Everything Sleeps.' Let's see how the author used her lead paragraph to set a smaller focus than all about sleep." I read aloud the lead.

> *Fruit flies sleep. So do giraffes. Some birds can sleep while they fly.*

"She just starts naming how everything sleeps." Lisa says, "That matches."

"So listing a few things can be a good lead," I say, "and it's also a way to bring our writing into focus."

"And it *matches* the title," Lisa repeats.

"True. Good observation, Lisa."

"I never really thought about fruit flies sleeping," Dwayne says.

"You're right, Dwayne. If the author listed *People sleep. Dogs sleep. Cats sleep,* who'd care? The author wouldn't have given the reader anything fresh or beyond the obvious. But here," I tap the page, "she's got me, and she has a focus."

## Focus Checkup

The next day, we review our discussion about focus and read the rest of the "Everything Sleeps" chapter, evaluating whether the chapter maintains its focus.

> *Green plants "sleep" at night by folding their leaves and closing tiny pores, called stomata, that are on the undersides of leaves. During the day, the stomata open to take in sunlight and carbon dioxide while they release oxygen. The sunlight, carbon dioxide, and water from the plant's stem combine to create sugar. At night, the process stops. While the plant "sleeps," the sugar gets turned into starch so the plants can store it. Later it will become fats and protein—plant food! This process is called photosynthesis, which is a Greek word that means "combining with light."*

Alicia notes how even the author's paragraphs have a focus. "That paragraph is all about plants," she shouts after I read this paragraph.

"But it's all about sleeping plants. Our books can have a focus, our chapters or sections or essays can have a focus, and so can our paragraphs," I say.

## Exploring Focus in Reading Workshop

Many reading skills mirror writing skills. For example, every time readers predict what a selection will be about, they are predicting the focus of the writing based on the clues the author provides.

Later in reading workshop, we extend the *All About Sleep* activity, applying what we'd discovered to our independent reading. "Before we read," I say, "let's first look at the title." I point to the title of my book by Neil Gaiman. "*The Graveyard Book.* Then, check out the lead of the book." I read the lead: "'There was a hand in the darkness, and it held a knife.' Does it match the title?"

We discuss. "Now you try." Students jot their observations about their books into their reading log. "Now let's look at another chapter the same way," I say, "the title, then the lead." We discuss these questions:

- Was the focus hinted at in the title, lead, and first few paragraphs? How?
- Did the writer stay on focus in this section?
- If the writer went out of focus, did he or she connect the information to the focus?

# Summarize to Hone Your Focus

Focus is found in summary. When we summarize, we cut away the clutter, honing writing down to a dominant thought or idea, the essential message. Main idea and controlling idea are synonymous with focus. This is another way reading and writing connect. We summarize what we read, and, in revision, we can use this same skill. Summarizing what we have written, or having others summarize it, illuminates how successfully we maintained our focus.

> The job of a headline is to give a tightly compressed summary.
>
> —David Eagleman

- What is the point of the writing?
- What message are readers receiving?
- Are readers getting the message we want?

## Summary Lovin': Focused So Fast

To make summary more concrete for students, I take a strong piece of nonfiction and model how being an interactive reader and taking notes helps us stay in tune with an author's focus.

"I am going to read a passage from Chapter 2, 'Armed to the Teeth,' in Russell Freedman's nonfiction book on World War I history, *The War to End All Wars*." I write both titles on the board while talking. "Based on the title of this chapter," I point, "and the title of this of the book," I point, "what do you think will be its focus?"

Students turn, talk, and predict. After a quick detour to look up the origin of the idiom "armed to the teeth" (see Figure 3.8), we agree that the focus of the chapter will be weapons in World War I.

"Can you imagine a time when I'd say to write less, write fewer words?" I ask.

"Well, you don't want us to write on the desk," says Diego, "I *know* that."

> Summary is one of the most powerful ways of teaching focus—and for teaching writing in general. It requires a writer to zero in on what matters most and to express that message in a condensed, no-wasted-words form.
>
> —Vicki Spandel

*Figure 3.8*

---

### Origin of "Armed to the Teeth"

According to the *American Heritage Dictionary of Idioms*, "armed to the teeth" means well equipped. In the fourteenth century, it referenced knights who wore head-to-foot armor. The expression gained its more figurative use as "well equipped" when referencing armies' weapon stock in the 1800s.

---

"That's right. But this isn't about writing on your desk." I scan the class's faces, waiting.

Faces scrunch. Bodies squirm.

"How many of you were taught to take notes while you read?"

"My teacher said you had to take lots of notes, so you'll pass the test," Tristan says.

"It is important to take a few notes," I say. "But sometimes we take so many notes, it stops being helpful. I want you to try something different."

I read a three-paragraph section, one paragraph at time, pausing after each paragraph for students to help me choose one word that best represents that paragraph, a summative word.

> European powers had been fighting one another for centuries, but as the summer of 1914 began, Europe was at peace. Alfred Nobel, the Swedish inventor of dynamite and founder of the Nobel Peace Prize, had predicted that his powerful explosives might very well put an end to all war. Rather than annihilate one another, the nations of Europe would have to settle future disputes through negotiation and compromise.

"What's an important word that sums up the focus of this paragraph?" I ask. After students turn and talk, we discuss possibilities.

"I can only use one word, right?" Shauna asks.

"Yep, one word that's in the passage or one that you think represents, synthesizes, or gives you gist of the paragraph."

"Can you say *un*-peace?" Terrance said.

"Oh, coining words, I like it, Terrance." Terrance looks like he thinks I'm displeased, or should I say unpleased. "No, I really like your answer. Tell me more about why that's your word."

"Well, they are talking about how dynamite will make peace, but I don't *think* so."

We list a few other one-word possibilities, but stick with Terrance's *un-peace.*

I display the next paragraph, reading it aloud.

> *Close economic ties among European countries also made a major war seem unlikely. Prosperity depended on international trade and cooperation.*

After some discussion, we select *cooperation* as our summative word or focus. I continually link the words *focus* and *summary*, highlighting their connection.

> *In addition, there were blood ties linking Europe's royal houses. Kaiser Wilhelm II of Germany and King George V of Great Britain, grandsons of Britain's Queen Victoria, were cousins. Czar Nicholas II of Russia was a cousin by marriage: His wife, Alexandra, was one of Victoria's granddaughters. Another granddaughter, Ena, was queen of Spain. Except for France and Switzerland, every nation in Europe was a monarchy, and almost every European head of state was related to every other.*

This time partners settle on and write a word on their own. We share, settling on *relatives* or *relationships*. It is a tie. Students try the next one on their own.

> *Most Europeans looked forward to a peaceful future. "The world is moving away from military ideals," declared the influential British journal* Review of Reviews, *"and a period of peace, industry, and worldwide friendship is dawning." It was easy enough to ignore the rivalries and suspicions among Europe's great powers that spelled trouble ahead.*

This passage is the most difficult, so it sparks interesting conversation. We decide they weren't stupid because they didn't know World War I was coming like we do. We settle on *hopeful*, but I also share the word *denial* with students. Some prefer that.

## Revise Writing with a One-Word Focus

Later, in writing workshop, we talk about how we could use this one-word focus activity to summarize as readers and to revise as writers. As we reread our writing, we ask what kind of promises we make with our titles as well as about our writing's overall focus. Do our paragraphs have a central idea or focus?

In a conference with Jasmine, she shows me a persuasive essay she is drafting to convince the principal that multiple piercings are not distracting. "So, read the first paragraph to me," I say.

"Don't run!"

"Hurry up!"

"Get to class!"

"Slow down!" This is the life of a middle school student. No matter what you do, it's wrong, right? I am barely a teenager, and already I can see that extra piercings are not the problem. Extra piercings make students happier so they can learn. Extra piercings probably make more blood flow and stuff. Next, we will be monitored for how much makeup we wear. I already have to tuck in my shirt. "Tuck it in! That's too tight." Is it any wonder kids skip school? I am sick of this place.

"I like your lead."

"You do?" Jasmine asks, shocked.

"It lets an adult see how you might feel about rules. You've got a lot of great ideas here, Jasmine."

"But I have to write more, right?"

"I wouldn't say more. Let's break up what you have and see what happens when we expand it. Remember the one-word focus. What's one word that would describe each of your paragraphs?

She reads. "One should be about how the piercings aren't hurting nobody."

"What's one word that says that?"

"No harm?" Jasmine asks, unsure.

"We try for one, but two can work. So you'll need a whole paragraph explaining *no harm*, and you don't start your other arguments until you finish that one." We review the things she knows about from our study of persuasion—anecdotes, examples, quotes—that might help her prove *no harm* to her audience.

At the end of writing workshop, she shares her revision and asks the other writers to give her one word. As Lisa would say, "They matched!" Jasmine beamed. Focus, a paragraph at a time, builds unity and coherence as well. It shows us where our details fit, and how many we need to communicate.

## What Was the Focus?

Questions help. And there is no question that narrowing our topics helps us focus, and simply writing helps too. Thinking about purpose, audience, and scope help too. When writers look for patterns and threads that make their writing one, patterns emerge. When we have our focus, writing works and our goal is reached.

# Detail

## Selecting the Concrete and Necessary

*The details always tell the story.*

—James McBride

With well-selected detail, writing transforms from the page to a movie in the reader's mind. Detail proves your point by illuminating your ideas with examples, providing the evidence readers need. Detail focuses on the concrete and particular rather than the abstract and general. It moves an idea from an abstraction to a concrete, well-drawn person, place, or thing, which readers can connect to their experiences in the world.

Detail appeals to the senses, making images readers can reach out and touch, see, smell, taste, and feel. In fiction and in nonfiction, detail creates characters or describes real people who appear three dimensional within the limitation of the two-dimensional page. Detail places a reader in a setting or location, creating the slant of light, weather, time period, condition, or topography—anything in the world that is relevant to establishing your point or telling your story.

Detail also logically supports what we say with evidence: facts, references, or quotations. When we write a literary analysis, detail may be the quotation from the text that illustrates exactly the point we assert about the writer or the selection. When we write expository text, we layer detail using

> There is no way to understand the world without first detecting the radar-net of our senses. Our senses connect us intimately to our past, connect us in ways that most of our cherished ideas never could.
>
> —Diane Ackerman

**61**

*Figure 4.1*

### Making DETAIL Work

- Show rather than tell.
- Come to your senses.
- Share not-what-everybody-else-would-notice details.
- Support with layers of facts, resources, and quotes.
- Select, summarize, expand, and delete.
- Use grammatical structures to embed detail in your writing.

> The emphasis of one detail of color or form or arrangement, the repression of another, make the difference between the poet's description of a landscape and the real-estate agent's.
>
> —Elsie Nutting

explanation and examples. As Henry James says, "An ounce of example is worth a pound of generalities."

Detail also needs to follow the Goldilocks rule—the rule of being "just right"—not too little or too much. We provide enough detail for readers to construct meaning in their minds, yet we don't overwhelm them with so much that it becomes weighed down and cumbersome. What we include and what we leave out, what we emphasize and what we suppress have incredible influence on readers' comprehension.

In this chapter, we will explore what writers do to make detail work (see Figure 4.1). Along the way, we'll see how these strategies come alive through reading, talking, and writing.

# Show Rather Than Tell

We know most students think "a little dab of detail will do ya," so I make detail concrete, moving it from the abstraction of explaining detail to real examples that show rather than tell. I start with what detail actually is and isn't.

## Show and Tell with *Factory Girl*

At the opening of class, I read aloud this rather brief piece of writing displayed on the whiteboard:

> She needed a job. A lot. She was hungry. She was poor. She went in a candy store to get a job.

After I read the passage, I ask, "What do you think?"
"Who's *she*?" Amanda asks.

> Details make stories human, and the more human a story can be, the better.
>
> —V. S. Pritchett

"A good question," I say. "Readers ask questions. Writers anticipate and answer them."

"Why is she hungry?" Anthony asks.

"So, this writing leaves us with more questions than answers. That's a problem," I pause. "What else do you see?"

"*A lot* shouldn't be two words."

It is interesting that students want to search writing for surface errors, often wanting to correct something that is already accurate. "I am glad you noticed *a lot*. A lot can be a problem word, but guess what? *A lot* is two words." Students continue commenting: it's boring; needs details; isn't making any pictures. They seem quite happy to rip it to shreds.

Next, I display the following passage from Barbara Greenwood's *Factory Girl*:

> *Emily Watson peered in through the shop window. The afternoon sun made a mirror of the glass, forcing her to shade her eyes to see inside. A long counter ran along one wall. On top were glass cases holding trays of candies—mounds of chocolate balls, butterscotch pennies, peppermint lozenges. Emily's mouth watered. Halfway along the counter stood a cash register, its gold paint glinting in the sunlight. The lady behind it was plump and motherly. And she was alone. Emily glanced again at the small sign in the window: Help Wanted.*
>
> *She tugged down her too-short jacket and smoothed her skirt. Then, taking a deep breath, she pushed open the door. The jingle of the bell startled her.*

After I read the excerpt aloud, I ask, "What do you notice?"

"She says more," Jackie replies.

"Tell me what you mean."

"It answers questions like you said," Sabrina says.

"Yeah, you know who the person is," Josh pauses. "She gives hints."

"Josh, you just hit on one of the biggest things we need to know about writing. When we share detail, sometimes we give hints instead of telling. It's called . . ." I write *Show rather than tell* on the board.

I make a T-chart on the whiteboard. On the right-hand side, I write the heading *Telling*. Underneath, I write *She was hungry*. "That's telling. How did Barbara Greenwood show that she was hungry?

"It says her mouth watered."

"Could you read me the quote exactly?" I write it on the chart under the heading of *Showing* on the left-hand side of the T-chart. (See Figure 4.2.)

Another student adds that looking for a job could indicate she was hungry. Students are inferring and involved.

We look again at the first two items on the list.

| Show, Don't Tell | |
|---|---|
| **Showing** | **Telling** |
| Emily's mouth watered. | She was hungry. |
| Emily glanced again at the small sign in the window: Help Wanted. | She needed a job. |
| She tugged down her too-short jacket and smoothed her skirt. Then, taking a deep breath, she pushed opened the door. The jingle of the bell startled her. | She was poor. |
| A long counter ran along one wall. On top were glass cases holding trays of candies—mounds of chocolate balls, butterscotch pennies, peppermint lozenges. Emily's mouth watered. Halfway along the counter stood a cash register, its gold paint glinting in the sunlight. | It was a candy store. |

*Figure 4.2*

"Isn't that interesting? The same amount of words shows rather than tells." Pointing to the sentences (*Emily's mouth watered* and *She was hungry*), I ask, "Which do you like better?"

"I like the mouth watering," Jackie says.

"Why?"

"Well, it makes you, experience it or something," Rodolfo says. "It helps you connect."

"Readers connect," I say. "Writers give readers something to connect to—an experience, like our mouth watering. We know that means we are hungry, yet we still have to be involved and do part of the work as a reader and make meaning. '*Emily's mouth watered*' asks readers to participate, to be a part of the process. '*She was hungry*' does all the work, which is sometimes boring for readers."

"But I like it when it just says what it means: She's hungry," Alberto says.

"Sometimes we need to tell it like it is," I say.

We continue adding other *telling* ideas from the first reading and the *showing* counterparts. (See Figure 4.2.)

## Characters Welcome: Selecting Detail

To continue refining our ideas about what effective detail is, I share these character descriptions from Rick Riordan's *The Lightning Thief*, one at a time. I display this paragraph on my whiteboard:

*Mr. Brunner was this middle-aged guy in a motorized wheelchair. He had thinning hair and a scruffy beard and a frayed tweed jacket, which always smelled like coffee. You wouldn't think he'd be cool, but he told stories and jokes and let us play games in class. He also had this awesome collection of Roman armor and weapons, so he was the only teacher whose class didn't put me to sleep.*

After reading the paragraph, I ask the kids what words or phrases stick with them. When Elena mentions the worn tweed jacket, I ask her why she likes it. "I can see it," she says.

Next I throw in something false to make a point. "He did a good job of describing his shirt, belt, pants, and shoes and how shiny they are."

Students' brows wrinkle. We look back. "Oh, wait, he didn't do that. Huh. So, I guess, focusing on one item of clothing is enough to make it visual. Our brain takes one well-selected and -described piece of clothing and we see a person who would wear that."

We discuss who Mr. Brunner is and how we know, pondering what it would be like if Riordan described every last detail. Next, we read the next paragraph about another character.

*Mrs. Dodds was this little math teacher from Georgia who always wore a black leather jacket, even though she was fifty years old. She looked mean enough to ride a Harley right into your locker. She had come to Yancy halfway through the year, when our last math teacher had a nervous breakdown.*

"This time the author tells it like it is," Ruby says.

Students note how the leather jacket is described, not her hair and everything about her. Something significant is chosen. Not all teachers wear leather jackets, and this may give us a hint at the kind of person she is. Students love Riordan's line, "She looked mean enough to ride a Harley right into your locker." They also see how that makes the leather jacket more important, just as he also contrasts it with her age. Another visual. I emphasize again how writers use a mix of showing and telling. Sometimes it is better just to tell the reader she's a math teacher; other times, as with Mr. Brunner, hints are given and the reader infers.

We continue reading the passages. In another passage, the author reveals their grade levels and tells us Grover has muscular disease. Yet when describing Mr. Brunner, Riordan only says he's in a motorized wheelchair.

*Grover was an easy target. He was scrawny. He cried when he got frustrated. He must've been held back several grades, because he was the only sixth grader with acne and the start of a wispy beard on his chin. On*

The more specific you are, the more universal you are.
—Nancy Hale

*top of all that, he was crippled. He had a note excusing him from PE for the rest of his life because he had some kind of muscular disease in his legs. He walked funny, like every step hurt him, but don't let that fool you. You should've seen him run when it was enchilada day in the cafeteria.*

The last detail is a favorite because of the humor. Humor is all about specifics. *Some days he runs to the cafeteria* isn't the same as, "You should've seen him run when it was enchilada day in the cafeteria." Specifics matter, but not everything should or could be described in exacting detail.

"Sometimes we just want to say, *There was a farmhouse on the hill* instead of, *A structure protrudes from the dirt, rocks, and prairie grass, sitting high atop the outgrowth of land. The rock and stone go from the ground to the tile roof.*" We discuss the nature of writing. Too much of anything is, well, too much.

The next day, I use the following paragraph from the same chapter in *The Lightning Thief*:

> *Anyway, Nancy Bobofit was throwing wads of sandwich that stuck in his curly brown hair, and she knew I couldn't do anything back to her because I was already on probation. The headmaster had threatened me with death by in-school suspension if anything bad, embarrassing, or even mildly entertaining happened on this trip.*
>
> *"I'm going to kill her," I mumbled.*
>
> *Grover tried to calm me down. "It's okay. I like peanut butter."*
>
> *He dodged another piece of Nancy's lunch.*
>
> *"That's it." I started to get up, but Grover pulled me back to my seat.*
>
> *"You're already on probation," he reminded me. "You know who'll get blamed if anything happens."*
>
> *Looking back on it, I wish I'd decked Nancy Bobofit right then and there. In-school suspension would've been nothing compared to the mess I was about to get myself into.*

The students notice that there is no physical description of Nancy. We discover other ways people can be described:

- What others say about the character (dialogue or thoughts)
- Actions of the character

After studying the models, students think about a person—a teacher, friend, relative, or neighbor—that they could describe. Students turn and talk about the person they chose and significant characteristics about them: their hair, or lack of it, clothing, voice, hands. We recall "focus" and "selection," picking one article of clothing that is most telling or, should we say, most showing?

Students write for ten minutes in their writer's notebooks. At their tables, they share a sentence or two about one significant thing about their person. A few read their pieces aloud, and we have fun listening for the defining feature.

# Come to Your Senses

We experience the world through our five senses. We take in information from what we hear, see, feel, smell, and taste. If we want readers to share our experiences—even our thoughts and opinions—we use sensory detail to communicate concretely.

> The senses feed shards of information to the brain like microscopic pieces of a jigsaw puzzle.
>
> —Diane Ackerman

## Hey, Where Am I?

Without identifying the author or title, I ask students to close their eyes and listen as I read aloud this passage from Eric Schlosser's *Fast Food Nation* twice.

> *Pull open the glass door, feel the rush of cool air, walk in, get on line, study the backlit color photographs above the counter, place your order, hand over a few dollars, watch teenagers in uniforms pushing various buttons, and moments later take hold of a plastic tray full of food wrapped in colored paper and cardboard.*

Students write where they think the narrator is, and give two reasons to support their claim. We talk about why they think so, highlighting that specifics and sensory details tap into their experiences.

Then, with a partner, students create another "Come to Your Senses" passage, describing an event, like a school dance, or a place, like the cafeteria or locker room. This writing activity kicks off a smorgasbord of inferring and showing rather than telling.

For a revision experience, students reenter a piece they are writing and find a passage where they can show a setting or another detail, rather than simply tell. Afterward, we discuss whether their changes improve the writing.

For more work on this idea of detail and inferring, use an audio recording of Andy Griffith's "What It Was, Was Football," parts 1 and 2. You can download it off iTunes. I play it for my students and ask them to take notes and try to figure out what he is describing. Of course, don't share the title with them or it will be ruined.

## The One Who Smelt It

"Nothing is more memorable than smell," writes Diane Ackerman (1990) in *The Natural History of the Senses.* "Cover your eyes and you will stop seeing, cover your ears and you will stop hearing, but if you cover your nose and try to stop smelling, you will die" (6). This essential sense is rarely included in student descriptions, but nevertheless, it is one of the most powerful for connecting to our readers. While smells can be hard to name, we can conjure them with specific identification. Many times, authors use smells to describe characters, settings, or even a season, as Patricia McLachlan did in *Edward's Eyes*:

> *Summer always smelled like heat, the ocean, and the spines of old books.*

Helen Keller said, "Smell is a potent wizard that transports us across thousands of miles and all the years that we have lived. The odors of fruit waft me to my southern home, to my childhood frolics in the peach orchard." Smells are an important sense that can truly bring our readers into a moment or memory.

I share a passage from Kathi Appelt's memoir *My Father's Summers*. I ask students what words or phrases stick with them, which leads to a discussion of the power of smells.

> *What I wasn't used to was having his smell back, the smoke from his Camel cigarettes, his Old Spice After Shave, the shoe polish he used on his boots. All those father odors, filling up the house. My mother opened every window, waxed the wooden furniture, sprayed room freshener in every corner. She scrubbed the tiles on the bathroom floor, scrubbed the dog's water bowl, scrubbed her hair, her hands, her face, shiny. Then she sat in her convertible and wept it all away, all but the smell. "I can't scrub the air," she said. And so he was there, but not really.* (2004, 29)

We discuss how authors select significant things to connect to their reader—not everything. "Think of a person or a setting and a certain smell you associate with them or it." Students talk with partners for one minute.

In their writer's notebooks, students write a quick description of the certain smells of a person or setting. We share some of the most powerful writing my students have written all year.

Here is an additional sensory mentor text from *Savvy* by Ingrid Law. Students read with a partner and highlight and label all the senses they can find and rate each one from least powerful to most powerful.

> *As we rushed out into the spring night, the air was crisp and cool, laced with the smell of diesel fumes and chicken fingers. After a noisy babble and bedlam inside the restaurant, being outside was a relief, a soothing hush of sky and pavement. I could hear cars on the road in front of the diner, each sounding like nothing more than a wave lapping shore.*

# Share Not-What-Everybody-Else-Would-Notice Details

What interesting, fresh, attention-grabbing, out-of-the-ordinary factoid would appeal to and fascinate readers? Masters of the craft, such as Bill Bryson, can make anything interesting because they have a nose for the novel and the unexpected. In *At Home: A Short History of Private Life*, as he describes the history of private life, we find details that are fresher than fresh. For example, Bryson's chapter about the bathroom offers constant interesting tidbits:

> *The ancient Greeks were devoted bathers. They loved to get naked—gymnasium means "the naked place"—and work up a healthful sweat, and it was their habit to conclude their daily workouts with a communal bath.* (2010, 345)

If students are asked to research and report information, they have to consider whether an idea is fresh (and related) or merely a bit of common knowledge. This isn't obvious to young writers. Before we take on a formal research paper, we do a few activities to identify the difference between what is novel and interesting and what is common knowledge.

## Out of the Ordinary

I read this first passage and ask students, "What do you think?"

> Vanilla is a flavoring. Flavorings make things have tastes. People put vanilla in lots of things. It tastes good. It comes from the grocery store, and is found on the spice aisle. It's a brown liquid. You put it in cakes to make them taste better. It's the opposite of chocolate. Vanilla! Yum!

"Is this writing strong or weak?"
"I think it's strong?" Belinda's voice goes up at the end, making it a question.
"I don't know," Philip says, "It says stuff . . . but . . . it's . . ."
"Boring!" adds Jonathan.
It is in the comparing and contrasting of a strong and a weak piece that students begin to analyze the writing (Spandel 2011), to see and name what's in front of their noses. Next, I share a stronger piece from Anne Byrn's *The Cake Mix Doctor*:

> *In the humid tropical forests of the world, a giant climbing orchid vine called* Vanilla planifolia *grows. But on only one day of the year do*

*the orchid blossoms open. When they do, they are quickly hand-polli-nated, for their only natural pollinator is the overworked and vanishing Melipona bee . . . In ten months, the orchid produces mature pods, which are hand-picked while green, boiled, dried, and fermented to take on the characteristic brown color that we know as vanilla beans. . . .*

*Pure vanilla is twice as expensive as artificial vanillin, which is used in cake mix formulation and comes from pin, fir, and other wood pulp by-products.* (1999, 382)

After comparing the two passages on vanilla, students' confidence increases. "The first one just kept saying the same thing," Tristan says. "I mean, I know it's a flavor."

"Yeah, I thought it came from a brown bottle, not a flower."

"So," I say, "you didn't know that. What do you think that tells us?"

"Be interesting. Don't just say stupid things that everyone already knows."

"As writers, we have to search for what's beyond the obvious—beyond what everyone might notice." I pause. "Writers look harder. They dig deeper, and readers are rewarded with something interesting."

A few days later at the library, students choose a topic with a partner on their own or from a list I provide. I give them a note card and twenty-five minutes to find two or three interesting facts about their topic that they don't think everybody would already know and details that not everybody would notice.

On our way back to the classroom, two boys can't wait to get back to the room to say, "Abraham Lincoln's wife had issues. Yeah, she was one taco short of a combination platter." Two girls countered that they found out about Texas Indians. When food was scarce, they would hunt through their feces for undigested food to eat again. "They called it second harvest!" Research had never been so interesting. They experience it through talk and sharing examples rather than my simply telling them procedures and rules.

# Support with Layers of Facts, Resources, and Quotes

Writers support what they say. If they say computers are harmful or helpful to kids, they back their assertions up with facts, citing resources or providing meaningful quotes. To justify, defend, or support what they write, writers weave layers of evidence, giving ideas weight, demonstrating this is some-thing beyond a shoot-from-the hip opinion.

What kind of support does a writer need to provide? It depends on the purposes for which we write. In any case, writers anticipate readers' ques-tions and answer them (mostly), save for the purpose of suspense. As a rule, we don't leave our reader with too many questions for too long—or they get irritated. Annie Dillard advises, "Spend it all" (1989, 78). She recommends holding nothing back. Use it all now and something better will come later.

## Answer Readers' Questions in Layers

Layering information in a text is crucial, but how do we demonstrate this to students? One way into revision is the Ask Three Sticky Questions method. Before students do this with their own writing, I model with a nonfiction passage from Susanna Van Rose's *Volcano and Earthquake*. I display the first sentence of the paragraph.

> *Immense flashes of lightning are often seen during [volcanic] eruptions.*

"What questions would we want the writer to answer in the next sentence?" I ask. "Talk with a partner for one minute."

Students share a few of their questions: What causes the lightning? How does it happen? Is there rain?

I reveal what Van Rose wrote in her next few sentences.

> *Immense flashes of lightning are often seen during eruptions. They are caused by a buildup of static electricity produced when the tiny fragments of lava in an ash cloud rub against each other. The electrical charge is released in bolts that leap through the cloud, as they do in a thunderstorm.*

"She told us what it was like. It's like a thunderstorm, but it's not one," Alicia says.

"When you're reading in social studies and science class, pay attention to the questions that come up as you read. See if the author answers them," I say. "Part of what writers do is consider their audience and what facts or details they need to know to understand what you are trying to explain."

Students then read another passage from Van Rose, which I have triple spaced so students have room to jot in the questions they see the author answering.

> *Volcanoes and earthquakes are more common in some parts of the world than others. This was known early in the 19th century, but it was not until the 1960s, when secrets of the deep ocean floor began to be revealed, that scientists found an explanation. This became known as theory of plate tectonics. Tectonic is a Greek word that means "building." The tectonic theory says that the Earth's surface is fragmented into huge slabs called tectonic plates. These chunks of the Earth's crust move*

*across its surface in response to forces and movements deep within the planet. The plate boundaries where plates collide, grind past each other, or move apart are areas of intense geological activity. Most volcanoes and earthquakes occur at these boundaries.*

We discuss and highlight the layers of the discovery: naming it plate tectonics, telling what the word *tectonic* comes from, and then explaining what the theory says while comparing it to something familiar. Students begin to see a purpose for research—to back up what we say.

## Quoting History

"Any time we make a statement as a writer, we need to consider a reader asking, 'How do you know that?'" I ask. In the following passage from *Children of the Great Depression*, Russell Freedman first states how kids in the 1920s felt. How does he know? More important for us, what does he do to show us he knows?

> *Kids who could not tune in to the popular shows of the 1920s often felt isolated and lonely. "We are just poor renters on a farm and there is no money for a radio or the books I like so much," a fourteen-year-old Texas girl wrote to Eleanor Roosevelt. "Dear First Lady, I have read of your kindheartedness and the cheer you have brought so many. Can't you suggest some way I can get a radio so I can hear the music and talk and news from outside my very small little world?"*

Students notice how the author uses a quote from a letter. Is one enough? Not for Newbery Medal–winning author Russell Freedman. Both quotes from the letter make us feel the pain and isolation of the Great Depression.

## Sticky Questions: Revising to Answer Readers' Questions

Students pull out either a notebook entry, a completed piece from their writing folder, or an in-process piece, and then form groups of three; I distribute large sticky notes or note cards.

- The first writer reads aloud from his or her writing to the other two writers who listen.
- When the first writer reads, the other writers listen, jotting three or more questions about the writing (Elbow 1998; Gallagher 2006; Lane 1993) on a sticky note.
- After the writer finishes reading, listeners share their questions with the writer, who may or may not discuss the answers.

- Now the writer knows what questions readers have, developing an ability to think about the reader.
- Writers consider the questions as they revise.

At this point, students have six questions as a starting point for revision the next day. More important, the abstract advice—readers should anticipate questions—is now more concrete. Now, writers will begin thinking about answering readers' questions as they generate and revise their own texts.

Of course, we can't answer every reader's question every time, but writers consider what's crucial to their message. Layered writing is what strong detail is made of, not a list of new detail after new detail. Instead, the writer takes an idea and expands it so readers understand it before moving on to the next idea.

# Select, Summarize, Expand, and Delete

Every teacher has read a student essay describing some big, important day or event. The detail is often exacting—in the beginning. It's almost as if the student is saying, "You want detail? I'll give you detail." We get the onomatopoetic beeps of the alarm clock as the writer awakens; we experience in real time the irrelevant details of the writer's morning routine. Instead of fast forwarding to the important part of the day—the focus—we get deep detail about how soft the carpeting feels on the writer's feet as she walks across the floor and touches the cold metal doorknob.

We trudge down the hall with the writer, waiting endlessly for her sister to get ready and relinquish the bathroom. Then, disappointingly, we get every excruciating, mundane detail of the writer's hygiene. Soon the young writer tires and wants to be finished and quickly summarizes the key part—or focus—of the big day.

Writers need to know which ideas we select to expand and which we select to summarize or delete. How do we help them figure that out?

To students, writing every detail is the answer to the pounding drum of feedback: "Write with more detail." It isn't just *more* detail that readers need, it's the *right* detail. Which ideas do we expand and which do we summarize or delete? And just how do we show students to add only just-right details?

Until writers have decided on their focus or scope, it is almost impossible to select the essential details necessary to communicate what they have to say. Focus narrows; detail expands. "Focus before detail" is a good banner to fly across the mind of writers as they begin projects.

> Words have to be crafted, not sprayed.
> —Norman Cousins

## Selecting the Best Picture

When the students enter the classroom, "Photograph" by Nickelback plays in the background. I turn the music down low.

"We've been talking about how the power of detail isn't in piling on more and more as much as it is picking the right details. And if we are going to paint a picture of person or a character, we consider things they do, the kinds of things they say, and what others say about them, but readers also long for some clues about the person or character's appearance."

I pull out a photo of my brother and me in front of the largest pecan in the world. "This is one of my favorite memories with my dad and brother captured in a photo," I say. "Even when I don't have the photo with me, I carry around the memory of that day in my mind."

Students insist I pass the picture around. As they pass it, I say, "Think of a favorite photograph you or your family has—either a real one or one you carry around in your mind.

"We can also write photos—or images frozen in our mind—with words. Look how Sharon Creech writes about a picture with words in her novel *Replay*":

> Alone in the room Leo shares with his brothers, he opens his father's blue leather-bound book, his Autobiography, Age of Thirteen, *and stares at the photographs pasted there: one of his father at age two (according to the notation below the picture), sitting on a porch, arms raised high, as if he is reaching for the sky; and one of his father at twelve, in shorts, barefoot, sitting on porch steps, smiling. The boy does not look like his father, but he seems vaguely familiar.*

"What's Sharon Creech doing in the passage? Talk with a partner."
Students discuss how Leo finds a photograph and looks at actual pictures.
"Do you think those pictures he described were the only pictures in the notebook?"
An argument ensues in every group.
"If there were more pictures, he would have described them," Shauna insists.
"No way!" Jonathan's head swings. "If there were like a hundred million pages and pictures like my sister's stupid photo album, we'd be here forever."
We discuss whether Creech just shares a few pictures or whether those were the only ones in the book. And since we can't know for sure, we conclude that it's probably a good idea to pick a few, because too much of anything is too much. "As we keep reading these written pictures or photographs," I say, "Pay attention to what you think Sharon Creech was trying to do with these passages. What was she trying to accomplish?"

*Papa slogs in through the door, pouchy bags under his eyes, a mustard stain on his shirt.*

"I can really see this one."

"What makes you see it?"

Robert rereads the sentence. "I can see Papa is tired and he probably works at McDonald's."

"Why do you say that?"

"Mustard on his shirt and he's tired." Robert says. "McDonald's is busy all the time."

"Those inferences make sense with the clues the author gave you, Robert." I turn to the class. "See, it's all about the clues we leave for our readers. We don't have to and should not describe everything. If we pick the right things, readers fill in the rest."

We discuss the three things Creech shows us about Papa: the mustard stain, pouchy bags under his eyes, how Papa moves (slogs).

"Wait a minute," Stephanie says. "This is more like a DVD!"

"Why do you say that?" I ask.

"Papa is moving through the door."

"Yeah," Shawna says, "but it's real short. It's like when you run it for a second then pause it."

"So is it still a picture with words?" The students decide it is. Then we read another paragraph from *Replay*.

*Each night Papa used to go into his children's rooms and say good night to them, one by one, sitting on the side of each bed, listening to whatever important things they had to tell him, and then he would smile and kiss them, and wish them* bello *dreams, no bad ones allowed.*

We reread each one and talk with a partner about what makes them visual, and we discuss the different ways we see the father, through actual pictures, frozen in time, his movements, his clothing, and what he used to do, as well as different layers of who he is. We talk in particular about which lines are the most visual and how not everything has to be described in minute detail. The writer gets to choose what's important in creating the picture for a reader.

At home, students look at photos or try to remember a time they wanted to capture like a photograph. They'll bring the photo or the picture they want to hold in their mind the next day. I explain that writing, like photographs, is a wonderful way to keep a memory.

## Six Pictures of My Father

The next day we take a few minutes to look at students' pictures. I play "Freeze Frame" in the background as they share their pictures. In fact, I have

*Figure 4.3*

| Top Ten Detail Playlist | |
| --- | --- |
| **Name** | **Artist** |
| ☑ "Box of Photographs" | Johnny Rodgers |
| ☑ "100 Years" | Five for Fighting |
| ☑ "Picture Book" | The Kinks |
| ☑ "Photograph" | Jamie Cullum |
| ☑ "Photograph" | Nickelback |
| ☑ "The Sun" | Maroon 5 |
| ☑ "Empty Sky" | Bruce Springsteen |
| ☑ "Sweet Old World" | Lucinda Williams |
| ☑ "Freeze Frame" | The J. Geils Band |
| ☑ "Family Photographs" | Erich Glaubitz Band |

a whole playlist of picture songs (Figure 4.3). After a few minutes, we put the photos in our notebook and I read "16 Pictures of My Father," found in the short-story collection *Telling: Confessions, Concessions, and Other Flashes of Light* by Marion Winik. Some of the "pictures" are written for more mature audiences, so I read only "pictures" 1, 3, 8, 13, 15, and 16.

To ensure students write pictures with details, I read "Picture 1" first and then say, "This wouldn't have been as interesting or easy for me to visualize if Marion Winik had just written, 'There is a picture of my dad and me.' If she had stopped there, would you have connected or visualized anything? Let me reread it and you tell me what sticks with you."

> *A small, square black-and-white photograph with a scalloped white edge on which the date May 1959 is printed in small type. I am the curly-headed baby in a white party dress sitting up on Daddy's shoulder eating a strawberry. Boyishly handsome in his crew-neck sweater and grown-out GI haircut, he smiles up at me, squinting into the sun. He is thirty, I am one, we are in love.*

I read the rest of the pictures from Winik's story, pausing for comments and what they notice or like.

"Let's use Marion Winik as a mentor for detail and try out in our writing what she did in '16 Pictures of my Father.'" We discuss that some pictures were actual pictures while others were memories that existed in the author's memory. Some of our descriptions may be actual photographs that we have, or they may be just moments in time that we "Freeze Frame." If we want to add movement and perhaps narrate an actual memory, we can do that as Winik did.

Students write in their writer's notebooks four to five pictures under the title they complete: Pictures of my _____.

It can be a person, a pet, a friend, or an object. It's up to the writer.

We write, share, and come to know detail's power.

# Use Grammatical Structures to Embed Detail in Your Writing

Most grammatical structures focus readers' and writers' eyes on detail. I selected the important structures in Figure 4.4 as the top five for ease in helping writers sharpen their ideas. These sentences can act as mini-lessons or quick lessons on sentence variety, but their main function is embedding detail.

*Figure 4.4*

## The Top 5 Grammatical Structures That Attract Detail

| Grammatical Structure | Function | Mentor Sentence |
|---|---|---|
| Prepositional Phrases | • Show relationships between nouns<br>• Orient reader in time and space (their position) | I just stood there **on** *the free throw line,* **in** *the shadow* **of** *that big orange sign* **above** *the scoreboard,* clutching the basketball tight **to** *my chest.* Outside, a wild October wind whipped **through** *town,* rattling the windows high **above** *the bleachers in the gym.* —L. D. Harkrader, *Airball: My Life in Briefs* |
| Serial Commas | • List items in a series<br>• List actions in a series<br>• Show both separation and connection among items | Ma sighed a great deal, an impatient noise usually accompanied with a frown at their *rough clothes, rundown house, or meager food.* —Grace Lin, *Where the Mountain Meets the Moon*<br><br>I had three places I wanted to visit, six things I wanted to make, and two conversations I hoped to have before dinnertime. —Katherine Hannigan, *Ida B*<br><br>*(continued)* |

| The Top 5 Grammatical Structures That Attract Detail *(continued)* | | |
|---|---|---|
| Colons | • Announces something is coming: a list or an important sentence <br> • Links ideas and sentences | This was the landscape whose every face we knew: giant saguaro cacti, coyotes, mountains, the wicked sun reflecting off bare gravel. —Barbara Kingsolver, *Animal, Vegetable, Miracle* |
| Appositives | • Pack information into one sentence <br> • Create rhythm and emphasis | Pedro, **a point guard**, was on Ned's team today. —Mike Lupica, *Long Shot* |
| Participial Phrases | • Add movement and action <br> • Show simultaneous action <br> • Act like an adjective | **Standing in a cow pasture near Dayton, Ohio**, he looked up and watched a flying machine circle in the sky above him. He could see the bold pilot lying facedown on the lower wing. —Russell Freedman, *The Wright Brothers* |

*Figure 4.4 (continued)*

## Hammering Out the Details

Writers select only the words and phrases that will reach out and grab readers with their intended message. As observers of life and the texts they read, writers notice, paying attention to the world around them, searching for the detail that will tell their story or make their point. Details are selected, not sprayed.

Did we nail detail? We did if our details are fresh, concrete, and necessary. We did if we support our nonfiction with facts, resources, and quotations. Did we summarize when appropriate, expand when appropriate, and delete when appropriate? If we carefully selected and pieced together our details, we nailed it.

# Form

## Organizing and Structuring Ideas

*Order is the shape upon which beauty depends.*

—Pearl S. Buck

For my eighth birthday, I got a paint-by-numbers set. Ecstatic, I could hardly wait to rip it open and paint the masterpiece pictured on the front of the box. This was going to be far better than the drawings I did on Manila paper. This would be a painting just like the one on the box. Five minutes in, I figured out I would have to painstakingly hunt down corresponding paint and carefully fill in numbered spaces. For a kid who hated coloring in the lines, this was pure torture. To my parents' dismay, soon I was painting my own picture with broad strokes right over the thin blue lines.

Is writing by formula any different? Fill in your thesis statement here, insert three reasons with exactly one supporting detail here and here and here, and conclude by repeating your main points. If you follow these directions, soon your writing will look like everyone else's. This kind of scaffolding is dangerous to student thinking. As Arthur Applebee said at a National Council of Teachers of English annual convention, "Composition is not a fill-in-the-blank exercise."

But some hear the word *form* and they leap to *formula*.

This is not my definition of form. When I say form, I mean something closer to format—options for organizing and combining ideas, a menu of

> A functional approach to language does not advocate teaching about language by handing down prescriptive recipes. Rather it is concerned with providing information about the development of effective texts for particular purposes.
>
> —Beverly Derewianka

> To be college- and career-ready writers, students must take task, purpose, and audience into careful consideration, choosing words, information, structures, and formats deliberately. They need to know how to combine elements of different kinds of writing—for example to use narrative strategies within argument and explanation within narrative—to produce complex and nuanced writing.
>
> —Common Core Standards for Writing

possible structures that will help writers communicate their message. A format is a basic, loose–tight template that defines the essentials of an orderly, coherent, and predictable structure. Form offers guidance and some established patterns without robbing the work of surprise, thinking, or originality. Form is an open-ended starting point for shaping and communicating a writer's purpose.

A great art teacher teaches students the basics of brushstrokes, perspective, light, and shadow and then invites young artists to experiment and muck about at making art. Likewise, great writing teachers show novice writers how to communicate with readers, how to use and combine forms that suit and enhance their message. Then they are released to muck about with prose. Form helps a writer bring order to his or her ideas, but structure should never act as a straitjacket, constricting freedom, ideas, or meaning.

In truth, form is *formative*. It's an ever-refining aspect of writing. With form's structure and malleability, writers are able to fit their particular purpose for a particular audience, in a particular pattern.

So what do young writers need to know about form?

Knowing basic information about genre, form, and mode gives students options to shape and organize their ideas. For this to happen students need to be immersed in the features of genre, as well as various forms each genre may take. Students need to explore real texts and analyze what they do and how they are put together. They need to see how writers use the modes of description, exposition, argumentation, and narration to clarify and expand their ideas and move their writing forward, deepening meaning, detail, and clarity. To do this, students explore the many forms that *form* may take (Figure 5.1).

To distinguish modes from genre and form, remember that modes are found within any genre or form. But don't get bogged down in the semantics: It's about identifying the patterns and the attributes that construct them. It's about making form work for your writing task (see Figure 5.2).

# Define Genre as a Type of Writing

The question of genre is most simply answered by asking yourself, "What type of writing are you trying to write?" (Ray 2006): Are you writing a letter, an essay, or a mission statement? Loosely defined, these are all types of writing. Now, you may say, I am writing fiction, but if you say that to a person, especially an inquisitive one, they will ask, "What kind?"

Fiction isn't enough. A novel or novella, you say. Well, that's the form. Still we want to know, "Is it fantasy, horror, realistic, adventure, true crime?" If you write nonfiction, is it a pamphlet, grocery list, editorial, or technical guide?

Confusing, isn't it?

## The Many Forms of *Form*

| Genre | Format | Mode | Expository Text Structures | Inventive Forms |
|---|---|---|---|---|
| *Fiction* | • Brochures | • Description | • Sequence | • Structured and organized with fresh combinations of genre, format, mode, and text structures |
| • Realistic | • Poetry | • Exposition | • Listing | |
| • Mystery | • Prose | • Argumentation | • Procedural | |
| • Historical | • Plays | • Narrative | • Classification | |
| • Fantasy | • Novel | | • Compare/ Contrast | |
| • Traditional | • Short Story | | • Problem/ Solution | • Designed to enhance a writer's message |
| *Nonfiction* | • Essay | | • Cause-and-Effect | |
| • Informational | • Speech | | | |
| • Biography | • Reports | | | |
| • Autobiography | • Literary Analysis | | | |
| • Memoir | • Summary | | | |
| | • Letters | | | |
| | • Instructions | | | |
| | • Manuals | | | |
| | • Twitter | | | |
| | • Blog | | | |

This list is not exhaustive. Note that many sources blend the first two columns—genre and format.

*Figure 5.1*

*Figure 5.2*

## Making FORM Work

- Define genre as a type of writing.
- Compare and contrast the organization and structure of text.
- Know your mode of operation.
- Immerse yourself in expository text structures.
- Discover the flexibility of form.
- Remember that imitation is the sincerest form.

If you pick up a stack of teacher resources on genre, you will find varying lists of what genre includes. Genres that everyone can agree on are illustrated in Figure 5.3.

*Figure 5.3*

## Genres We Can All Agree On

| Fiction | Nonfiction |
| --- | --- |
| Realistic | Informational |
| Historical | Biography |
| Fantasy | Autobiography |
| Traditional | Memoir |
| Mystery | |

Some sources list forty-seven genres! Are they all subgenres or are they forms? For example, procedural texts are a form of informational nonfiction writing. Some argue procedural texts are a form or text structure, while others argue it's a genre. We can all agree procedural texts are a type of writing with certain features we expect to see.

If you insist on a distinction between genre and form, you might be interested in this *American Heritage Dictionary* definition.

> gen•re *n*. 1. A type or class. 2.a. A category of artistic composition, as in music or literature, marked by distinctive style, form, or content.

Arguing over distinctions isn't our goal. Whether someone calls argumentation a mode, a genre, or a text type doesn't matter. What matters is that writers know the common elements that construct argumentation before they are asked to write it:

- Both supporting ideas and opposing ideas on a debatable issue are presented (pros and cons).
- Evidence supports propositions (sufficient relevant statistics and examples).
- Logical reasoning builds the argument based on finding the best solution.

We learn the pattern of success through exposure to real texts and our analytical discussion of them. The template is what matters. Knowing the common characteristics of a form or genre is the point—whatever you want to call it.

Understanding form helps students comprehend and compose text. Genre and form are guideposts, not a rule or formula but a pattern of success that might be helpful in communicating with readers.

I want my students to observe form as they read text. I want them to pay attention and notice the key elements. I want them to be able to alter those elements for their own intents and purposes. The goal is to give students options and guideposts in the land of text. The value is the act of thinking, classifying, and naming attributes. The brain longs for random items to be grouped or classified.

> That form ever follows function. This is the law.
>
> —Louis Sullivan

## Tap into What the Digital Generation Knows About Genre

If I list all the different genres to launch my instruction, students will tune out. Instead of providing lists, it's better if students actively create the lists, using their own background knowledge, discovering all that they already know about genre.

> Miss Lupescu taught in lists, and Bod could not see the point to it.
>
> —Neil Gaiman

Students know media, so I take advantage of this to show them what they already know about genre. "In your writer's notebook, list as many of the TV shows and movies you watch as you can. Online, TV, or at the theater. They all count."

Students' pens scratch across the page for three minutes (see Figure 5.4).

After groups brainstorm, they share their responses with their group. Students combine their generated lists, writing one title per sticky note. They categorize all the sticky notes in an open sort, discovering on their own, putting like with like. After they have settled on their categories, students label each of them. We share our categories, noting similarities and differences.

If no group categorizes the shows and movies into genres, then I ask, "Are there any you'd consider comedies? Are there any sitcoms, which is short for situation comedies?"

Students start scanning their lists. "Yes!"

"How do you know a show is a comedy or drama?" I ask. "How are they different?"

"Well, comedy is supposed to make you laugh," Samantha says.

*Figure 5.4*

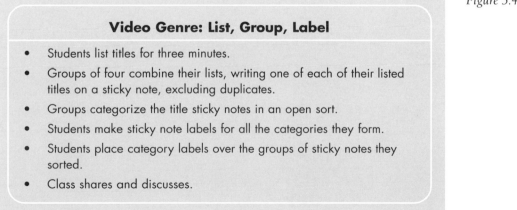

**Video Genre: List, Group, Label**

- Students list titles for three minutes.
- Groups of four combine their lists, writing one of each of their listed titles on a sticky note, excluding duplicates.
- Groups categorize the title sticky notes in an open sort.
- Students make sticky note labels for all the categories they form.
- Students place category labels over the groups of sticky notes they sorted.
- Class shares and discusses.

> **Art is nothing without form.**
> —Gustave Flaubert

"Yeah, you can hear laughing by the audience in the background," Julian says. "But that never happens on the serious shows."

"Okay, before we move on to dramas, let's make a list of all the things we know are in comedies," I say. I record answers on the chart tablet. Students look at TV shows and movies through an analytic lens. Plus, they will view these shows with a different eye for pattern and form long after this discussion ends.

I ask other questions to keep the conversation going:

- How can you tell if shows are true?
- What kinds of things usually happen on those shows?
- How do the producers and directors set the tone (music, lighting, and pace)?
- How is this kind of show different from and the same as others?

Students help me generate categories, all of us thinking together. After we've come up with labels for our categories: Drama, News, Reality, Comedy, Cartoons, we make a chart on a long piece of butcher paper (Figure 5.5).

You can continue this investigation by moving into the subgenres. My students were so engaged in talking about something of high interest for which they had sufficient background, they made me use more butcher paper. I took the extra time with subgenres, because these charts are going to act as schemata as we discuss books and gather more and more sophisticated

*Figure 5.5*

| Genre | Comedies | | Drama | | | |
|---|---|---|---|---|---|---|
| **Subgenre or form** | **Sitcom** | **Stand-Up** | **Police/ Detective** | **Dramedy** | **Science Fiction** | **Soap Opera/ Telenovella** |
| | | | | | | |

**Using What We Already Know About Genre**

We make a chart like this one on a long piece of horizontal butcher paper.

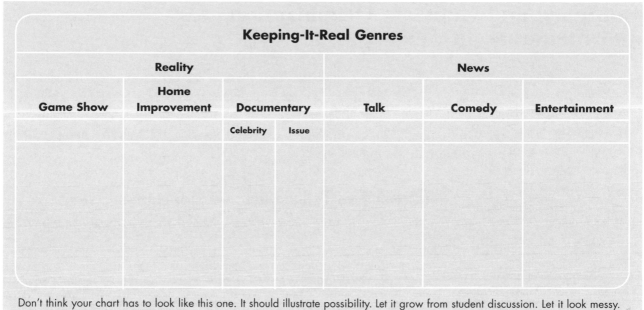

**Keeping-It-Real Genres**

| Reality | | | | News | | |
|---|---|---|---|---|---|---|
| Game Show | Home Improvement | Documentary | | Talk | Comedy | Entertainment |
| | | Celebrity | Issue | | | |
| | | | | | | |

Don't think your chart has to look like this one. It should illustrate possibility. Let it grow from student discussion. Let it look messy. Allow for hybrids or multigenres like dram-edy and real-edy.

*Figure 5.6*

answers about the essential features of each genre and how we can use this knowledge to help us write. Figure 5.6 is a chart we made for the subgenre of reality/real-life shows.

Later, in reading workshop, we start a chart that grows into something like Figure 5.7. I ask students to write down the title of the last three things they've read. Some have read their science textbook, magazines, Web pages, or novels. Whatever they've read, they write the title and then post it in a category on the chart. Students continue to list titles and authors in corresponding categories as they read and notice. When students have ownership in the process, they become addicted to charts.

*Figure 5.7*

**Genre Chart for Reading Workshop**

| Fiction | | | | | | Nonfiction | | |
|---|---|---|---|---|---|---|---|---|
| Realistic | Fantasy | Mystery | Historical | Science | Traditional | Informational | Biography | Autobiography |
| | | | | | | | | |

The class had a real argument about where social media should land. Though we decided that social media fit best under the three nonfiction genres, others insisted that many online postings are pure fiction.

# Compare and Contrast Organization and Structure of Texts

How do we make students aware of all the text structure possibilities? We do what real writers do. We read, compare, and contrast structures (Marzano, Pickering, and Pollack 2004) and take what we need to shape our own writing. We orchestrate lessons in which students talk, notice, and pay attention to text in new ways.

## Nonfiction Can Tell a Story and Entertain

I want students to notice that genres are about as neat as a sixth-grade boy's backpack.

To do this, I take them to the Dust Bowl for a few days.

I hold up the book *The Worst Hard Time* by Timothy Egan and explain that in our U.S. history a catastrophic national disaster devastated a large part of the United States, including our home state of Texas.

I explain that the Dust Bowl occurred in the 1930s: the rain stopped, crops and grass died, the ground dried up and started blowing the earth into the sky, plunging farms and cities into darkness. Cattle were blinded. People suffocated. Farm equipment and homes were buried—all by piles of dust carried by painful and strong winds.

"And what people *were* able to grow, the rabbits ate. The rabbits multiplied like a curse. There were thousands of them," I explain. "People felt a rage at the land, the lack of rain, the dirt in their homes, in their eyes, and in their mouths. Rage. And there was one thing they felt they could do something about—the rabbits."

Because of the challenging nature of the text, I read aloud an excerpt from the National Book Award winner.

> *Rabbits had the run of the land, crowding fields, yards, streets. They were an easy source of food, but they also took away food, gnawing en masse in places where some farmers still hoped to raise a crop. People saw rabbits as a scourge, a perpetual motion of mastication, indifferent to the human alterations that were blowing away.*
>
> *"BIG RABBIT DRIVE SUNDAY—BRING CLUBS"*
>
> *In the pages of the* Texan, *John McCarty thought it was time to get rid of the big-eared menaces. People gathered in a fenced field at the edge of Dalhart, about two thousand folks armed with baseball bats and clubs. The atmosphere was festive, many people drinking corn*

*whiskey from jugs. At last, they were about to do something, striking a blow against this run of freakish nature. They spread to the edge of the fenced section, forming a perimeter, then moved toward the center, herding rabbits inward to a stacked enclosure. As the human noose tightened, rabbits hopped around madly, sniffing the air, stumbling over each other. The clubs smashed heads. The bats crushed rib cages. Blood spattered, teeth were knocked out, hair was matted and reddened. The rabbits panicked, screamed. It took most of an afternoon to crush several thousand rabbits. Their bodies were left in a bloodied heap at the center of the field. Somebody strung up a few hundred of them and took a picture.*

I stop and reread parts of the text to get students' responses. Many are outraged, disturbed. We discuss how the writer got us to feel those reactions through the words he used.

In the first paragraph of the excerpt from *The Worst Hard Time*, how do the verbs affect the horror and movement of the piece? The deeper into the massacre, the more verbs or verbals (shown in bold for emphasis) Egan uses:

> *As the human noose **tightened**, rabbits **hopped** around madly, **sniffing** the air, **stumbling** over each other. The clubs **smashed** heads. The bats **crushed** rib cages. Blood **spattered**, teeth were **knocked** out, hair was **matted** and **reddened**. The rabbits **panicked**, **screamed**.*

The onomatopoetic quality of a few verbs increase the horror: *smashed, crushed, spattered, knocked, screamed.* In five sentences, the author adds a panicked energy by piling on the verbs.

A few students wonder how Egan knew about it if he wasn't there.

"Egan did research: He interviewed survivors and read old newspapers. For this information, he interviewed Melt White, who was a boy at the time." I explain. "Using his interview with Melt, the writer reconstructed a narrative or story of what happened." I read another excerpt:

> *Melt White had disobeyed his daddy and gone to the rabbit drive. He did not take part, but he watched at the edge of the slaughter. As the citizens of Dalhart closed in, the boy cringed at the sounds: swinging clubs, whoops and hollers, and the anguished howls—he told his mama he heard the rabbits cry—as they died. He ran to his house with the tarpaper roof and carried with him nightmares that never left.*
>
> *The rabbit drives caught on and became a weekly event in some places. In a single square mile section, people could kill up to six thousand rabbits in an afternoon.*

I distribute a copy of the excerpt to pairs. They reread, looking for clues to identify the genre. We chart what makes this nonfiction, discussing who the audience is and what decisions the writer made based on genre and to keep the reader interested:

- Facts/statistics
- It's true
- Writer talks to witnesses and researches old newspapers

Students are interested in how the writer can make a true event interesting. "He made it like a story!" We discuss how description, detail, and drama make literary nonfiction—or, as one student mistakenly called it, "literally" nonfiction.

As part of this lesson, I also share a few books about the Dust Bowl written at their level—for example, *Years of Dust: The Story of the Dust Bowl* by Albert Marrin. As a bridge to the next discussion, I share some excerpts from *Rose's Journal: The Story of a Girl in the Great Depression* by Marissa Moss.

## Fiction Can Use Facts and Inform

The next day, we review what we noticed about *The Worst Hard Time*: the nonfiction genre, its purpose and audience, the retelling of actual events and people based on newspapers and interviews.

To show students the difference between genre and form, I share a contrasting example, recounting a similar event of the same era in the same county. I display an excerpt titled "Rabbit Battles" from the Newbery Award winner *Out of the Dust* by Karen Hesse.

> ### *Rabbit Battles*
> *Mr. Noble and*
> *Mr. Romney have a bet going*
> *as to who can kill the most rabbits.*
> *It all started at the rabbit drive last Monday*
> *over to Sturgis*
> *when Mr. Noble got himself worked up*
> *about the damage done to his crop by jacks.*
> *Mr. Romney swore he'd had more rabbit trouble*
> *than anyone in Cimarron County.*
> *They pledged revenge on the rabbit population;*
> *wagering who could kill more.*
>
> *They ought to just shut up.*
> *Betting on how many rabbits they can kill.*

*Honestly!*
*Grown men clubbing bunnies to death.*
*Makes me sick to my stomach.*
*I know rabbits eat what they shouldn't,*
*especially this time of year when they could hop*
*halfway to Liberal*
*and still not find food,*
*but Miss Feeland says*
*if we keep*
*plowing under the stuff they ought to be eating,*
*what are they supposed to do?*

"What do you notice about how this text looks?" I ask.

"It looks like poetry," answers Jonathan.

"Ah, so it's poetry rather than prose. It's a different form. We know this event really happened because of what we read yesterday, but what would we call this if it's based on a true event, but some of it is made up?"

"Plus it's a poem," Randy adds.

We look at the genre chart we started in reading workshop (see Figure 5.7). "It's something true that happened in history, but it's fictionalized. We call that . . ."

"Historical fiction."

To wrap up, we discuss the differences between fiction and nonfiction by looking at copies of the excerpts from *The Worst Hard Time* side by side with a copy of *Out of the Dust*.

## What's Your Point of View?

It would seem children never talk about point of view in school. When you mention it, eyes glaze over, because the discussion of point of view is brief. Instruction usually stops at identification of first person or third person (I was out of college before I even realized a second-person point of view existed). But there is more to it. Point of view affects how the story is told. What's left in; what's left out. It can even cue you to genre, and certainly, it has an effect on what writers do and how they do it.

The next day students reread both Egan's and Hesse's excerpts and identify the point of view of each. We explore both texts through as many questions as I can get away with:

- Do we know who narrates each?
- Are the writers talking about themselves or someone else?
- What point of view is each in?
- Does point of view matter for the focus of these two pieces?

- Which one of the excerpts feels the closest to the rabbit drive?
- Which one has the most distance? Why?
- What's the difference when we write using the *I*-voice, first person, and the *he/she/it*-voice, third person?
- What affect does the point of view have on genre?

I often follow these questions up with, "How do you know?"

After our initial observation and discussion about the kind of narration we find in each piece, I choose a moment when the kids need more information to keep the conversation going and I distribute the chart in Figure 5.8.

When we look at Hesse's excerpt, we have a lot of discussion. After I clarify for students that even in the first person you can name other characters or people's actions, we settle on the first-person point of view. We talk about how the first column of the chart applies and doesn't apply to the *Out of the Dust* excerpt.

"How is the Egan excerpt different in terms of point of view?"

We discuss the fact that this is told from a third-person point of view. An outsider is telling the story because he wasn't there. He didn't witness it, but even though third-person narration can give a sense of being removed from the subject, it feels closer than the *Out of the Dust* excerpt because Egan inter-

Figure 5.8

| What's the Writer's Perspective? | | |
|---|---|---|
| **Point of View** | First Person | Third Person |
| **Who's the Narrator?** | *I*-voice | *He/She/It/They*-voice |
| **How It Looks** | I am in charge. | Charles is in charge. |
| **How It Affects Attitude** | The narrator is a participant—emotionally involved. The first-person narrator reveals only his or her own thoughts and those expressed aloud by others. Considered less formal.<br><br>Personal and subjective | *Third-Person Limited*: Narrator is limited to one person's thoughts as an outside observer. Considered more formal.<br><br>*Third-Person Omniscient*: Narrator is all knowing and can reveal more than one character's thoughts.<br><br>Objective observer |
| **Distance** | Involved<br>(The insider) | Removed<br>(The outsider) |

There is a point of view called second person—the *you*-voice. Besides greeting cards and songs, second-person point of view is used less and usually in tandem with the first-person point of view. Second person is used from time to time to invite the reader into the discussion: What do you think?

viewed an eyewitness. The author was able to conquer this distance and get rich information through extensive interviewing and research, taking in multiple perspectives or viewpoints to strengthen the story.

We suppose why Hesse chose to be more removed from the rabbit war. They just had different purposes. One is primarily to entertain—historical fiction—and one is nonfiction with the primary purpose of getting accurate facts to the reader.

In the end, the chart shows a primary pattern, but as in most cases with writing, rules are text dependent. We can expect certain patterns, but good writers are always looking for a just-right mix to make their message sing.

# Know Your Mode of Operation

The word *mode* finds its roots in customary fashion and music. In a way, modes of writing—description, exposition, argumentation, and narration—are like customary things writers do, and each mode hits certain notes. Students need to understand modes in isolation and in combination to help them communicate meaning to a reader.

Modes are found within any genre or form. Modes are active tools, which may alternately help a writer *describe* the elements of a problem in a letter, *explain* character background information in a novel, *persuade* readers in an editorial, or *narrate* an event in an anecdote or short story. It all depends on the author's purpose. What is the author trying to say? Which mode will help the author achieve that end?

Particular modes lend themselves to certain genres or forms, but just as writers mix genres, we mix modes to communicate ideas and information within any form or genre. It's almost an impossible task to use only one mode in any developed piece of writing.

Modes help us formulate our thinking in clear ways for our readers. To help writers remember the modes for making meaning, I use a mnemonic: DEAN (see Figure 5.9).

For my students, I transform these abstract-sounding words—description, exposition, argumentation, narration—into verbs, actions writers can do to help readers understand and visualize their message. Once a writer knows what he or she wants to write (purpose), then they need ways to express their ideas (see Figure 5.10).

Modes come alive when we look at real texts.

## Benjamin Franklin à la Mode

*Benjamin Franklin's Almanac: Being a True Account of the Good Gentleman's Life* is a great book to kick off a discussion about modes. I put the text in front of

> Too often in schools, the concept of mode is grossly oversimplified.
> —Katie Wood Ray

Figure 5.9

| DEAN Complicated | | |
|---|---|---|
| **D** | Description | Images and analogies help reader visualize a setting, character, or process. |
| **E** | Expository | Information and examples in a variety of structures aid readers' understanding by showing relationships among ideas: classification, comparison/contrast, cause/effect, problem/solution. |
| **A** | Argumentation | Propositions are supported through relevant statistics, anecdotes, and examples that help your audience think through multiple perspectives on an issue or controversy. |
| **N** | Narration | Time and events are arranged in an order that is easy to follow and focuses on what is important to the story or message. |

Figure 5.10

| DEAN Simplified | | |
|---|---|---|
| **D** | Describe | Use images to help reader visualize a setting, a character, or a process. |
| **E** | Explain | Share information and examples in a variety of structures to aid your readers' understanding by showing relationships among ideas: classification, sequence, compare/contrast, cause/effect, problem/solution. |
| **A** | Argue | Make propositions and give support with statistics, anecdotes, and examples that help your audience understand the issue. |
| **N** | Narrate | Take your reader through time and events in an order that is easy to follow and focuses on what is important to your story or message. |

my students and let them observe, notice, name, and discover the modes. Candace Fleming, the biography's author, uses all but one of the modes in a mix, leaning on a dominant mode from time to time.

In the first excerpt, Fleming describes the setting of Franklin's early life:

> *Boston wasn't particularly pretty either. Narrow, winding streets full of bumps and holes climbed the low hills above the harbor. On either side of the streets stood square, weathered-gray houses, about a thousand of them. Geese honked on the Common, and pigs roamed the trash-strewn streets.*

"What is the writer doing here?" I ask. "How is she explaining? Reread, and then turn and talk to your neighbor."

In our discussion, students list sounds, how things looked, where things were, who or what was there. Finally, Beatriz uses the word *describe*, and I am on it like brown on rice.

I ask, "When Beatriz says *describe*, I look at all the things you said this writer did—does describing cover all of them?"

We agree it does.

"That's one way writers inform us: They describe. Writers also use a few other structures. Let's see whether we can find them in this text."

In writing, authors use modes to make meaning and clarity. We dive into another excerpt to see how Fleming shares information:

> *Josiah [Franklin's father] hoped his youngest son would become a clergyman. Since clergymen needed to be well educated, Ben was enrolled in this school at the age of eight. He did well, rising quickly to the head of his class. But Ben's father changed his mind about his son's future. Training for the church, he claimed, was too expensive. Yet the school was free, charging only six shillings for "fire money" (money used for wood to heat the school)—and even that was waived if students could not afford it. So what was Josiah's real problem? Many historians believe that although Ben qualified for the school when it came to intelligence and scholarship, his father knew the boy was not pious enough to become a minister.*

"What's the author doing here?"

We discuss how she explains that Ben is the youngest and is destined to be a minister, but he didn't have what it takes. After I define the word *pious*, I ask how the author shares information. In this case, her purpose was to explain Ben's background and character. She even used punctuation (parentheses) to explain what "fire money" meant.

The next day, instead of moving on to argumentation, we look at the mode of narration. Argumentation is less familiar and will make more sense after they've seen the other modes. After all, we use narration, explanation, and description in effective argumentation or persuasion. Fleming narrates this next excerpt.

*Ben once invited a group of friends to an "electrical picnic." He planned to kill a turkey by "electrical shock," then roast it with "electrical fire." Unfortunately, he became so engrossed in conversation he forgot to pay close attention to what he was doing. He touched two wires together and* zap! *Ben received the shock instead of the turkey. His body vibrated from head to toe, and smoke curled from one buckled shoe. Luckily he escaped with just a few bruises and a sore chest.*

"How is Fleming getting this information to us?" I ask.

"It's like when you tell a joke," Beatriz says. "You tell a story by saying what happened."

"But it's the facts, so it's explaining," Ralphie says.

I nod.

"She tells how stuff happens in order."

"A sequence?"

He nods.

"I think you are all right, but what is the primary mode? What's the mode she uses most? I think it's narration—taking us through time," I say. "Describing: yes. Explaining: yes. But she's doing it in the structure of a narrative or story."

The modes of description, exposition, argumentation, and narration underlie text patterns that support larger organizational structures such as genre and form. Fleming wrote a nonfiction book in the subgenre of biography in the form of an almanac. She wrote in three of the modes, giving her writing variety and interest. She matched her purpose and the type of information she wanted to share with appropriate modes. Modes are there for writers to add detail, to expand, to inform, and to tell the story. Quite simply, modes are options that help writers communicate.

## Argumentation

Argumentation is the mode most likely to be referred to as a genre. I don't start my discussion of argumentation with the word *argumentation*. That's deadly. I wait to introduce the word until students start to identify the elements of it in this editorial by Leonard Pitts (see the appendix):

**Offramp to Fame Pitted with Potholes**
*"I want to be famous."*
*My grandson told me that when he was six. I repeat: six.*

*It has always struck me as a vivid illustration of the way we've been transformed by the omnipresence of media. Time was, little boys dreamt of being cops, cowboys and superheroes. But that was long ago.*

*Fame itself is the dream now, the lingua franca of the media age, democratized to such a degree that every Tom, Dick and Snooki can be a star. If you're not famous, you're probably not really trying.*

*Fame, the thinking seems to be, is an end unto itself. It solves all problems, fixes all shortcomings, makes all things OK. Except that fame actually does none of those things. Fame does not change what you are; it only magnifies it.*

*Here, then, is Ted Williams, who is now famous. And if you think I mean the Hall of Fame baseball player, you've likely been out of the country a few days. That brief time span encompasses the entirety of this Ted Williams' fame.*

*It began Jan. 3 when a videographer for* The Columbus Dispatch *posted online a startlingly incongruous video. This wild-haired homeless man with a hand-written sign is panhandling at a freeway offramp. But when he speaks, it is in the trained and manicured baritone of a professional announcer. Which, it turns out, he once was, before alcohol, crack, homelessness and petty crime reduced him to what the video captured.*

*That video went viral and made Williams, 53, a literal overnight sensation. By Jan. 6, he was on* Today. *He's done* The Early Show, *Jimmy Fallon, Dr. Phil, Entertainment Tonight and has job offers from Kraft Foods, the Cleveland Cavaliers and MSNBC.*

*Then came Jan. 10. Williams was in L.A. to tape an episode of* Dr. Phil *reuniting him with the family he abandoned. He and one of his adult daughters were briefly detained by police following a violent argument at a hotel. Williams has said he was two years clean and sober, but his daughter said he was drinking again. He denied it. Until two days later, when he canceled all his engagements and announced that he was entering rehab.*

*And was any of this not sadly predictable?*

*One is reminded of how divers who ascend too quickly from the depths sometimes get the bends. To go from a freeway offramp to the* Today *show in three days is the metaphoric equivalent.*

*"It's almost choking me," he told the* Dispatch.

*"People in rehab," he told ET, "we're fragile. ... You jump out of this car, there's a camera there, you roll down your window just to flip a cigarette out the window, and there's somebody that points at you. . . . Remember, I, a week ago, was holding a sign where people wouldn't give me the time of day."*

*Not that it's surprising his story resonated. This is a nation of long shots and second chances; it is in our DNA to root for underdogs.*

*So Williams has become a sort of national reclamation project. But some of us, I suspect, unconsciously believe that fame—and its frequent companion, fortune—are enough to get the job done.*

*Williams himself seemed to buy into this. Consider a sequence from Dr. Phil where he faced the 29-year-old daughter he later had the argument with. Having left her behind for the joys of coke and booze when she was a child, he now promised to buy her a Louis Vuitton purse.*

*You don't get to where Ted Williams got in his life unless you have some serious, as they say, issues—questions of character, dependency and emotional health. It is naive to believe those things can be fixed—for Williams or anyone who faces similar challenges—in a single lightning strike of overnight sensation.*

*Let us be glad Williams now has a second chance. But let also hope his decision to go into rehab means he, at least, now understands better what fame can and cannot do.*

*It is nice to be famous. It is better to be whole.*

We read Pitts's editorial aloud and discuss what his purpose was in writing the essay. As the students identify Pitts's argument, I expand on those answers, building toward the idea that argumentation deals with something that is debatable—such as *fame solves all your problems.*

"I want to be a famous basketball player," Jordan says.

"Yeah, a lot of people want to be famous," I say, "Why do you think Pitts started the essay that way?"

"He wanted to show you that fame isn't that good," Ramon says.

We discuss the effective use of a quote or dialogue to start his argument. I write *argumentation* on a chart and we record the attributes we see in the essay (Figure 5.11). I name the informational genre as well as identify this form as an editorial. "The purpose of an editorial isn't just to say this is what I think; it's meant to make you think too, even if you disagree. It's like starting a conversation."

*Figure 5.11*

### Argumentation Chart

- Uses quotes as evidence
- Addresses both sides (argument and counterargument)
- Gives examples and anecdotes to make your point
- Builds a case to make the reader see your point of view (logical versus emotional)

As we read several persuasive pieces from editorials and other sources, we continue to build this chart of critical attributes. Once we've constructed this understanding through analyzing models, students are ready to begin experimenting with argumentation.

We note how Pitts acknowledges both sides. And the real argument comes at the end: "It's better to be whole."

## Argumentation at Work in Fiction

Although it is much harder to find argumentation in fiction, it's there, especially in Kate Klise's mixed-genre book, *Regarding the Fountain*. Here is a quote from Sally Mander in a newspaper article, excerpted from this fictional work:

> *Okay, so it [the fountain] leaks a little bit. Big deal. We can fix it. But noooo! We've got to buy a new fountain! What kind of lesson does this send to our children? When something breaks, do we just get rid of it? This is one more example of how we have become a throwaway society. It's a sad day for the town of Dry Creek.*

This is an editorial within a novel, so it makes sense that it employs elements of argumentation, though it may seem a tad emotional and one-sided.

# Immerse Yourself in Expository Text Structures

"What's *suppository* writing?"

Indeed.

Several students have actually asked me that. While expository writing can be a pain, it's less so when you show students that text structures, such as modes, provide writers a variety of ways to explain.

Readers use text structures to understand. To help students understand and remember the purpose of expository text structures, I make a simple EX factor wall chart (see Figure 5.12) to highlight that the first two letters of expository and explain are the same.

Under the umbrella of expository text structures, we have several patterns: sequence, procedural, listing, classification, compare and contrast,

*Figure 5.12*

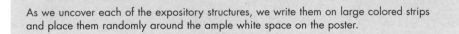

The **EX** Factor Wall Chart

**EX**pository text structures

**EX**plain

As we uncover each of the expository structures, we write them on large colored strips and place them randomly around the ample white space on the poster.

## Expository Text Structures

| | |
|---|---|
| Sequence | Organize events in a chronological way. |
| Procedural | Organize a process so another may follow and either do or understand the process. |
| Listing | Organize actions, events, or specific points with bullets, commas, or numbers. |
| Classification | Organize a subject into categories or explain the category into which an item falls. |
| Compare/Contrast | Organize information by highlighting similarities and differences. |
| Problem/Solution | Organize information by defining a problem and then suggesting possible solutions. |
| Cause and Effect | Trace the results of an event or the reasons an event happened. |
| Graphics | Use graphs, charts, diagrams, photos, and icons to aid readers' understanding. Titles and captions are often necessary. |

While it's possible for a piece of writing to be entirely in one of these text structures, most authentic texts use a mixture to communicate ideas with clarity. Although textbooks often create entire essays based on these text structures, most writers lean primarily on one or two, because it is almost impossible not to call on several text structures to help express a string of ideas in the same piece of writing (see the appendix).

*Figure 5.13*

problem/solution, cause and effect, and graphics. These text structures support the writer's ideas. At some point I share a list (see Figure 5.13), but only after we've explored a lot of model texts.

## Explaining Text Structures with a Three-Ring Circus

Again, I can't just give students the definitions; they need to experience the text patterns and discover their attributes for themselves. Intentionally showing the connection between reading and writing, I share over a few weeks all the expository structures in texts. I use the award-winning *The Great and Only Barnum: The Tremendous, Stupendous Life of Showman P.T. Barnum*, written by my favorite biographer, Candace Fleming, to kick off the discussion.

"I've been reading this book by Candace Fleming. She writes a lot of biographies, like the Ben Franklin one we've read. I am addicted to them." I show the book. "This one is about P. T. Barnum. Have you ever heard that name, Barnum?"

Alicia raises her hand. "It's that thing with the, you know, greatest show on earth or whatever, with all the animals and stuff."

"A circus," Brian interrupts. "Did he invent circuses?"

"That's a good question. How would we find out?"

The class, deflated, says, "Read."

"C'mon, it's fun if you're interested." I scan the class's disbelieving eyes. "I have been noticing that Candace Fleming does a lot of things to make sure I understand who P. T. Barnum is—and stay interested." We discuss that this book is nonfiction because it's a biography, and we expect certain elements in a biography, which we list on a chart:

- Tells about his whole life (sequence and narration)
- Describes who he was as a person (character)
- Includes things he did (significant or interesting accomplishments)

I add information in parentheses as I list student responses, not in a corrective way, but to augment student-generated ideas: "That's great and it makes me think of . . ." Also, I add two more bullets, highlighting how biographies are really more than just things the subjects did, or their whole life story, but those important events that contributed to who they are.

- Events that shaped the subject
- Events that define this person in history

For example, I show them Matt de la Peña's picture book *A Nation's Hope: The Story of Boxing Legend Joe Lewis*, which focuses on one particular event that was significant to the boxer's life.

## Comparing and Contrasting Information

"Writers have options on how to organize their writing. We try to make it clear and interesting to readers. Look at this part. I didn't know this, but before circuses P.T. Barnum ran museums."

I show the sidebar. "In nonfiction, there are callout boxes or sidebars that highlight additional information. This sidebar is titled 'Museums Now and Then.'" I write the subtitle on the whiteboard as I continue, "What's the author doing for us with her subtitle?"

Students turn and talk.

We share our thinking: She's telling us this will be about museums now and then. I question them about whether she is hinting at a text structure and they twist their faces.

"Let's read it and see how Fleming structures or organizes information in this sidebar." I read the excerpt aloud:

> *Nowadays, most museums are public institutions created for the*
> *purpose of educating people about specific areas of interests such as art,*

*science, and natural history. Experts run these museums. They are well organized. And their information is accurate.*

"What does the word *nowadays* tell us?" We discuss how organizationally, this transition tells us this paragraph (or category) will be all about museums *now*.

"And look how this next part starts: 'But in Barnum's day.' What can we predict?"

"It's going to change," says Ruby.

"How do you know?" I ask.

"When my mom says 'but' I know she isn't going to let me go to the mall: *I was going to let you go, but you didn't clean your room.*"

"'*But*' says a contrast is coming—a difference."

I read.

*But in Barnum's day there were no large public museums. Instead, museums were owned by individuals who set up their own display, then charged the public an admission price.*

I read the entire excerpt to my students. We learn that museums originated with scientific and educational exhibits at first, but then other entertainment venues almost bankrupted them and they had to keep customers. Therefore, museums changed their purpose and content.

*Fun came first, and the showman looked for displays that appealed to popular tastes, adding to his collection in a hodgepodge: giant balls of string next to fossils; ancient coins next to a flea circus. Some artifacts were fake, others were labeled incorrectly, and none included any information about their historical or cultural significance. Later, to compete with theaters and traveling artists, he added live performances, a zoo, and even an aquarium. Americans had never seen anything like it. Wrote the historian A. H. Saxon, "Barnum changed the meaning of the word* museum.*"*

We reread the paragraphs and name that the author categorized using *now and then* as a structure, giving us more information on the *then*. The author uses compare and contrast. She classifies information into categories: what happens now and what happened then. But she also compares and contrasts. Students wonder if it can be both. Worksheets look for one right answer; conversations help students own concepts. Classification is, after all, the kissing cousin of compare and contrast, and we'll get to that next.

With classification, the author's purpose is to categorize information, for example, the way we have separate classes in middle school: one class for math, one for social studies. However, when we compare and contrast, our purpose is to highlight differences and similarities, like this excerpt from *A Drop of Water* by Walter Wick:

> Ice is solid, like metal or rock. But unlike metal or rock, ice is solid only at temperatures of 32 degrees Fahrenheit (0 degrees Celsius) or colder. At room temperature, ice melts, changing back to liquid.

Students also see compare and contrast in this excerpt from Sid Fleischman's *Escape! The Story of the Great Houdini*:

> Like most boys, Ehrich had picked up a magic stunt or two. Unlike most boys, who master a secret or two and move on, his fascination with tricks took hold.

Figure 5.14 lists words and phrases that authors use to compare and contrast within text.

*Figure 5.14*

| | **Compare and Contrast Text Structure** | |
|---|---|
| **Structure** | **Author's Purpose:** **To highlight similarities and differences** |
| Compare | And, as well as, compare to, likewise, similarly, in the same way, either, or, like |
| Contrast | But, contrary, despite, although, however, nevertheless, yet, instead, rather, otherwise, on the other hand, unlike |

## Classifying Information

Later, we expand our discussion about classification. I show them a few pages from *Don't Know Much About the Pilgrims* by Kenneth C. Davis. It's easy to see that it's organized around a question-and-answer format. We discuss how each part of the text can be classified as a question or an answer. I preview another book, *The New Way Things Work* by David Macaulay. Each chapter is a classification or category:

- The Mechanics of Movement
- Harnessing the Elements
- Working with Waves
- Electricity and Automation
- The Digital Domain
- The Invention of Machines

> The mind cannot handle very many unrelated ideas, objects, or events. It is necessary to find some pattern, some common property in order to catalog many separate things into a smaller number of types.
>
> —Frank O'Hare and Dean Memering

Then, we look at Chapter 4 of *The Great and Only Barnum*, "A Visit to the American Museum." This chapter is organized as a room-by-room tour, starting with "The Entrance Hall." It's fun reading, but students also see that each subheading—in this case, room—classifies what is in each section.

Later, in pairs, students look at another stack of nonfiction books and articles I've pulled from the library and other sources to discover how chapter titles and subheadings are all ways we classify—even paragraphs!

Because students make the discoveries, they tell me—I don't tell them. We record text structures on a chart to capture our thinking, which we add to over time. Figure 5.15 lists some ways authors use categories to organize information.

When students are reading nonfiction in reading workshop or in other courses, such as science and social studies, this explanation of expository texts helps them construct meaning. We are raising their awareness first and then we invite them to try out these structures in paragraph responses, in small revisions of writer's notebook entries, and later in longer works.

*Figure 5.15*

### Classification Text Structure

| Structure | Author's Purpose:<br>To categorize, separate, and group information |
|---|---|
| Classify | • Information is sorted into categories like biological classification or parts of speech<br>• Arrange groups based on shared characteristics<br>• Use category words such as: What are the types of . . .? Question/Answer, Living/Nonliving, Good/Bad, Best/Worst, etc.<br>• Subtitles and paragraphs classify and group |

## Time and Order: SCU (Sequence/Chronology Unit)

I point at our expository text structures chart.

"We know writers can compare and contrast or classify to share their thinking. We can also organize our writing in other ways. I read another excerpt from *The Great and Only Barnum*, asking only, "What's Fleming doing here? What organizational structure or pattern is she using to explain?"

> *After renaming the place Barnum's American Museum and borrowing what he called "start up funds" from his friends, he developed a three-part business plan. First, he would renovate, making the museum*

*Figure 5.16*

| Sequence or Narration Text Structure | |
| --- | --- |
| **Structure** | **Author's Purpose:** <br> **To narrate events or actions over time** |
| Sequence | First, second, last, then, as, while, before, after, afterward, as soon as, during, finally, following, immediately, initially, later until, meanwhile, next, now, today, when |

*cheerful and interesting. Second, he'd advertise so people would be intrigued enough to visit. And last but not least, he would fill the museum with fascinating, exciting, ever-changing exhibits.*

After reading the passage twice, we name that this excerpt moves though time and narrates the order in which events happened, and we name some of the ways the writer leads the reader through the passage. For our first exploration, I chose an excerpt with rather obvious transition words, such as *first, second,* and *last but not least,* but now that we are aware of the structure, we find less obvious, yet guiding examples. See Figure 5.16 for words that may indicate a narrative structure.

## How to Find More Procedural Mentor Texts

Like sequence, procedural text structures narrate processes or give directions on how to do something. It's not a huge surprise that I found no procedural text in a biography of Barnum. That structure didn't fit Fleming's purpose.

That's not to say a procedural structure couldn't be used. In fact, in *King George: What Was His Problem?*, Steve Sheinkin's first chapter is "How to Start a Revolution." The next subheading reads, "Step One: Kick Out the French," and the next "Step Two: Tax the Colonists." This text is an outlier, but that's its strength.

"There is another expository text structure—or one more way nonfiction writers can explain," I say. "This expository structure is called procedural text. You've all heard of how-to texts and instructions. Procedural structures describe, narrate, and explain how to do something, how to complete a process, or how a process works."

I put out a call for students to bring in examples of texts that explain or tell us how to do things. Now they are more adept at noticing form and structure. The goal is to get students to pay more attention to the texts they encounter in the world. We brainstorm several possibilities:

- Recipes
- Directions
- Instructions found in magazines, newspapers, online, electronics, etc.

Of course, I always have a few of my own to share. Here are some highlights:

*How to Talk to Your Dog* by Jean Craighead George
*The Worst Case Scenario Survival Handbook* by Joshua Piven and David
    Borgenicht (Several students point out this is also set in the
    problem-solution structure.)
*The Dangerous Book for Boys* by Conn Iggulden and Hal Iggulden
*The New Way Things Work* by David Macaulay
*How to Lose All Your Friends* by Nancy L. Carson
*The Girls' Book: How to Be the Best at Everything* by Juliana Foster
*How to Talk to Girls* by Alec Greven
*Show Me How: 500 Things You Should Know. Instructions for Life from the
    Everyday to the Exotic* and *More Show Me How* by Lauren Smith and
    Derek Fagerstrom
*My Anxious Mind: A Teen's Guide to Managing Anxiety and Panic* by
    Michael A. Tompkins and Katherine A. Martinez

Not to mention all the gaming, how-to-fix guides, recipes, piles of how to draw this and that, and appliance instructions that kids bring in. Some are from newspaper articles, the Internet, and magazines such as *Ranger Rick*.

Students choose one procedural text they want to study closely. "Table Football" from *The Dangerous Book for Boys* was most popular and gave many boys and a few girls the opportunity to work in the mode of argumentation to convince me why they had to experience the game to see if the instructions were accurate. I am a pushover for enthusiasm toward writing and reading.

The mentor text from *The Dangerous Book for Boys* includes much-needed diagrams—something students notice—as well as the supplies you'd need. I include only a small section here:

1. *Place the coins on the close edge of the table, as in the diagram. The first blow must be struck with the heel of the hand against the coin half over the edge. The three coins will separate. From then on, only the coin closest to the player can be touched.*
2. *The aim of the game is to pass the coin up the table by firing the closest through the two farther up. If you don't get the coin through, that's the end of your go and your opponent begins again from his side of the table. Just one finger is usually used to flick the coins. They should always be in contact with the table, so a great deal of the skill is in judging the force as well as planning ahead.*

Without pictures, directions are hard to follow. We discuss what that means to us as writers.

One student finds it particularly interesting to see a procedural structure in a fiction book. She shares an excerpt from Kathy Appelt's fantasy-mermaid novel, *Keeper*:

> *The job of [surfboard] waxing is more complicated than it sounds.*
>
> *Step 1: Keeper had to wash the salt water off the board. Because there was no running water at the Bus, Dogie had attached a string of water hoses from his house all the way down the road to the Bus. This meant that Keeper had to run back and forth from house to Bus to turn the water on and off. It wasn't that far, maybe fifty yards, but she had to hurry anyway. "N-n-no n-n-need to waste water," Dogie always told her.*
>
> *Step 2: She had to remove the old wax. First she had to scrape the whole deck of the board with a thing called a "comb," which looked a little like a hair comb, but instead of long, thin teeth, it had small, squatty teeth, perfect for jabbing underneath the old wax. This was the hardest part, especially when the wax was majorly caked on and gunky. Keeper had to press down on the comb with both hands to pry the wax off.*

Students note how the author returns to the story quickly because her purpose is not to describe how to clean a surfboard so the reader would be able to do it. Instead, it's just part of the story that reveals setting and character.

## Problem-Solution

Sometimes a sentence or two can be a good place to start a discussion about text structure. I display these sentences from *Henry Aaron's Dream* by Matt Tavares:

> *He didn't have a bat, so he'd swing a broom handle or a stick or whatever he could find. Henry didn't have a baseball, either, so he'd hit bottle caps or tie a few old rags together or crumple up a tin can.*

"What's the writer doing?" I ask.

Students answer that the author is explaining, describing Hank Aaron's beginnings and how he didn't have baseball equipment.

"How is the writer organizing his ideas?" I ask.

Students note in the first half of both sentences we find out what he didn't have, and in the second half, we find out how he got around that. We discuss the possibilities of a problem-solution or cause-effect structure. "What word signals a relationship between the two sentences?" I ask.

"So," April says.

"He didn't have this, so he did this instead—problem then solution," I say. "Can *so* show a cause-effect relationship too?" We discuss, notice, and argue. The learning lives in the discussion.

Here's a longer example I show them from another piece of text from D. B. Johnson's introduction to the graphic biography *Thoreau at Walden* by John Porcellino:

> *After graduating from Harvard at twenty years old, David Henry Thoreau returned home to Concord, Massachusetts. Like many recent graduates, he was forced to ask himself: What am I going to do with my life?*
>
> *He toyed with the idea of being a minister, a lawyer, a doctor, and a businessman. He decided to teach public school, but that didn't last long—he quit when he was ordered to flog his students. People in Concord thought Thoreau was crazy to throw away a good job just because he was against beating a student; kids had always been whipped in school.*

Sharing lists of questions is one way to get students to start thinking about the problem-solution text structure. Here is a list of questions from Doug Buehl's *Classroom Strategies for Interactive Learning* (2001, 12):

- What is the problem?
- Who has the problem?
- What is causing the problem?
- What are the effects of the problem?
- Who is trying to solve the problem?
- What solutions are recommended or attempted?
- What results from these solutions?
- Is the problem solved?

I also share that we can be more intentional about our problem-solution structure, as in an essay about a school- or family-related issue, but it's interesting to find this pattern in virtually everything we read at one time or another. For example, students may identify a problem around the school and then describe possible solutions for the issue. We add problem/solution to our chart of expository text structures, and the students add it to the list of texts they scour for examples of and how these structures help them compose and construct meaning. Figure 5.17 addresses the purpose of the problem-solution organization as well as words and phrases that cue the structure.

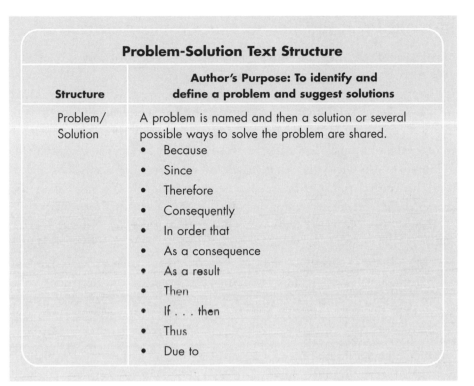

*Figure 5.17*

| **Problem-Solution Text Structure** | |
| --- | --- |
| **Structure** | **Author's Purpose: To identify and define a problem and suggest solutions** |
| Problem/ Solution | A problem is named and then a solution or several possible ways to solve the problem are shared. <br> • Because <br> • Since <br> • Therefore <br> • Consequently <br> • In order that <br> • As a consequence <br> • As a result <br> • Then <br> • If . . . then <br> • Thus <br> • Due to |

# Discover the Flexibility of Form

If learning form is not a fill-in-the-blank exercise, what is it? Learning about form is noting what works in texts, what shapes meaning, and then taking the bits and pieces we need to create a structure and organization that helps our writing communicate with a reader for our purposes. For example, I use bullets in an expository piece for the purpose of highlighting multiple items, but it also simplifies and separates with more punch than a comma. But can I use a bulleted list in fiction, a book review, or a literary analysis?

Maybe.

It depends on your purpose and audience.

The point is, genre study is like a supernova. At any moment, a genre can explode—either breaking into parts or combining in new ways. We don't want our writers to write straight off the form; we want them to see the attributes and patterns and tailor what they need for their particular purpose. To do that, they need to see form and genre through writers' eyes. Writers pay attention to all the text they see. How can we replicate this in our classrooms?

> Students should first have experience with the various text forms and features before being expected to read or write similar forms.
>
> —Margaret Mooney

# Inspiring Creative Thinking with Inventive Structures

Mostly, learning form and genre are as simple as Katie Wood Ray's question: "What have you read that is like what you're trying to write?" If the answer is nothing, then how do we find it? I want to produce kids who, when faced with a challenge, look to a text to show them the way. They browse books like writers, reading like writers, looking at how each book is organized. I want them to think, "Isn't that a fresh idea to arrange a biography of Mohammad Ali's life with *rounds* instead of chapters?" The new lens makes it fresh. The relationship between boxing and his life are evident in the arrangement, and yet somehow, this obvious choice isn't that obvious.

Genre and form are about categories, but categories have a way of shifting over time. Think about how the categories "politician" and "celebrity" have changed. At one time, it would have been unthinkable that a TV stunt wrestler or cinema's *The Terminator* would be the governor of one of our fifty states. However, after Jesse Ventura and Arnold Schwarzenegger did just that, the categories evolved (or devolved!). Will reality stars or talk show hosts run for president some day?

I am addicted to finding new forms of writing that show me a variety of ways to organize my thoughts—not as imitation, but to borrow something from one form and make it work for my new purposes. What does it inspire in forming my ideas and focus? I have read memoirs organized around a mother's answering machine messages (Amy Borkowsky's *Amy's Answering Machine*) and many books structured around song titles. In the following charts (Figures 5.18–5.20) is a sampling of a few fresh takes on genre and form, which will spark creative and inventive structures. Just seeing the options opens up possibilities. Form can follow function, but only if students have an awareness of all the options for form that exist.

One way to encourage new forms is a book pass: piles of books everywhere for kids to browse or read for two to three minutes, then pass on and look at something else. Activities like this nudge students to think more creatively about how they organize their prose.

Let's grow students' ability to browse like writers, getting inspired not only by standard form but also by those innovations on form that bring the next fresh idea. Combining and customizing for an exact fit helps them shape—or form—their next piece of writing. It may not always work, but by attempting, young writers discover and, sometimes, stumble into their style.

We've seen biographies told in fresh ways. How do *you* measure a life?

# Remember That Imitation Is the Sincerest Form

As students start paying attention to these interesting forms, they will eventually try them, although you may want to start them off with a few small directed responses:

- Respond to today's reading in a poem (or newspaper article or letter).
- Take a section of your memoir and give the DK treatment (callout boxes, extra information, etc.) to something important in your memoir, using a sidebar to do it.
- Use any of the text that inspires you to look at your life or a research project through a new lens.

*Figure 5.18*

| **Who Are You? Biographies** | |
|---|---|
| *Twelve Rounds to Glory: The Story of Muhammad Ali* by Charles R. Smith, Jr. | This book is written in poetic verse, but the interesting aspect was the choice to make each chapter of Ali's life a round. Sometimes brilliant organizing features have obvious links. How wonderful for kids to see simple and elegant choices that can inspire the form their next writing takes. |
| *Ben Franklin's Almanac: Being a True Account of the Good Gentleman's Life* by Candace Fleming | What is Benjamin Franklin famous for? Many things, of course, but his almanacs were a staple of his time and are still available today. An almanac is an innovative way around which to organize his life. The text is accessible and interesting and has many text types and forms within it. |
| *How to Think Like Leonardo da Vinci: Seven Steps to Genius Every Day* by Michael J. Gelb | This title framework for nonfiction has been used before: *How to Think Like a Scientist* by Stephen P. Kramer and scores of others. Just type in "How to Think Like" in the Amazon.com search engine. It's not necessarily about reading the book as much as inspiring a fresh form. Could you see your students writing a literary response about a character in a fiction book they're reading using the "How to Think Like (Character's Name)"? A social studies research paper on "How to Think Like Abraham Lincoln"? |
| *A River of Words: The Story of William Carlos Williams* by Jen Bryant (illustrated by Melissa Sweet) | The story of William Carlos Williams is told in simple text with his poetry all around, linking to and deepening the narrative. Although its form is somewhat straightforward, no one could consider Melissa Sweet's scrapbook illustrations ordinary. |
| DK biographies, various authors (Helen Keller, Mohandas Gandhi, Abraham Lincoln, Amelia Earhart, Harry Houdini) | Using pictures and charts to tell stories are quite appealing to today's digital generation. Students are more inspired to write a report knowing they can use some of their skills as an artist or a graphic or media designer to make it sparkle. It's still about finding what's significant. |

## Tell It Like It Is: Memoir

| | |
|---|---|
| *Encyclopedia of an Ordinary Life* by Amy Krouse Rosenthal<br><br>List Poems: "I Am Waiting" by Lawrence Ferlinghetti and "Where I'm From" by George Ella Lyon, both found in *The United States of Poetry*, edited by Blume, Homan, and Pellington | Though we often tell our children to never write in lists, wouldn't they miss out if they never tried a list poem, and felt, for a moment, like a poet? That all the randomness that is their life and their thinking comes together, organized in a moment of art. Amy Rosenthal's memoir uses the structure of an encyclopedia. She lists her life, alphabetically. And it's an extraordinary yet ordinary form. Taking something old and making it new again is fresh. |
| *My Life in Dog Years* by Gary Paulsen<br><br>*A Three Dog Life* by Abigail Thomas | Are we truly living a dog's life? Paulsen and Thomas both use their dogs as organizing or focusing principles. The difference between a memoir and an autobiography is how we focus. An autobiography is a chronology, and a memoir focuses on an aspect of our lives and seeks to make meaning of it. Anyone who's had pets knows the relationship with your animals certainly could act as an organizing pattern for your writing—even a brief essay. |
| *Neighborhood Odes* by Gary Soto | This collection of poems borrows from Pablo Neruda's inventive verse form of odes. We see raspas and sprinklers and other ordinary neighborhood things. These poems invite young writers to think about what's significant and what really makes anything what it is: neighborhood, home, family, school, or group of friends. It reminds me of William Carlos Williams: No idea, but in things. |
| "Nothing to Eat but Food: Menu as Memoir" by John Dufresne, found in *We Are What We Ate* (Mark Winegardner, editor) | This essay is designed around what the author's family regularly ate on each day of the week. An inventive lens that helps us see inside his family and their interaction, ever focused on what happened at the dinner table, Monday through Sunday. |
| *Songbook* by Nick Hornby<br><br>*Love Is a Mix Tape* by Rob Sheffield | Built around lists of songs, these books aren't merely catalogs or descriptions of songs. They focus more on how music brought meaning to certain times or experiences in our lives. In one class, some eighth graders imitated this form and went as far as to burn a CD of the songs that were significant to them at this point in their lives. Although none of the eighth graders drive, the part in Nick Hornby's book recounting driving with Springsteen blasting and the wind blowing though his hair got them to write about experiences intertwined with the music instead of a simplistic review or description of the song. Sheffield's is more about relationships and the honor of the mix tape, which has now given way to a digital song list. |
| *Stitches* by David Small<br><br>*To Dance: A Ballerina's Graphic Novel* by Siena Cherson Siegel | The form of graphic novels had escaped me until I started reading graphic memoirs. David Small's award-winning, painful account of his childhood is at once heartbreaking and affirming. The art and text help us know all it is to dance. |

*Figure 5.19*

## What's the Story? Fiction

| | |
|---|---|
| *The Fruit Bowl Project: 50 Ways to Tell a Story* by Sarah Durkee | A rock star visits an eighth-grade classroom and assigns students to write one story in any genre, form, point of view, and style they choose: instant message, rap, monologue, screenplay, poetry, horror, letter, lyric, fairy tale, newspaper article, etc. Inspired by the classic French book *Exercises in Style* by Raymond Queneau (translated by Barbara Wright). |
| *Regarding the Fountain: A Tale, in Letters, of Liars and Leaks* by Kate Klise<br><br>*Dying to Meet You: 43 Old Cemetery Road, Book 1* by Kate Klise | A narrative romp though many text forms (yes, I am meaning to imply it's fun): memos, letters, phone messages (from people without phones), announcements, writing assignments, acrostics, write-arounds, newspaper articles, postcards, telegrams, receipts. You get the idea. |
| *How I Became a Pirate* by Melinda Long | Long shows or categorizes the good and bad about choosing pirating as a career. Classification is not an original idea, but applying it to a picture book on pirates is. |
| *Monster* by Walter Dean Myers | A mixture of screenplay and journal, this adolescent novel combines forms to create a riveting, disturbing novel about knowing your identity no matter what the outside world says. |
| *Diary of a Wimpy Kid* series by Jeff Kinney<br><br>*Amelia's Notebook* series by Marissa Moss | I almost didn't include these choices, because I am not sure how fresh the diary or notebook as organization is anymore. Yet, I feel that this is a clear place where a genre of sorts was created by the popularity of using something kids are supposed to be writing. Of course, the integration of drawing and doodles also are part of the allure. |
| *The Naked Mole Rat Letters* by Mary Amato | Epistolary books have grown in popularity. They're not just for letters anymore. They could be e-mails, as in *The Naked Mole Rat Letters*, or text messaging, as in Lauren Myracle's *TTFN*. Text messaging as narrative is surging in this genre. |
| *Ophelia Joined the Group Maidens Who Don't Float: Classic Lit Signs onto Facebook* by Sarah Schmelling<br><br>*Twitterature: The World's Greatest Books in Twenty Tweets or Less* by Alexander Aciman | Can status updates be enough to tell a story? Inference anyone? Can it be that one of the biggest time wasters of all time was preparing us for a new form—Facebook literature?<br><br>What about Twitter? Is it literature worthy? Keep your eyes peeled for these new forms that can bring a little bit of our kids' world into old world literature. |
| *Yummy: The Last Days of a Southside Shorty* by G. Neri | Books based on events and seen through a character's eyes are nothing new, but the observer in this book is particularly intriguing, and the graphic novel nature of it adds to its accessibility. This is a form for the more visual student of the digital age. |

*Figure 5.20*

Combining and using different genres are the only ways for students to become fluent with them. To begin, they have to see, study, analyze, and emulate them (Graham and Perin 2007).

## Form Here to There

Form evolves, shapes, and helps writers structure and organize their thinking. Structure is not stagnant or formulaic. Form serves the writer's purpose, not the other way around. To use form effectively, we read and analyze—really taking apart texts we read, putting them back together, and noting all that works and doesn't. Only then will our writing take form.

# Frames

# Exploring Introductions and Conclusions

*Art consists of limitation. The most beautiful part of every picture is the frame.*

—G. K. Chesterton

A few years ago, I chose a frame for one of my favorite works of art, Van Gogh's *Room at Arles*. I deliberated on what would be the best frame for this special print. What would reflect my feelings when I look at it? How would it fit with the décor of my home? I could easily shove it in any old frame and be done with it, but I thought about the frame, what it was made of, how it affected the print. Would it enhance or distract? I searched for the right medium, the appropriate thickness. Okay, fine, I obsessed.

We make choices with our leads and conclusions as well. We could slap something on the beginning and end that would function as a frame—or we could custom frame it. We could craft a lead that reveals what is to come. We could construct a conclusion that will linger long after it's read.

But what are the options beyond the standard Dollar Store frame? That black metal one-size-fits-all frame that tells readers what you're going to tell them, tells them, then tells them what you told them. Young writers long for ways to begin and end their writing. How many times do we hear students plead for a clue?

"How do I start? What do I say first?"

*Figure 6.1*

## Making FRAMES Work

- Frame your writing with a *lead* and *conclusion*.
- Connect your *lead* and *conclusion*.
- Capture your readers' attention with a lead.
- Collect and categorize leads.
- Wrap up your writing with a conclusion.
- Collect and categorize conclusions.
- Explore creative nonfiction conclusions.

Okay, so they don't ponder endings as much. Mostly, they stop at the end of the sentence when they run out of steam. Young writers need more options. And while they need not obsess over their frames like I did, they should be able to generate a few leads and conclusions, try them out, and pick the best.

In this chapter, we will explore what young writers can do to become custom framers of their writing with attention-grabbing leads and just-right conclusions (see Figure 6.1).

# Frame Your Writing with a Lead and Conclusion

I pull two paintings from behind my desk and place them on the tray beneath my whiteboard. "I brought two paintings from home."

"They're the same thing," Jamaica says. "Why do you have two of the same picture?"

"Hey, that's that guy who cut his ear off, isn't it?" Javier asks.

"Yes, Javier, it is Vincent Van Gogh's room," I say. "Now, to answer Jamaica's question, why do I have two framed paintings? Before I answer, turn to your partner and discuss how the two paintings are alike and different."

After a few minutes, we come together to discuss the differences and similarities.

"Really the only difference is the frame," Ruby says.

"Yeah, one goes with the picture and the other one doesn't," Jamaica says.

"Do the frames make the picture look different?" I ask.

Squinting eyes focus.

"Yeah, I mean the colors look different and stuff."

"What do you mean?"

Once we discuss the various differences and similarities, I bring them back to the subject. "Just like these paintings have different frames, your

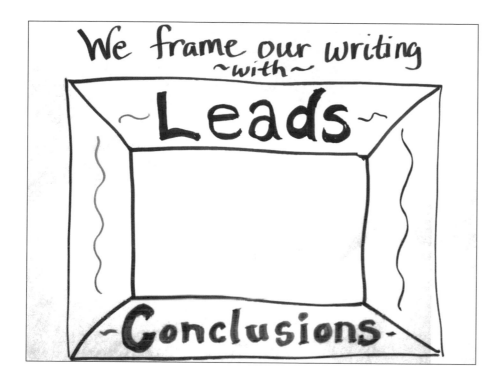

*Figure 6.2*
Framing Writing with a Lead
and Conclusion

writing can too. The frame of your writing defines where it starts and where it stops. It gives your writing a border."

I move to the board and write *Lead* and then several inches below, I write *Conclusion*. I draw a rectangular box, or frame, around the words (see Figure 6.2).

"I can make my frame any way I want, but I have to think about what's within the frame," I say, "and that my lead and conclusion should enhance what I have to say." To explain this further, I bring back an old childhood favorite.

## Connect Your Lead and Conclusion

I used to dive right into to teaching leads, but now I start by showing how leads and conclusions can be, and should be, connected. Conclusions that echo an image or idea from the lead are powerful. Instead of explaining this, I share models so students can discover it.

"You can learn a lot about leads and conclusions from *If You Give a Mouse a Cookie*. That's right. That circular story you heard over and over models a secret about leads and conclusions."

I read a few lines. "And what's it go back to at the end?"

They chant the title.

"Right. We've come full circle, as they say."

As writers, we can achieve this same balance in more sophisticated ways. Echoing an idea or an image from the lead in the conclusion is both subtle and satisfying to the reader. Like the German proverb says: "The beginning and end shake hands with each other." The lead and conclusion bookend our writing.

## Is There an Echo in Here?

I display the lead and conclusion from sports columnist and author Mike Lupica's novel, *Travel Team* (Figure 6.3). Before we read, I explain, "Just so you know, Danny is the *he* named in the first lines." We read Lupica's lead and conclusion, and then I ask, "How does the writer connect the lead and conclusion?"

Students turn and talk.

*Figure 6.3*

| | **Connecting Your Lead and Conclusioin** |
|---|---|
| | ***Travel Team* by Mike Lupica** |
| Lead | He knew he was small.<br>He just didn't *think* he was small.<br>*Big* difference. |
| Conclusion | The two of them shook hands the regular way.<br>The old-school way.<br>Then Ty kept holding on to Danny's hand and somehow lifted him up in the air in the same motion. Then Will was there, and Bren, putting Danny up on their shoulders, carrying him around the court, the way the old Vikings had carried his dad once.<br>Danny looked down on the day and thought:<br>So this is what it looks like from up here. |

Of course, I didn't pick this because characters should shake hands. I share it because Lupica connects us to a huge issue in the book, Danny's smallness. Students notice the lead promises us that there is a big difference between Danny's being small and thinking of himself as small. The conclusion not only connects back to the lead but also hints at the friendships we assume he has throughout the book, and how we, quite literally, lift each other up. In a way, Lupica lifts his reader up with a literally higher point of view, looking at our world in new ways.

Additional examples of leads and conclusions are presented in Figures 6.4–6.6 (nonfiction) and Figures 6.7–6.10 (fiction).

*Figure 6.4*

| ***Kitchen Confidential* by Anthony Bourdain** | |
| --- | --- |
| Lead | Don't get me wrong: I love the restaurant business. |
| Conclusion | I'll be right here. Until they drag me off the line. I'm not going anywhere. I hope. It's been an adventure. We took some casualties over the years. Things got broken. Things got lost.<br>But I wouldn't have missed it for the world. |

*Figure 6.5*

| ***Make Way for Sam Houston* by Jean Fritz** | |
| --- | --- |
| Lead | All his life Sam Houston liked to do things in a big way or not at all. |
| Conclusion | But Sam Houston had already given Texas all he had. |

*Figure 6 6*

| ***Every Bone Tells a Story: Hominin Discoveries, Deductions, and Debates* by Jill Rubalcaba and Peter Robertshaw** | |
| --- | --- |
| Lead | The boy died face down in the shallow lagoon. His body bobbed gently in the near motionless water close to the shore. Sand washed over him. Days turned into weeks; his flesh rotted. Months turned into years; his teeth fell out . . . |
| Conclusion | There is no doubt that the next generation will have superior tools and techniques at their disposal. Turkana Boy, Lapedo Child, Kennewick Man, and Ice Man will continue whispering their secrets into the ears of tomorrow's archaeologists. Their stories have just begun. |

| | *A Fine White Dust* by Cynthia Rylant |
|---|---|
| Lead | I've got these little bitty pieces of broken ceramic in my hands, and some of that fine white dust is coming off them, like chalk dust. There are some flecks of green paint on a few of the pieces. And some blue here and there. You'd never know to look at it that this mess used to be a cross.<br><br>I've been trying to forget it, keeping it in a paper bag in my bottom drawer for nearly a year now—since the summer of seventh grade. |
| Conclusion | And finally, I know too. That throwing away this mess doesn't mean I'm giving something up. Or losing something I can't get back.<br><br>It's that there are too many pieces and too much dust.<br><br>I'm just ready for something whole. |

Figure 6.7

| | *The Tiger Rising* by Kate DiCamillo |
|---|---|
| Lead | That morning, after he discovered the tiger, Rob went and stood under the Kentucky Star Motel sign and waited for the school bus just like it was any other day. The Kentucky Star sign was composed of a yellow neon star that rose and fell over a piece of blue neon in the shape of the state of Kentucky. Rob liked the sign; he harbored a dim but abiding notion that it would bring him good luck. |
| Conclusion | He lay in bed and considered the future, and outside his window, the tiny neon Kentucky Star rose and fell and rose and fell, competing bravely with the light of the morning sun. |

Figure 6.8

| | *The Sky Is Everywhere* by Jandy Nelson |
|---|---|
| Lead | Gram is worried about me. It's not just because my sister Bailey died four weeks ago, or because my mother hasn't contacted me for sixteen years, or even because suddenly all I think about is sex. She is worried about me because one of her house-plants has spots. |
| Conclusion | I don't know how the heart withstands it.<br><br>I kiss the ring, put it back into the cabinet next to the notebook, and close the door with the bird on it. Then I reach into my pack and take out the houseplant. It's so decrepit, just a few blackened leaves left. I walk over to the edge of the cliff, so I'm right over the falls. I take the plant out of its pot, shake the dirt right off the roots, get a good grip, reach my arm back, take one deep breath before I pitch my arm forward, and let go. |

Figure 6.9

| | *Storytime* **by Edward Bloor** |
|---|---|
| Lead | Kate was flying. |
| Conclusion | When the building was completely out of sight, Kate could no longer contain herself. She let go of their hands and took off running on her own. She threw back her head to feel the breeze in her hair and the sunlight on her face. Then she stretched out her arms and let the swirling river winds envelop her. They seemed to lift her up and pull her along as if she were weightless; as if she were sprinkled with fairy dust; as if she were flying. Quite involuntarily, she opened her mouth and began to sing. |

*Figure 6.10*

This conclusion also *echoes* its lead—another strategy—which we'll discuss in the next section. The lead to *Storytime* is "Kate is flying." Which brings up the question: Is she really? And, here, though it never says she is flying in the conclusion, I had to read it to make sure it didn't, and yet she flies.

## ECHO! Echo! E-c-h-o!

Sometimes conclusions echo more than an image from the lead. They also capture significant events that happen throughout the book (for examples, see Figure 6.11). Noticing how authors select events for the echo-echo-echo conclusion is a great lesson on determining importance. Students can write a conclusion before we read a conclusion and then compare it. It's an ancient activity, but it primes their conclusion awareness.

Once students see that the connection between the lead and conclusion hold a piece of writing together, we focus specifically on strategies for leads and then, later, strategies for conclusions.

# Capture Your Readers' Attention with a Lead

Let's start at the beginning.

The first few words of your writing will either capture readers, bore them to sleep, or send them running. Examples of successful leads fill the books, articles, and short stories already in your classroom. As a class, we discover and name those patterns and possibilities, unlocking the mysteries of what works.

## Endings That Echo!

### Nonfiction

| | |
|---|---|
| *Margaret, Frank, and Andy: Three Writers' Stories* by Cynthia Rylant | E. B. White—Andy—once said, "All that I hope to say in a book, all that I ever hope to say, is that I love the world."<br><br>He wrote one more children's book, *The Trumpet of the Swan*, and then his beloved wife, Katharine, died and he did not write any more books. He planted an oak tree at her grave and went back to his farm, where he tended the animals, fixed things, and wrote letters to old friends and young readers.<br><br>Then, after eighty-six years of worrying that he would die, E. B. White at last let go of the world he loved so much. He left having known "the glory of everything." And, like Charlotte, having made it more radiant. |

### Fiction

| | |
|---|---|
| *Harris and Me* by Gary Paulsen | The deputy spat out the window. "Nice people, the Larsons. You have a good summer?"<br><br>And it was all there. The horses and the pigs and Ernie and the pictures and Louie and swimming and going to see the Gene Autry movie—all there at once, filling me so that I had to look out the window and hide my eyes.<br><br>"Yes. I did. I had a nice summer." |
| *Carlos Is Gonna Get It* by Kevin Emerson | I was sitting back in my tub and still having the shivery June, last-day-of-school, first-day-of-summer feeling of being so small I was big, like I could look down over everything and enjoy the view—<br><br>Of five bodies stretched out in the bathtubs in a circle like flower petals.<br><br>Of a silvery train catching the afternoon sun as it headed home.<br><br>Of a little figure sitting on top of one roof out of hundreds, kicking his heels against the side of the house and staring off into the summer shimmer.<br><br>Of distant hills wrapped in a haze that always remind me of chances. |

*Figure 6.11*

## Stacks of Leads

I distribute a bunch of randomly selected novels and nonfiction books, placing them on tables and asking students to pick one. I also have a stack of sentence strips ready to go. Then I invite students to read only the first line of the book in their hands. Volunteers read aloud some of their selections.

As we share the leads, a few of us write them on sentence strips and begin categorizing them on several colored sheets of butcher paper hanging around the room. In the discussion that follows, the leads are italicized to indicate the authors' text.

Shibahn reads her lead from *The Graveyard Book* by Neil Gaiman: *"There was a hand in the darkness, and it held a knife."*

"What does that lead do?"

"It makes me want to read it."

"Why?" I place a sentence strip and a marker at Shibahn's desk.

"I want to find out what's going to happen." Shibahn records her lead on the sentence strip.

"So, Neil Gaiman's lead makes us want to read."

"Not me," says Chloe.

"Ah, not everyone's going to like every lead."

"Yeah, I don't like those kind of books."

"Shibahn and Chloe noticed the lead hints at genre—those kinds of books," I say. "Besides promising something scary, we get a shocking detail of the hand holding a knife. We know something will happen. This makes us predict; it gives us a question we want to know the answer to. Let's put this lead on this chart and see if we find any other leads like it." Shibahn tapes her lead on a piece of butcher paper.

"I have one," Javier volunteers. He reads the lead from *Schooled* by Gordon Korman, "*I was thirteen the first time I saw a police officer up close.*"

"Is Javier's lead like *The Graveyard Book*?" I ask.

"It hints at trouble. I mean, why'd he have to see a cop up close?"

"It doesn't have to be bad," Chloe insists.

I jump in after I hand Javier a sentence strip. "The text leaves us with questions again." I shrug my shoulders. "We don't know yet, which may make us want to read on, but we have to think about the text that comes after it. We can't put a false lead on our writing. It has to match what we write about. We wouldn't use these leads to begin an expository piece on how to make a peanut butter sandwich."

"Mine's better," Ruby says, and she reads the lead to *Dovey Coe* by Frances O'Roark Dowell: "*My name is Dovey Coe, and I reckon it don't matter if you like me or not.*" Ruby continues beyond the first line and I let her. "*I'm here to lay the record straight, to let you know them folks saying I done a terrible thing are liars. I aim to prove it, too. I hated Parnell Caraway as much as the next person, but I didn't kill him.*"

The class wants Ruby to repeat the title. This game sparks interest in books, getting students to pay attention to how a lead either hooks you or it doesn't. "Does this lead go with *The Graveyard Book* lead?"

After some discussion, we decide it does. Ruby copies the lead onto a sentence strip and then tapes it on the butcher paper beneath *The Graveyard Book* lead.

"I have another," Samantha says before she reads the lead from the National Book Award winner *Godless* by Pet Hautman. "*Getting punched hard in the face is a singular experience.*"

As we decide this one can go (for now) with the other leads, Chloe expresses worry. "Do all the beginnings have to be all violent or scary?"

"Hmmm," I say. "Trouble or controversies do pique a lot of people's interests. Why do you think reality shows run next week's fight as a teaser to get you to watch again?" I play a bit of the song "Trouble" by Ray Lamontagne on my iPod. The kids decide we should label these leads "Trouble."

Switching gears, I say, "What are some other leads you have that are different—less blood and murder?" I point to Chloe. "What do you have, Chloe?"

She reads from Joan Bauer's Newbery Honor book, *Hope Was Here*: "*Somehow I knew my time had come when Bambi Barnes tore her order book into little pieces, hurled it in the air like confetti, and got fired from the Rainbow Diner in Pensacola right in the middle of lunchtime rush.*"

"What's that lead doing?"

"It's telling you there's trouble because someone quit."

"What else?"

"You know someone was a waitress and she needs anger management," Jonathan says.

"You know she's in some place . . ."

"Setting," I say, then I let the students battle it out.

"Yeah, a diner."

"No."

"Pensacola . . . in Florida."

"So this lead has trouble, but it's not gory or scary. It's just an everyday kind of problem." I survey the class. "Should this lead go with these or is it a new category? We discuss and decide it needs a new piece of butcher paper and maybe we need to revise "Trouble" to "Shocking Detail" or something like that.

"Remember, if you don't like the first sentence, you can look at how other chapters start, and like Chloe said, they don't have to be violent." Real wall charts grow through revision. Using sentence strips makes it easier to change things around—both sentences and categories.

"Mine's not scary," Jose says. "Listen: *The way I figure it, everyone gets a miracle*" (John Green, *Paper Towns*).

"What's that lead promise?" I ask.

"He's gonna need a miracle."

"That's not hopeful," says Chloe.

"It is if he gets it," Jose replies.

We start a new category. Jose places his sentence strip on yet another piece of butcher paper, leaving space for a heading later.

"This one's bad. It gets you all seeing it by the words."

"Read it, Robert."

Robert reads the first sentence of Matt de la Peña's novel *Mexican WhiteBoy*: "*Dressed in a well-worn Billabong tee, camo cargo shorts and a pair of old-school slip-on Vans, Danny Lopez follows his favorite cousin, Sofia, as she rolls up on the cul-de-sac crowd with OG swagger.*"

Robert puts down the book. "Oh, man he's gonna be in trouble."

"Why do you say that?"

"I read on, and he's staying with his cousin who's all gangsta and he's not gonna fit in."

After I calm them down, I ask Robert to reread the lead and students talk with their partners about all they see this lead doing: It sets up Danny's character with his clothes, and even the author's voice tells us it's casual with "rolls up" and "OG swagger" (OG is "original gangster"—I had to ask).

"Let's start a new chart that's character or visuals or something."

Since we hadn't heard any nonfiction yet, I encourage students who have some at their desks. Kevin is reading *The Best American Sports Writing 2009*, edited by Leigh Montville. When I interrupt Kevin's reading, he says, "It was so good I couldn't stop."

"What hooked you Kevin?" I ask.

He reads from "Life and Limb" by Bruce Barcott, *"On the day he decided to pay a man to cut off his leg with a power saw, Tom White woke up with a powerful yearning to run."*

"I had to see where that was going," Kevin says.

"Did it fulfill its promise?" I ask.

"Huh?"

"Did the words that follow fit with that lead?"

Kevin squints.

"Kevin, how would you have felt if the article ended up being about decorating your Croc sandals with pins?"

"I'd have been mad and put it back."

"But you kept going because it fulfilled the promise."

"Whatever," Kevin says. "I just liked it."

"I want us to notice why we like things and try some of those things in our own writing. But you don't have to give a shocking detail to have a lead. Let's hear more."

We end up with a few more categories and discussions over the next few weeks. The key is to immerse writers in models that show what's possible, what they might try. The names of categories may change. We add or delete them. But what's important is that we construct meaning together.

## Collect and Categorize Leads

We could distribute lists of leads to students, but it's better if students discover those leads and we name them together. Students search, evaluate, share, read, categorize, and construct meaning.

Following are the lead categories my students came up with over the first semester of the year, a little at a time. It is the constructing of the lists, the discussions and discoveries, that make this activity work. The value is in its organic nature. If I merely give them the lead lists, meaning isn't made, and it won't stick. We follow a general process:

- Collect
- Categorize
- Imitate
- Celebrate

## The Name of the Frame

In the end, what we call the leads or strategies doesn't matter. What matters is the students are engaged in collecting them and processing their attributes. The lists of leads that follow aren't designed to limit writers but to expand their options. What I want to develop in my writers is an I'll-try-this-and-see-what-happens attitude. Each time they try, even if they fail, the strategy or possibility is imprinted and may work for another writing task. Here are some basic strategies—or things writers do—to make their leads part of a dynamic and meaningful frame (see Figure 6.12).

*Figure 6.12*

### Lead Strategies

- Zoom in on one of the five senses.
- Hint at something to come.
- Describe a searing image.
- Make a fresh comparison.
- Set a context with a few of the five Ws.
- Begin with what it's not.
- Stack information in lists.
- Ask questions.
- Reveal thoughts.
- Start in the middle of the action.
- Introduce a character or person.
- Let the people (or the sources) speak.

You don't need to teach all of these lead patterns. Start with those you discover through inquiry. Monitor student interest and involvement, and plan to revisit and add leads over time. What's crucial is that students begin paying attention to leads and emulating successful ones in their own writing.

## Zoom in on One of the Five Senses

As humans, our senses give us feedback helping us make sense of our world by taking in information through our eyes, nose, ears, and skin—even our mouths. This is how we come to know the world. Using sensory detail in your lead is a concrete way to draw a reader in, transporting readers into your piece of writing (Figure 6.13).

*Figure 6.13*

| **Sensory Leads** | |
|---|---|
| **Nonfiction** | |
| "Quarterbacks Built Here" by Paul Solotaroff in *The Best American Sports Writing 2009* (Montville) | The perfectly thrown football, moving at a high rate of speed, makes a ripping sound as it leaves the hand, something between a whoosh and a mortar launch. |
| *Lincoln: A Photobiography* by Russell Freedman | Abraham Lincoln wasn't the sort of man who could lose himself in a crowd. After all, he stood six feet four inches tall, and to top it off, he wore a high silk hat. |
| **Fiction** | |
| *Fever 1793* by Laurie Halse Anderson | I woke to the sound of a mosquito whining in my left ear and my mother screeching in the right. |
| *Moon Over Manifest* by Clare Vanderpool | The movement of the train rocked me like a lullaby. |
| *Catching Fire* by Suzanne Collins | I clasp the flask between my hands even though the warmth from the tea has long since leached into the frozen air. |
| *Eragon* by Christopher Paolini | Wind howled through the night, carrying a scent that would change the world. |
| *Reckless* by Cornelia Funke | The night breathed through the apartment like a dark animal. The ticking of a clock. The groan of a floorboard as he slipped out of his room. All was drowned by its silence. But Jacob loved the night. He felt it on his skin like a promise. |

## Hint at Something to Come

Everyone likes having their curiosity piqued. Suspense and wanting to find out what will happen next keeps us reading. We can't give readers too much.

| Hint Leads | |
| --- | --- |
| **Nonfiction** | |
| *Great Big Book of Tiny Germs* by Bill Nye, the Science Guy | We're outnumbered! They are everywhere, but you can't see them. |
| *The Frog Scientist* by Pamela S. Turner | The sun is just peeking over golden Wyoming hills as Dr. Tyrone Hayes wakes his team. |
| *The Trouble Begins at 8: A Life of Mark Twain in the Wild, Wild West* by Sid Fleischman | Mark Twain was born fully grown, with a cheap cigar clamped between his teeth. |
| **Fiction** | |
| *The Fire-Eaters* by David Almond | It all starts on the day I met McNulty. |
| *Things Not Seen* by Andrew Clements | It's a Tuesday morning in February, and I get up as usual, and I stumble into the bathroom to take a shower in the dark. Which is my school-day method because it's sort of like an extra ten minutes of sleep.<br>It's after the shower. That's when it happens. |
| *Let The Great World Spin* by Colum McCann | Those who saw him hushed. |
| *Tinkers* by Paul Harding | George Washington Crosby began to hallucinate eight days before he died. |

Figure 6.14

Instead, we hint that something interesting is about to happen, like Hansel dropping bread crumbs, we leave enough behind to pull our reader onward (Figure 6.14).

## Describe a Searing Image

Giving readers a visual can establish the focus of your writing in the first sentence. A surprising image can use the power of description to capture your reader from the very first words they read (Figure 6.15).

## Make a Fresh Comparison

When we want our reader to see or appreciate something that may not be familiar to most readers, we compare it to something more accessible to

| Shocking Image | |
|---|---|
| **Nonfiction** | |
| *Stiff: The Curious Lives of Human Cadavers* by Mary Roach | The human head is of the same approximate size and weight as a roaster chicken. I have never before had occasion to make the comparison, for never before today have I seen a head in a roasting pan. |
| **Fiction** | |
| *The Midwife's Apprentice* by Karen Cushman | When animal droppings and garbage and spoiled straw are piled up in a great heap, the rotting and moiling give forth heat. Usually no one gets close enough to notice because of the stench. But the girl noticed and, on that frosty night, burrowed deep into the warm, rotting muck, heedless of the smell. |

*Figure 6.15*

them. For example, we may not know the texture of a brain, but we know the consistency of jelly and cold butter. Comparisons make writing concrete (Figure 6.16).

*Figure 6.16*

| Comparison Leads | |
|---|---|
| **Nonfiction** | |
| *The Human Brain Book* by Rita Carter | The human brain is like nothing else. As organs go, it is not especially prepossessing—3lb. or so of rounded, corrugated flesh with a consistency somewhere between jelly and cold butter. It doesn't expand and shrink like the lungs, pump like the heart, or secrete visible material like the bladder. If you sliced off the top of someone's head and peered inside, you wouldn't see much happening at all. |
| "Diatoms" in *Ubiquitous: Celebrating Nature's Survivors* by Joyce Sidman | Diatoms are single-celled microscopic organisms that drift through the ocean by the billions, like tiny snowflakes. |
| **Fiction** | |
| *Turtle in Paradise* by Jennifer L. Holm | Everyone thinks children are sweet as Necco Wafers, but I've lived long enough to know the truth: kids are rotten. |

## Set a Context with a Few of the 5Ws

Readers want to know who or what this writing is about, where and when it takes place, and at some point find out why. Writers can make use of the reporter's formula (Carroll and Wilson 2008) in anything they write: who, what, when, where, and why? Giving readers an answer to one or more of these questions gives them the meaning and clarity they need to follow our writing (Figure 6.17).

*Figure 6.17*

| **Context Leads** | |
|---|---|
| **Nonfiction** | |
| *The Hive Detectives: Chronicle of a Honeybee Catastrophe* by Loree Griffin Burns | Put on your veil, grab your hive tool, and light up your smoker . . . we're going into a beehive. |
| *The Wave: In Pursuit of the Rogues, Freaks, and Giants of the Ocean* by Susan Casey | The clock read midnight when the hundred-foot wave hit the ship, rising from the North Atlantic out of the darkness. |
| *What's the Big Idea, Ben Franklin?* by Jean Fritz | In 1706 Boston was so new that its streets were still being named. For five years the town officials had been thinking up names and they hadn't finished yet. . . . Luckily Milk Street had been named early, because that's where Benjamin Franklin was born. So right away he had an address. That was handy since he turned out to be famous and people like to know where and when famous men are born. |
| *A History of US: From Colonies to Country, 1735–1791* by Joy Hakim | In England, July 4th, 1776 seemed to be just an ordinary day. But if King George III had put an ear to the ground, he surely would have heard the earth trembling. |
| *Unbroken: A World War II Story of Survival, Resilience, and Redemption* by Laura Hillenbrand | All he could see, in every direction, was water. |
| **Fiction** | |
| *Waiting for Normal* by Leslie Connor | Maybe Mommers and I shouldn't have been surprised; Dwight had told us it was a trailer even before we packed our bags. |
| *The Hunger Games* by Suzanne Collins | When I wake up, the other side of the bed is cold. My fingers stretch out, seeking Prim's warmth but finding only the rough canvas cover of the mattress. She must have had bad dreams and climbed in with our mother. Of course, she did. This is the day of the reaping. |
| *Masterpiece* by Elise Broach | Home, for Marvin's family, was a damp corner of the cupboard beneath the kitchen sink. Here, a leaking pipe had softened the plaster and caused it to crumble away. |
| *The Tale of Despereaux* by Kate DiCamillo | This story begins within the walls of a castle, with the birth of a mouse. |

# Begin with What It's Not

One of the most interesting and most productive lead patterns we came across is what my students affectionately refer to as "The Snot Lead" (Figure 6.18). Telling us what someone or something is *not* is an interesting way to

*Figure 6.18*

| It's Not Lead | |
|---|---|
| **Nonfiction** | |
| *Hitler Youth: Growing Up in Hitler's Shadow* by Susan C. Bartoletti | This is not a book about Adolf Hitler. |
| *Eleanor Roosevelt: A Life of Discovery* by Russell Freedman | Eleanor Roosevelt never wanted to be the president's wife. |
| "Baby Ruth Candy Bar" in *The Kid Who Invented the Popsicle: And Other Surprising Stories About Inventions* by Don L. Wulffson | The Baby Ruth candy bar was not, as is commonly believed, named after Babe Ruth, the famous baseball player. |
| "Pelé: Coffee, Boxer Shorts, and Pajamas" in *Lives of the Athletes: Thrills, Spills (and What the Neighbors Thought)* by Kathleen Krull | No one, including Edson Arantes do Nascimento, knows how he got the nickname Pelé or what it means. |
| *Extreme Animals: The Toughest Creatures on Earth* by Nicola Davies | We humans are a bunch of wimps! We can't stand the cold, we can't stand the heat, we can't live without food, or water, and just a few minutes without air is enough to finish us off. Luckily, not all life is so fragile. All over the planet there are animals (and plants) that relish the sort of conditions that could kill a human quicker than you could say "coffin." |
| *The Good, the Bad, and the Barbie: A Doll's History and Her Impact on Us* by Tanya Lee Stone | Ruth Handler looked absolutely nothing like a Barbie Doll. |
| **Fiction** | |
| *The 10 p.m. Question* by Kate De Goldi | Tuesday the fourteenth of February began badly for Frankie Parsons. There was no milk for his Just Right. There was no GoCat for the Fat Controller, so the Fat Controller stood under the table meowing accusingly while Frankie ate his toast.<br><br>The newspaper hadn't arrived, which meant Frankie couldn't take a headline and article for Current Affairs and so would earn one of Mr. A's sardonic looks. |
| *Maniac Magee* by Jerry Spinelli | Maniac Magee was not born in a dump. |

set up the reader. Sometimes in knowing what something isn't, we know what it is.

## Stack Information in Lists

Sometimes we want to flood readers with detail. A spray of sentences may not work as well as packing the information into a sentence or two using the power of listing. Giving readers scads of information early in your piece can help them visualize and make sense of your text—and keep them reading (Figure 6.19).

*Figure 6.19*

| List Leads | |
|---|---|
| **Nonfiction** | |
| *Steven Caney's Invention Book* by Steven Caney | When people think of an "inventor" they probably conjure up an image of an absent-minded, wild-haired professor, working in a laboratory filled with bubbling test tubes and elaborate electronic machines, or at a blackboard filled with intricate mathematical calculations. |
| *Lives of the Athletes: Thrills, Spills (and What the Neighbors Thought)* by Kathleen Krull | Roberto Clemente's first baseball games in Puerto Rico made use of a stick cut from a guava tree (the bat), old coffee sacks (the bases), and knotted bunches of rags (the balls). |
| *Mistakes That Worked* by Charlotte Foltz Jones | Call them accidents. Call them mistakes. Even serendipity.<br>If the truth were known, we might be amazed by the number of great inventions and discoveries that were accidental, unplanned, and unintentional. |
| **Fiction** | |
| *Rules* by Cynthia Lord | Rules for David<br>Chew with your mouth closed.<br>Say "thank you" when someone gives you a present (even if you don't like it).<br>If someone says "hi," you say "hi" back.<br>When you want to get out of answering something, distract the question with another question. |
| *The True Confessions of Charlotte Doyle* by Avi | Not every thirteen-year-old girl is accused of murder, brought to trial, and found guilty. |

## Ask Questions

Readers have questions, but writers can use them too. Engage your reader with a question (Figure 6.20). Be careful though. Make sure it's a real question. One you might want to answer. At times, this strategy becomes stale or cliché: "Have you ever met an important person? Well, I have." It's almost as bad as the abhorrent "I'm going to tell you about. . . ." lead. However, question leads are indispensible for nonfiction writers, so I warn students to be careful. We should only ask real questions, not simply restate a prompt in question form—or we've put our lead in *Jeopardy*.

*Figure 6.20*

| Question Leads | |
|---|---|
| **Nonfiction** | |
| *Elizabeth Leads the Way: Elizabeth Cady Stanton and the Right to Vote* by Tanya Lee Stone | What would you do if someone told you you can't be what you want to be because you are a girl? What would you do if someone told you your vote doesn't count, your voice doesn't matter because you are a girl? Would you ask why? Would you talk back? Would you fight . . . for your rights? Elizabeth did. |
| "Wedding Ring" in *The Kid Who Invented the Popsicle: And Other Surprising Stories About Inventions* by Don L. Wulffson | Have you ever wondered why people wear wedding rings, or why the ring is always worn on the third finger of the left hand? |
| *Being Wrong: Adventures in the Margin of Error* by Kathryn Schulz | Why is it so much fun being right? |
| **Fiction** | |
| *Any Which Wall* by Laurel Snyder | Have you ever stumbled onto magic? Maybe while you were trudging to school one drizzly day, or in the middle of a furious game of freeze tag? Has anything odd ever happened to you? |

## Reveal Thoughts

Some of us like to read because we feel like we're being let in on a secret, the writer's or character's deepest thoughts. Don't underestimate the power of sharing a bit of what you as a writer are thinking or what a character may be wondering to bring your reader into your writing (Figure 6.21).

| Thought Leads | |
|---|---|
| **Nonfiction** | |
| *The Abracadabra Kid: A Writer's Life* by Sid Fleischman | I am astonished, when I pause to think about it, to discover myself to be an author of humorous novels for children. Or an author at all. |
| **Fiction** | |
| *So You Want to Be a Wizard* by Diane Duane | *Part of the problem,* Nita thought as she tore desperately down Rose Avenue, *is that I can't keep my mouth shut.* |

*Figure 6.21*

## Start in the Middle of the Action

Is your lead boring? An old writer's trick is to cut the first page and start with the action. Sometimes too much background information or fictional exposition about a setting can send a reader running. Start in the middle of the action—*in medias res*—and you'll hook readers (Figure 6.22).

*Figure 6.22*

| Action Leads | |
|---|---|
| **Nonfiction** | |
| *Candy Bomber: The Story of the Berlin Airlift's "Chocolate Pilot"* by Michael O. Tunnell | Nine-year-old Peter Zimmerman searched the sky for airplanes. |
| *Houdini: Art and Magic* by Brooke Kamin Rapaport | On the eve of a 1917 performance at New York City's Hippodrome, Harry Houdini was cinched into a straightjacket and hoisted upside down from his ankles by a subway derrick. Thirty feet above Forty-Sixth Street and Broadway, he convulsed, wriggled, and swayed. |
| **Fiction** | |
| *The Wild Things* by Dave Eggers | Matching Stumpy pant for pant, Max chased his cloud-white dog though the upstairs hallway, down the wooden stairs, and into the cold open foyer. |

## Introduce a Character or Person

Joy Hakim has made a career of making American history and science interesting. She argues that when we make history about memorizing dates and battles, we lose our connection. In her History of US series, she makes history a story about people, which hooks students. Writers use people to focus their leads (Figure 6.23).

*Figure 6.23*

| People Leads | |
|---|---|
| **Nonfiction** | |
| *The Orchid Thief* by Susan Orlean | John Laroche is tall guy, skinny as a stick, pale-eyed, slouch-shouldered, and sharply handsome, in spite of the fact that he is missing all his front teeth. |
| **Fiction** | |
| *Scat* by Carl Hiaasen | The day before Mrs. Starch vanished, her third-period biology students trudged silently, as always, into the classroom. Their expressions reflected the usual mix of dread and melancholy, for Mrs. Starch was the most feared teacher at the Truman School.<br><br>When the bell rang, she unfolded stiffly, like a crane, and rose to her full height of nearly six feet. In one hand she twirled a sharpened Ticonderoga No. 2 pencil, a sure sign of trouble to come. |

## Let the People (or the Sources) Speak

Citing sources or giving readers insight through dialogue can pull readers in (Figure 6.24). On the surface, it seems dialogue is for fiction and quotes are for nonfiction, but my students and I discovered that fiction often starts with quotes. For example, in the historical fiction novel *Chains*, Laurie Halse Anderson leads with a quote. And along the same lines, nonfiction often starts with dialogue from the subjects being written about or from an observer of the situation about which the piece is written.

| **Dialogue and Quotation Leads** | |
|---|---|
| **Nonfiction** | |
| *The Calculus Diaries: How Math Can Help You Lose Weight, Win in Vegas, and Survive a Zombie Apocalypse* by Jennifer Ouellette | **Xander:** Giles lived for school. He's actually still bitter that there are only twelve grades.<br>**Buffy:** He probably sat in math class thinking, *There should be more math. This could be mathier.*<br>Dialogue quoted from "The Dark Age," *Buffy the Vampire Slayer* |
| *Years of Dust: The Story of the Dustbowl* by Albert Marrin | Every blade of grass has its angel that bends over it and whispers, "Grow, grow."<br>Quoted from the *Talmud* |
| *The Shallows: What the Internet Is Doing to Our Brains* by Nicholas Carr | "Dave, stop. Stop, will you? Stop, Dave. Will you stop?"<br>Dialogue quoted from HAL the computer in Stanley Kubrick's *2001: A Space Odyssey* |
| **Fiction** | |
| *Notes from a Liar and Her Dog* by Gennifer Choldenko | "I don't even know what I did this time," I say to my best friend, Harrison Emerson. |
| *Chains* by Laurie Halse Anderson | Youth is the seed of good habits, as well in nations as in individuals.<br>Quoted from Thomas Paine's *Common Sense* |

*Figure 6.24*

## Lead Them On

Just because the lead list ends here doesn't mean yours does. Leads are ever evolving, and with your particular grade level or writers, you may want to do a bit more or significantly less. This list gets the hunt started. In any case, your students' lists of options should keep growing and changing. See the appendix for lead charts to involve students in collecting and imitating.

In addition to the leads in the preceding lists, I have seen a few other innovations worth noting:

- **Newspaper articles** in *Tears of a Tiger* by Sharon Draper and *Wringer* by Jerry Spinelli
- **Notes to reader** in *The Thing About Georgie* by Lisa Graff
- **Notes to characters** in *Swindle* by Gordon Korman
- **Advice** in *A Whole Nother Story* by Dr. Cuthbert Soup

- **Warnings to not read** in the A Series of Unfortunate Events series by Lemony Snicket and the Pseudonymous Bosch series
- **Reproductions of real newspaper headlines and pamphlets** from a period of time in which the novel is set, such as *Countdown* by Deborah Wiles

Perhaps there is a young writer in your classroom today who will combine something in an innovative way or create an original category. What works is the only rule. Figure 6.25 provides a few strategies I use to prompt new ways of working with leads.

*Figure 6.25*

## Strategies for Using Lead Charts in the Writing Process

While we can wait for the kids to naturally evolve, sometimes we need to give them a nudge. The following activities do that. Students use writing they are currently working on or past writings in their folders or writer's notebooks.

- **Lead Like a Writer**—Find a lead that you like and copy it in the chart (see appendix sheets) or on the top half of a sheet in your writer's notebook. Try the strategy at least twice in your writing, seeing whether you can create a better lead. Read the new leads to three people and see what kind of response you get.

- **Lead Between the Lines**—Hunt through your own writing for an exciting line that mirrors any type of lead you've studied, for example, images, dialogue, or "it's not" statements. Is the lead hiding in your fourth paragraph? Your notes? Have you thought about starting in the middle of the action? Look through what you've already written for a lead.

- **One Mistake Leads to Another**—Sometimes when we work at generating leads, we come up with a few good ones. And sometimes the leads can end up working somewhere else in your writing. There is no wasted writing. Whatever you write, even if it doesn't see the light of day, makes you a better writer. Save everything.

- **Mis-Lead**—Watch out for leads that don't fulfill their promise. When rereading your writing in the revision stage, see whether your lead matches the tone and content of the rest of your writing. Can you make any links, like an echo in the conclusion?

- **Follow Your Lead**—Bring three leads that you like to class. Add your leads to the discussion and continue categorizing, labeling, imitating, and celebrating.

- **You Can Lead a Source to a Writer**—Don't forget the power of quotations. Sometimes when I am generating writing, looking at famous quotes gets my ideas in motion. If I am writing an essay on procrastination and I come across Eleanor Roosevelt's quote, "You must do the thing you think you cannot do," I've got a lead and a focus. Remember that quotes don't have to come from books or famous people; characters use dialogue, and you can quote what interview subjects say. Don't hold on to your sources. Use them. Let them do the work for you.

- **Three Little Leads**—I borrowed this activity from my friend and colleague Vicki Spandel (2011), who asks writers to generate three new leads when revising their work. She also points out that on standardized tests, leads and conclusions are the most important part of your writing: the first impression and the last—the frame. My students write the three leads, using models as inspiration, on a separate piece of paper. Then students circle the one they like best and write a sentence or two about why they chose it. Voilà. I have something to grade.

- **A Stack of Leads**—Sometimes to kick off my lead studies or to inject a shot of freshness, I simply pick up a stack of new books or articles and read the leads aloud, one at a time, asking students what each lead is doing. After discussing them, students copy the leads on the appropriate list, or we add them to our class wall charts.

- **Actions Lead to Action**—Sometimes we do lead instruction and students still don't use them in their writing. That's why we revise. But when I want to ensure they remember and use their options for a timed, high-stakes writing test on the horizon, I pick the top three leads, and, as a class, we make a pantomime or charade for each one. Once we get down the actions, I yell out, "Sensory lead! Strike a pose!" Students scramble to touch their fingers together, then touch their ears, then their nose, then near their eyes, and stick out their tongue. They don't have to be this complex. When I yell, "Dialogue lead! Strike a pose!" students do air quotes. Of course, they can always use the mute actions to answer the question, "What kind of lead is this?" Sometimes we just have to laugh and move to learn and remember.

- **Lead Themes**—I love music, and so do my students. Searching for songs that match leads can be fun. For our "Snot" leads, we can use "Nobody but Me" by The Human Beinz, or for dialogue our theme could be "What I'd Say" by Ray Charles.

# Wrap Up Your Writing with a Conclusion

I often struggle with conclusions in my own writing. I know a good conclusion when I hear one, but how do I help students see what works to end a piece of writing and what doesn't? Beyond a simple formula of repeating or recycling the introduction, customizing conclusions doesn't get the same depth of discussion as leads. Even so, students know their writing has to end; that's why young students tack on "THE END," when they are finished—a frame, yes, but customized or original or thought provoking, no.

We can't blame them. They've seen THE END modeled, and they are borrowing it. We've also seen them borrow what I call the *Dallas* ending, from the early 1980s TV series (everything was a dream), or worse, the even more worn out "it all worked out in the end." In academic circles, this is called *deus ex machina*, meaning "God from the Machine." A penniless family receives a letter in the mail, informing them that a long-lost uncle died and left his fortune to them. Voilà! Anything that's too magical, too formulaic, or too mundane disappoints readers who stuck with you 'til the end.

Let's face it: readers favor certain kinds of endings. Some like endings that are tied up neatly in a bow. Others like things being left up in the air, deciding for themselves how things turned out. A case in point is Lois Lowry's Newbery Award-winning *The Giver*. When my eighth graders read this dystopian novel, we debate over exactly what happens as Jonas's toboggan slides into the cold, harsh winter. Did he escape? Did he die? Students look back at the text and compare it to other texts to insist on how it actually ends. A few years later, in a speech, Lowry ruined the ending for me because she said what happened. Since she was wrong, I continue to debate it.

Think about what happened when *The Sopranos* series finale aired. The entire episode built tension that something awful was about to happen to Tony and his family. The tension builds higher and higher until the screen goes black and mute for a full minute. People complained to their satellite and cable companies that they had missed the conclusion of the drama they'd watched for years. But it was the writer's intention to not tie up everything neatly. The ending was heaven for those of us who love being jarred into discussion and supposition.

Even Dr. Seuss displeases some readers with his conclusion to *The Butter Battle Book*. In the last scene, a representative from each side of the butter battle stands at the wall ready to drop a bomb and blow the other side to smithereens. Dr. Seuss leaves it unresolved (even his end punctuation leaves us in the air with an ellipsis).

> You can't tell the reader what it means at the end. The reader has to know what it means, and feel what it means. The reader has to be there experiencing the text.
>
> —Don Murray

*"Who's going to drop it, Will you . . .? Will he . . .?"*
*"Be patient, said Grandpa. "We'll see.*
*We will see . . ."*

I warn you: I prefer subtle conclusions to obvious ones. I have to put that preference aside while teaching. As evaluators of student writing, the samples we'll highlight in our lessons, we need to acknowledge our own prejudices and judge conclusions on their construction and how they work, not on how they fit into our personal likes and dislikes for resolution or resonance. I love living in questions; some prefer to be done with it. We have to show students the full range of possibilities writers can use.

A formula for the perfect ending doesn't exist, but writers have a few broad patterns to consider for wrapping up their writing. As with leads, writers need options. The process of reading, discovering, naming, and categorizing continues with the other half of the frame: conclusions. After all, experiencing conclusions is the best way to learn the feel and sound of a powerful ending.

Conclusions are an essential part of the frame. Editor Jack Hart explains that the conclusion is "the reader's last taste" that "colors [the reader's] perception of everything that came before." (Hart 2006, 68). This is your last contact with the reader. You leave an impression about your whole piece with those last few words. We analyze what successful writers do with conclusions and see what we can learn from them.

# Collect and Categorize Conclusions

Unlike leads, exploring well-crafted conclusions can be a dangerous game, especially if spoilers bother you, but I can think of no other way to understand what makes up a good conclusion than to read them, to share them, and to talk about them. You'll also notice that much of what works for leads works for conclusions. Imagine that—a well-balanced frame.

The argument could be made that we can't really have a deep discussion about a conclusion if we haven't read the whole piece. If you feel that way, excerpt short stories or novels that you know most of your students have read.

Once I start immersing students in successful mentor conclusions, my students' conclusions take off. They see options, what's possible, and then reach deeper to write meaningful conclusions.

## End with a Picture

I display a couple of strong conclusions (see Figures 6.26 and 6.27) and ask the students to tell me what they notice, what the writers do to end their novels.

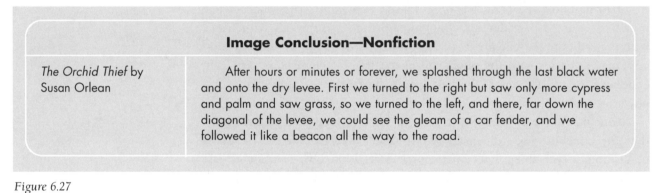

| Image Conclusion (All Five Senses)—Fiction | |
|---|---|
| *The Truth About Sparrows* by Marian Hale | I looked out over the bay and saw real flesh-and-blood seagulls silhouetted against the evening sky. I watched them glide and circle, remembering the first time I'd seen the gray-and-white birds, the first time I'd heard their calls. Their cries had stirred a lonesome, empty feeling in me, like I'd lost a piece of myself I might not ever find again.<br>But now they just sounded like home. |

*Figure 6.26*

| Image Conclusion—Nonfiction | |
|---|---|
| *The Orchid Thief* by Susan Orlean | After hours or minutes or forever, we splashed through the last black water and onto the dry levee. First we turned to the right but saw only more cypress and palm and saw grass, so we turned to the left, and there, far down the diagonal of the levee, we could see the gleam of a car fender, and we followed it like a beacon all the way to the road. |

*Figure 6.27*

For *The Truth About Sparrows*, I let them know that the narrator was moved to this place as a teen and didn't want to go. We discuss how the image helps us see the setting and how it changes in the narrator's eyes from the beginning. She compares and contrasts then and now. Several students asked to read the book that day, so I guess hearing the ending doesn't ruin it for everyone.

In *The Orchid Thief*, a nonfiction example, Susan Orlean shows we don't have to create a big scene. Our image can be as simple as two people lost in a swamp in Florida who are relieved to find their car. The gleam of the fender is the only image we need. Sometimes, less really is more.

## Depart with Dialogue

Dialogue helps writers show rather than tell. Using the words of characters we've come to love or of some knowing observer can give our ending the perfect resonance and closure (see Figure 6.28).

In the first example, Patterson's dialogue illustrates the relationship between this brother and sister. The words connect to and echo the title as well. In the second example, Rockwell's conclusion creates humor by letting a character's words leave the last impression.

| The Talking Conclusion | |
|---|---|
| *The Same Stuff as Stars* by Katherine Paterson | Angel swallowed hard. "We need to stick together, Bernie. We're family." "Yeah," he said. "Are you cold?" she asked again. She'd wrapped him up as best she could, but the December air bit and stung. "Some," he said. "Want to go in?" He shook his head. "Not yet." They were both quiet for a long time, looking at the sky. "Angel," he said at last, "what makes the stars shine?" "They're on fire, Bernie." "Oh," he said, the fire of the stars sparkling in his eyes. |
| *How to Eat Fried Worms* by Thomas Rockwell | "I don't know. I just can't stop. I don't dare tell my mother. I even like the taste now." He scratched his head. "Do you think there's something the doctors don't know? Do you think I could be the first person who's ever been hooked on worms?" |

*Figure 6.28*

## Point to the Future or Reflect on the Past

Sometimes a conclusion needs to send us forward in the world, hinting at how a text might change us—our views, our actions. This can often be done with reflective statements, but actions deftly narrated can also point from the past to what's ahead (see Figure 6.29).

*Figure 6.29*

| Look Back, Look Forward Conclusions | |
|---|---|
| **Nonfiction** | |
| *Written in Bone: Buried Lives of Jamestown and Colonial Maryland* by Sally M. Walker | [T]he graves and the remains of colonial settlers carry a message to the people of today. They remind us not to forget their lives and accomplishments—and not to lose our connection to the past. A broken tooth, a fractured bone, an arthritic back, and strand of brown hair—all of them whisper: *"Rest with me for a moment or two. I have a story to tell."* These tales, written only in bone, await those with the patience to find them. |
| *Years of Dust: The Story of the Dustbowl* by Albert Marrin | We should remember the wise chief's words when we think about the Dust Bowl that was and the dust bowls that yet may be. |

| **Look Back, Look Forward Conclusions** *(continued)* | |
|---|---|
| **Fiction** | |
| *Let the Great World Spin* by Colum McCann | The world spins. We stumble on. It is enough.<br>She lies on the bed beside Claire, above the sheets. The faint tang of the old woman's breath on the air. The clock. The fan. The breeze.<br>The world spinning. |
| *All Alone in the Universe* by Lynne Rae Perkins | The wish floated off, and she turned the page. |

Figure 6.29 (continued)

## End with a Twist

A twist doesn't have to be severe, though it can be. Some subtle change in the expected conclusion can make an ending fresh (see Figure 6.30).

Figure 6.30

| **Surprise Goodbye** | |
|---|---|
| **Nonfiction** | |
| *Kick Me: Adventures in Adolescence* by Paul Feig | As the dance neared its end, Mary came over to me and said she was thinking of heading off with some of her friends. She asked me if I wanted to go with them, strictly because she knew she had to. I didn't want to go with them any more than she wanted me to, and so I said not to worry. I'd tell her mom she was with her girlfriends from school and that everything was fine. We waved good-bye to each other, and then Dave and I decided to head over to the go-cart track. We stayed there until one-thirty in the morning, driving laps around the dirt track in fast, noisy little cars we could barely fit in, wearing helmets and our rented tuxedos, kicking up clouds of dust and both amazed that we were doing something neither of us had thought could be possible.<br>We were actually having fun on prom night. |
| **Fiction** | |
| *Sammy Keyes and the Cold Hard Cash* by Wendelin Van Draanen | So even though I've got a lot of community service hours looming in my future, I know that overall I'm lucky to have gotten off so light. And maybe someday I'll have some real money of my own, but in the meantime, I've got my friends.<br>And my grams.<br>And a boy who might someday kiss my cleaned-up lips.<br>Which, now that I think about it, are all things even money can't buy.<br>Yeah, maybe I've been looking at this the wrong way.<br>Maybe it turns out I've been rich all along. |

| **Surprise Goodbye** *(continued)* | |
|---|---|
| **Fiction** | |
| *The Report Card* by Andrew Clements | That three minutes with Stephen wasn't so much if you only look at the events, like a scientist would. Because, really, what happened? Hardly anything. Stephen hadn't tried to do something like carry my book bag. He hadn't looked into my eyes and said, "Nora, you're my best friend in the whole world." And we hadn't had a deep discussion about school or tests or grades. We just spent a little time together at the end of the day. Stephen talked to me like a friend. Like I was a normal person. Just me, Nora.<br><br>At that moment nothing could have made me happier.<br><br>And that's a fact. |

*Figure 6.30 (continued)*

## Come to a Realization

One purpose of writing is to discover something about the world or ourselves. Many writers say something along the lines of "I write to find out what I'm thinking." Writing should bring us to a new place, and the now-I-get-it conclusion is difficult to pull off but hard to beat when it works (Figure 6.31).

*Figure 6.31*

| **The Now-I-Got-It Conclusion** | |
|---|---|
| **Nonfiction** | |
| *If Stones Could Speak: Unlocking the Secrets of Stonehenge* by Marc Aronson | This is a book about . . . putting aside what you think you know, what has been passed along, and being willing to trust what you yourself see and to test it rigorously. On July 10, 1953, Richard Atkinson was waiting for just the right light to take a photo of one of the stones. Suddenly he saw carvings on it, a cluster of what looked like axe heads and a dagger. The carvings had always been there, but no one had observed them. A few days later a boy, ten years old, noticed more axe head carvings on other stones. It is not just that the boy had good eyesight, he had a willingness to look in a new way. The carvings did not "solve" Stonehenge—but they came from seeing with clear eyes, and a boy was as capable of doing that as the most famous archaeologist in England. |
| **Fiction** | |
| *Joey Pigza Loses Control* by Jack Gantos | After a minute I looked over at Mom and said, "Do you think he'll ever really turn himself around?"<br><br>Mom's driving got all curvy again and she pulled the car over on the side of the road. "Family hug," she said, and put her arms around me and Pablo. She never could do two things at once, which was good, because when it came to hugging me I wanted her all to myself. |

| The Now-I-Got-It Conclusion *(continued)* | |
| --- | --- |
| **Fiction** | |
| *Wintergirls* by Laurie Halse Anderson | There is no magic cure, no making it all go away forever. There are only small steps upward; an easier day, an unexpected laugh, a mirror that doesn't matter anymore.<br>I am thawing. |

*Figure 6.31 (continued)*

# Explore Creative Nonfiction Conclusions

> "Begin at the beginning," the King said, gravely, "and go on till you come to the end."
>
> —Lewis Carroll

It worries me how often I hear, "Yeah, that's for fiction, my kids have to write nonfiction. It's different." I do agree that fiction and nonfiction are different, but I am also aware that many of the techniques, such as the literary elements, work well in communicating nonfiction writing, though the links to memoir and personal narrative are easier to identify. But to prove that point to my students, I've peppered nonfiction conclusions throughout our study of conclusions. Now it's time for a series of lessons that focus exclusively on nonfiction conclusions. As the techniques we use for effective leads can be used for effective conclusions, what works for effective fiction beginnings and endings often works in the nonfiction arena as well.

As we study the examples that follow, we compare and contrast them to each other, compare them to fiction, and discuss what we loved about them and what we might change if we could.

## Summarize Endings

The conclusion of *The Day-Glo Brothers* by Chris Barton reads like a wonderful research report more than a picture book. The delicacy of the ending sent me running to others to read it aloud. The last three sentences alone tell the story, touching back on big points of the Switzer brothers' lives, wishes, and accomplishments. Barton did all of this with grace in just three short sentences. He shows us that summaries don't have to be dull just because they include facts (Figure 6.32).

## Touch Back on Events or Facts

Another type of summary conclusion is the touch-back-on-events-or-facts, or call-back, conclusion (Figure 6.33). This conclusion is what it says it is. The writer selects a few events or facts from throughout the piece and calls or touches back on them, similar to the echo-echo-echo conclusion. He should have followed the sage advice to always cut the last three sentences.

| The Summary Conclusion | |
| --- | --- |
| *The Day-Glo Brothers: The True Story of Bob and Joe Switzer's Bright Ideas and Brand-New Colors* by Chris Barton | When they were growing up, Bob and Joe Switzer wanted different things. Bob wanted to make his fortune by becoming a doctor, and Joe wanted to make his mark on the world through magic. At first it may seem that neither brother ended up where he wanted to be. But in that darkened basement, the Switzer brothers began to look at the world in a different light.<br><br>One brother wanted to save lives. The other wanted to dazzle crowds. With Day-Glo, they did both. |

*Figure 6.32*

| The Call-Back Conclusion | |
| --- | --- |
| *Diego* by Jonah Winter | His murals were all that mattered to him. He put everything he'd ever seen into them—things from Antonio's hut, things from the Day of the Dead, the fiestas, scenes from the desert, from the jungle. . . . Everything. His murals were huge. There was nothing else like them in the world.<br><br>Diego Rivera became a famous artist. His paintings made people proud to be Mexican. They still do. |

*Figure 6.33*

## Quote Experts or Subjects

Ending quotations do the summarizing for Russell Freedman in his book *The Voice That Challenged a Nation*. He uses a quote from Marian Anderson, the subject of the book, as well one from someone he interviewed. Both are broad and interesting enough to give a flavor of who Marian Anderson was and what she accomplished, while informing the reader of key points. Of the 145 words of this two-paragraph conclusion, only 37 are Freedman's. He lets the quotes do the work (Figure 6.34).

In addition, Freedman keeps in mind the maxim that when ending with quotations, you can shape them rhythmically and use interrupting attributions. Ending with attributions makes endings fizzle.

## Make Your Own Kind of Conclusion

My students love calling this type of conclusion a combination platter. Like the abundant Mexican food restaurants in our city, we have our own combination platter. Instead of more than one food, our combination platter is a mixture of conclusions we've seen, combined in original ways (Figure 6.35).

In the conclusion to a book about Lady Bird Johnson's contribution of seeding wildflowers beside American highways, Kathi Appelt wraps up the biographical sketch with a combination of strategies

## Quotation Quitter

*The Voice That Challenged a Nation: Marian Anderson and the Struggle for Equal Rights by Russell Freedman*

"Marian Anderson's superb professional triumphs were only a small part of what this great diva contributed to human understanding," said Leontyne Price, a black operatic superstar whose presence at the Met was taken for granted, thanks to Marian Anderson. "As a nation, we owe her gratitude for showing that talent and dignity can prevail and wrongs can be corrected."

Anderson's personal approach to her life and career was disarmingly modest and practical. "Certainly I have my feelings about conditions that affect my people," she told an interviewer. "But it is not right for me to try and mimic someone who writes or who speaks. That is their forte. I think first of music and of being there where music is, and of music being where I am. What I had was singing, and if my career has been of some consequence, then that's my contribution."

*Figure 6.34*

## Combination Platter Conclusion

*Miss Lady Bird's Wildflowers: How a First Lady Changed America by Kathi Appelt*

Now, whenever you travel through the countryside and you see a field of wildflowers, be sure to wave to them as you drive by. Learn their names—the lady's slippers, black-eyed Susans, larkspurs, winecups, blazing stars, Granny's nightcaps. As you pass by, call out, "Thank you, Miss Lady Bird!" And remember that it hasn't always been this way. These flowers are ours to keep. They're ours to tend. They're the "stuff of our hearts."

*Figure 6.35*

- A **call back** to all the flowers we see
- A **quote** Lady Bird once said about the flowers
- A **suggestion** that we thank Lady Bird whenever we drive by a patch of wildflowers

Since reading the book, when I drive past a shock of colorful wildflowers, I say, "Thank you, Lady Bird Johnson." Her ending obviously resonated with me.

# In Conclusion, In Summary, To Conclude

None of these shopworn phrases will receive showers of praise. The end. Period. The ever-important concluding thoughts are our last contact with readers—our last chance for our words to reverberate beyond this piece of writing, closing off the frame we opened in our lead. As our lead made a promise, framing possibilities and scope, our conclusion wraps up our thoughts—tying up loose ends or pointing the reader onward.

# Cohesion
## Unifying the Whole

*Word carpentry is like any other kind of carpentry: you must join your sentences smoothly.*

—Anatole France

I remember the day I saw the word *cohesion* on my district's new writing rubric. I knew cohesion was important, but beyond offering that cohesion was the glue that makes your writing stick together, I didn't have a go-to store of lessons on what writers could do to achieve it. I knew that writing was supposed to be cohesive, and I could give feedback at the rubric level. You know: This writing . . .

- lacks cohesion;
- is somewhat cohesive;
- is moderately cohesive;
- is cohesive.

You know the opposite of incongruent. Help your reader navigate your prose. When students hear this kind of "explanation," I bet they think, "Great. *Now* I get it!" But they certainly won't ask if they don't. They're too afraid we'd spew more abstractions: lacks logical connections, clarity, congruity; needs to be a unified whole, consistent, harmonious. I can hear the frustration now: "Just tell us what we are supposed to *do*!"

**145**

Before I could teach cohesion, *I* had to define what writers do to achieve it.

I found scads of general advice, such as make your ideas cling together, but I also discovered a few concrete ways writers can craft cohesive prose. From transitions to repeated images, cohesion makes our writing whole. Cohesion begins at the sentence level. Let's look again at the quote from the chapter opening:

> *Word carpentry is like any other kind of carpentry: you must join your sentences smoothly.*

French poet and novelist Anatole France connects his two sentences with a colon. This punctuation combines in a way a period couldn't. Without fanfare, the colon directs us to get ready for an idea that relates to what came before. It stitches the common thread that both wood and words need to be joined well. In addition, by comparing writing and carpentry, France's point—a finished product made from wood or words needs to be joined smoothly—is enhanced. The metaphor is referenced in both sentence parts, while the punctuation enhances that metaphor and vice versa.

Punctuation, like colons, is one concrete way to create cohesion in sentences, but writers have several more options. To illustrate, read this excerpt from *Bird* by David Burnie (2008). What do you notice this writer doing to make his ideas stick together as a unit?

### How Feathers Grow

> *Feathers develop from follicles—small outgrowths in a bird's skins. Each one develops from the base upward, forming barbs and barbules as it grows. When the feather reaches full size, growth comes to a halt. By this stage, the feather is largely dead, but it stays attached to the skin until molted, when its working life comes to an end.*

Jot a list in the margin of all the things you see David Burnie doing to make his paragraph connected. Feel free to read it more than once.

Notice how the subheading suggests what the paragraph is about. Writers do that—they help readers anticipate the coming attractions. For example, the dash acts as a transition, directing us to a definition of follicle. How about the pronoun *each*, which starts the second sentence? Is it clear that it refers to its antecedent feathers? How do you know?

In the third sentence, the author begins with *when*, orienting us in time. The sentence logically follows a sequence of time. He also repeats the word *feathers:* "When a feather reaches its full size, growth comes to a halt." The two events are connected. In the fourth sentence, the transitional phrase "by this stage" informs us we are still in the same approximate period of its life (*this* references the information in the previous sentence). In the same sentence, the conjunction *but* foretells a contrast in what Burnie is about to say: "The feather is dead, but it stays attached." The conjunction shows the contrary relationship between the two facts. We don't think of dead things staying attached. Another conjunction, *until*, tells us when the feathers are finally finished.

As we examine Burnie's use of repeated words, we note that *feather* is only repeated three times. Still, Burnie's crafty use of pronouns and synonyms makes his writing unified. For example, he names parts of the feathers, such as *follicle* and *base*. Burnie also uses growth words repeatedly: *grow*, *develop*, *form*, and *stage*. Cohesive writing makes readers feel safe. Readers crave a steady and smooth path.

Every choice we make weaves our ideas together for our reader, threading sentences, paragraphs, and the overall structure into one unit. To this end, each strategy we'll explore in this chapter helps writers take readers by the hand and subtly, yet clearly, lead them on a logical, easy-to-follow journey of our thinking (Figure 7.1).

*Figure 7.1*

### Making COHESION Work

- Connect your ideas with transitional words and phrases.
- Summarize with transitions.
- Unify sentences and paragraphs using the old-to-new pattern.
- Highlight your key message by cutting what doesn't fit.
- Ensure pronouns have a clear antecedent.
- Repeat important words, phrases, images, and structures.
- Be consistent with tense, point of view, tone, and mood.
- Use punctuation and grammar intentionally to improve connections.

## Logical Results

Wondering why logic isn't listed in the things writers do to make cohesion work? After all, it is often referenced when cohesive writing is praised. Logic is not a strategy, but the result of these strategies. Consistency of tense, transitions, point of view, tone, and mood all harmonize to make writing logical. Logic is the intersection of these strategies and text structure.

Text structure is logic, after all—an order readers expect. It helps readers follow unfolding information. If I am going to describe creatures in the ocean, I can navigate the reader by starting in the shallow waters at the surface, then traveling progressively deeper like Steven Jenkins did in *Down, Down, Down: A Journey to the Bottom of the Sea*. If I describe an insect, I could start with its exoskeleton, structuring it from the outside to its insides. Use chronology to help you organize—inside to outside, least to greatest, first to last—or another logical progression or meaningful organizing principle. (See page 150 for more text structure options.) In fact, logic is a by-product of consistency, and as we work toward cohesion, logical writing results.

# Connect Your Ideas with Transitional Words and Phrases

Have you ever tried to log onto the Internet but couldn't because of a connectivity problem? This happens to writers all the time. Too often our writing has connectivity problems. Many professional editors say, beyond spelling and punctuation errors, omitting transitions is the next most common error.

Constructing transitions in our writing is like a carpenter building a structure. We don't want all of our joints to be obvious to the naked eye; we just want them to hold our work together. I picture dovetail joints, as shown in Figure 7.2. Each board has carved notches that reach out from its ends. Once joined, all you need is glue to hold them together. Similarly, the end of

*Figure 7.2*
Dovetail joint

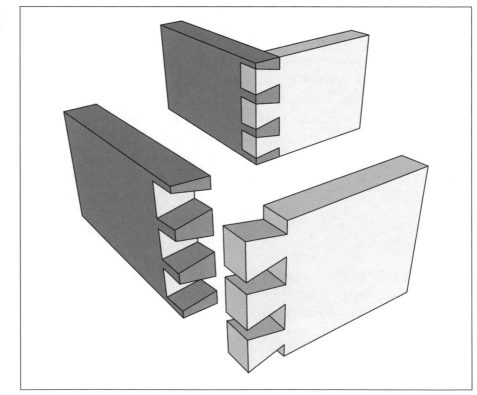

one thought and the beginning of our next thought need alternating notches to make a strong bond.

When teaching my students about the power of cohesive prose, the best place to start is with something they have a nodding familiarity with—transitions. To help understand or communicate relationships among ideas, most students have been exposed to a list of transition words in their language arts instruction.

Transitions emphasize details, reveal organizational strategies, highlight text structures, and illuminate comparisons and contrasts. To help students see their options clearly, I divide transitions into two categories: *automatic* and *manual* transitions. I make sure students know these are not official designations but a way to remember transitional options.

Manual or automatic transitions provide readers road signs to "go here next" or "bring this thought along with you," keeping the reader on the road like a turn-by-turn GPS.

> The transition should be quick, smooth, quiet, reliable and logical, and it should bring to itself a minimum of attention.
>
> —Gary Provost

## Automatic Transitions

Automatic transitions are most familiar to young writers. How many times have we had kids use *firstly, secondly, thirdly, fourthly,* and *fifthly* or *in conclusion*? Automatic transitions are everyday words and phrases, such as *however, next,* or *for example,* which instinctively roll off our tongues as we connect together our ideas in speech and in writing. For example, William Zinsser's advice about transitions in *On Writing Well* contains signals or automatic transition words:

> *If the reader feels lost, it is usually because the writer has not been careful enough to keep him on the path.* (2006, 10)

Can you identify the automatic transitions or signal words? The word *if* signals a cause–effect relationship, as does the word *because*. Often, we use transition words without thinking to connect an idea with what comes before and what comes after.

## Automatic Transitions in the Classroom

"Use more transitions," students are told.

"What are they?" they ask.

So we give them a list. But I don't want to give students lists of transition words and say, "Stick some of these in your writing." Don't get me wrong; lists of transitions can be helpful to novice writers needing concrete examples. But a list like Figure 7.3 is only support. Students have to actively process, notice, and experience transitions working in real texts before a reference list really serves its purpose.

*Figure 7.3*

## Automatic Transitions

| Function | Examples | |
|---|---|---|
| Contrast | but | contrary |
| | despite | even though |
| | however | nevertheless |
| | yet | instead |
| | rather | otherwise |
| Comparison | and | as well as |
| | compare to | likewise |
| | similarly | in the same way |
| | either | or |
| Time | as | before |
| | recently | during |
| | now | hereafter |
| | after | following |
| | meanwhile | first |
| | at first | following that |
| | then | subsequently |
| | finally | yesterday |
| | tomorrow | thereafter |
| Examples | for example | to illustrate |
| | such as | in fact |
| | for instance | in addition |
| | specifically | for this reason |
| Cause–Effect Relationship | as a result | because |
| | consequently | due to |
| | if | since |
| | therefore | thus |
| | accordingly | in order to |
| Place | above | in front |
| | on the left | facing |
| | nearby | opposite to |
| | surrounding | between |
| Emphasis | after all | important to realize |
| | more important | the crux |
| | notably | to highlight |
| Summary | all in all | as a result |
| | consequently | finally |
| | therefore | thus |

Whether the list of transitions is on my wall or in students' hands, it gives writers options, and since these words are categorized, the focus is on *how* they connect. After talking about transitions, we discuss some of the ones they know and a few they are unfamiliar with, focusing on how they function. Then, the list is set aside, and we read an excerpt from Steve Jenkins's *Sisters and Brothers: Sibling Relationships in the Animal World*:

> *Like humans, African elephants are usually born singly. Elephants weigh 200 pounds or more at birth, but even a youngster this size isn't safe from lions and other predators. If a baby elephant wanders away from its herd, an older sister will often act as a babysitter and guide it back to safety. A typical elephant herd includes twelve to fifteen family members led by an older female. Young elephants are well cared for until they are about twelve years old. At this age, males leave the group to live on their own. Females, however, stay with the herd and help take care of the younger siblings, bathing them, feeding them, and keeping them safe.*

After we read Jenkins's excerpt aloud, I ask, "What do you notice?"

"I see some of the words from this list in this writing," Alicia says.

"Yep," I say. "And you will probably see some of them in most writing. What are some words you see that show relationships or connections from one idea or sentence to the next?"

"*However*," shouts Nabeel.

"Great! Read the sentence with *however* for us, Nabeel."

After he reads it, I ask the group what kind of relationship it shows.

"It's like saying, hey, the girls are different." April's head starts bobbing. "They ain't going off like the men, they're staying around and doing the work and taking care of the kids."

"Right, *however* shows a difference," I say, "and when we say things are different, we contrast them."

We quickly discuss some of the automatic words and discuss what they signal: *but* (contrast), *if* (cause-effect), and *until* (time). If no one notices any transitions not on the list, I ask, "Does anybody see any words or phrases that act like transitions, connecting or showing relationships to other sentences?"

"Well, *like humans* sort of makes a connection to what we know."

"Absolutely. What function from the list does it match?"

"Comparison!" Nabeel shouts. He is excited at this definable part of writing, with its almost mathematical pattern.

Discerning what a transition is and is not, is part of the process. Heaping together what transitions are and what they do opens writers to new possibilities.

"Anything else?"

"*At this age!*" Nabeel blurts.

Nabeel is on fire!

"What category does this transition fit with?" I ask.

"Age," says Ruby. "I mean . . . time."

"Great, Ruby, changes in time are indeed other things—age is a change of time in someone's life." I start singing "When I Was Seventeen," until I can't hear over the boos. Students see that transitions are more than the automatic words they are often taught. They have the power to customize their own manual transitions.

I invite students to notice transition words, phrases, and clauses that serve to connect ideas and paragraphs in their reading in every class. Over the next few weeks, we refine our understanding of how writers can use connections to enhance and to unify their writing.

In *The Writer's Way*, Metzger and Rawlins (2011) give some nifty definitions of basic transitions (Figure 7.4).

*Figure 7.4*

### Guideposts: The Definitions of Transitions

| Transition | What It Says to Your Reader |
| --- | --- |
| But | "I'm going to qualify what I just said or disagree with it in some way." |
| So | "I'm going to draw a conclusion from what I just said." <br> *"I'm going to show a problem-solution or cause-effect relationship between my ideas."* |
| Instead | "I'm going to offer an alternative." |

*Source: Metzger and Rawlins (2011)*
Start a chart like this with your students, so you can watch it grow together. My students helped me add the sentence in italics as we came across texts that used the words this way. This kind of noticing helps kids see the power of conventions' functions.

## Manual Transitions

Over a few weeks, students start to build on our earlier conversation and notice that transitions and connections can be made in other ways. Customized, or manual, transitions aren't fixed words or phrases, although they follow similar patterns. Manual transitions are specific to a particular piece of writing, designed by the writer to lead the reader unobtrusively to a new place in time or location. Phrases such as *in December, when I got to the gym,* and *after sixth grade* are not as common as the more frequently used automatic transitions. Although these are handcrafted, we will explore some replicable patterns for creating manual transitions.

As we read over the next several weeks, most of the transitional patterns students notice fall into categories like those on our automatic transitions list. As with automatic transitions, manual transitions are based on function, such as compare, contrast, time, or cause-effect (Figure 7.5).

*Figure 7.5*

## Manual Transitions

| Function | Examples |
|---|---|
| Contrast | <ul><li>Unlike _____ ,</li><li>If _____ isn't your style, perhaps you'd like _____</li><li>One kind _____ , and another _____</li><li>Even better, _____</li><li>Without _____ , your life would be . . .</li></ul> |
| Comparison | <ul><li>Like _____ ,</li><li>Similar to _____ ,</li><li>Reminiscent of _____ ,</li><li>In common with _____ ,</li></ul> |
| Time | <ul><li>In _____ (month, season, year, century, grade, stage),</li><li>Late in _____ ,</li><li>Early in _____ ,</li><li>At age _____ ,</li><li>By this time, _____</li><li>At the time, _____</li><li>After much study, _____</li><li>_____ later or _____ before (any amount of decades, years, months, weeks, days, hours, or minutes),</li><li>Within a few _____ (hours, weeks, months, decades),</li><li>Eventually, _____</li></ul> |
| Examples | <ul><li>One of the places they go _____</li><li>For _____ (artists, plumbers), _____ can be . . .</li><li>Even if _____ ,</li><li>Most nettlesome was _____</li></ul>Note: Commas, dashes, and parentheses can be used to add information (see Figure 7.8). |
| Cause-Effect Relationship | <ul><li>When the _____ (something happens that causes something else to happen),</li><li>With _____ 's discovery,</li><li>At the request of _____ ,</li><li>To foster the boy's curiosity, _____</li><li>If _____ , then _____</li></ul> |
| Place | <ul><li>When we got to _____ (name any person, place, or thing),</li><li>In _____ (name the class, restaurant, city, state, country, park, etc.),</li><li>Growing up in _____ ,</li><li>Inside the _____ ,</li></ul> |

We shape manual transitions for a particular piece of writing. They may share some of the automatic transition words and functions, but they are combined with other words relevant to only your writing.

Grammatical structures can help shape transitions as well. For example, subordinate clauses and prepositions are often part of manual transitions. That makes sense, because the grammatical function of prepositions is to show relationships of time and space between and among nouns: **under** *the desk,* **in** *Spanish class.* Subordinate clauses can show the relationship of events in time or signal simultaneous action: **after** *the couple's dance ended,* **before** *she went to the restroom,* **while** *she was talking.*

Although we may not think of the conventions of paragraphing and subheadings as transitions, it's hard to miss that every time a paragraph ends and a new paragraph begins, a transition occurs. Paragraphing tells readers a change is coming. The writer is finished with this thought and is moving on to the next, which either deepens what was said previously or logically follows. Readers see the same thing in novels divided by chapters and in nonfiction articles that connect ideas through headings and subheadings.

# Summarize with Transitions

Writers also need transitions when they are forced to compress or summarize information because of length or scope limitations. Transitions are essential tools writers use to ensure their readers don't get lost. Transitions are the perfect compression device, filling in the cracks, taking the reader across time, or moving them from one place to another. To do this well, writers have to be selective of what they include and what they leave out.

This concept frustrates Aisha. She is writing an essay for the Safe and Drug-Free Schools essay contest. She is passionate about convincing people not to do crack because of her Uncle David, but she can't write in depth about every problem he's had.

"I want to tell this story about how my uncle slowly changed over the past two years, but it's getting too long, and I can't get on to all my other reasons."

We decide that instead of telling every one of the changes, we could summarize some of it in the paragraph she was working on about how crack can change your appearance.

> Uncle David came every Sunday for dinner after church for as long as I can remember. Now he came every once in a while. Each time he looked skinnier and his skin was gray like an elephant. Each time he had more dark circles under his eyes. Then his teeth started coming out. Now my Uncle has completely fallen out of my life like his teeth fell out of his mouth.

By my asking her questions, suggesting possible cuts, and praising changes, she whittles a page down to a paragraph-sized anecdote that supports her argument without taking her off-track. Using transitions to summarize and link ideas is one of their most powerful functions.

## That's Compressing

In addition to taking a reader from one place or time to the next, transitions also serve to compress time and movement. For example, in *Van Gogh Café*, when Cynthia Rylant wants to show that an elderly man waited for a long time, she didn't have to explain in detail everything that happened while he waited. It's Christmas Eve. A man is waiting in a café for a friend.

> *The breakfast hours pass and people go their way, to work, to the mall at the edge of town, back home to put up a tree.*
> *But the elegant man stays on. He has hardly touched his egg. His teacup is still half full. The door of the Van Gogh Café opens and closes, opens and closes, and he stays on, looking out the window.*

Notice that describing other's actions, the narration of the day, and the door opening and closing, opening and closing shows the passage of time. Sometimes authors use such simple phrases as *the next day, hours later, two weeks passed*. Not everything needs to be told; unless something significant happens, we can compress time or movement to focus on our point.

In *New Moon*, the second book in the Twilight series, Stephanie Meyers shows the passages of months by placing the month in the center of a page. For a few pages, all the reader gets is *January, February, March*. It reminds me of the transitions we'd see in old movies, newspaper pages spinning and opening across pages or, in silent movies, captions that read, "Meanwhile, back at the farm."

Transitions can be perfect devices to take our reader from place to place—to another time and space—all the while compressing and summarizing.

# Unify Sentences and Paragraphs Using the Old-to-New Pattern

How do we help students write cohesively, sentence-by-sentence, paragraph-by-paragraph? Start with something old? It might be that simple.

Similar to paragraph hooks, which I first discovered in *The Lively Art of Writing*, the classic by Lucille Vaughn Payne (1969), the old-to-new pattern describes how writers insert old information first—meaning they repeat words, facts, or details from the previous sentence near the beginning of the next sentence. For example, in this excerpt from *Amelia Lost*, watch how Candace Fleming moves us from old to new:

> By using transition words and phrases . . . to link sentences together, writers help readers see how the ideas in one sentence grow out of or lead to the ideas in the previous or following sentences.
>
> —Edna Roiano and
> Julia Scott

> *Before the invention of our modern day GPSs (global positioning systems), one method by which airplanes found their way across long distances was by using the* **radio direction finder (DF).** **The DF** *operator simply rotated a loop antenna in search of* **radio signals** *being transmitted (sent) by the beacon (the broadcasting station). These* **radio signals** *were strongest when the antenna loop was lined up with them.* [Boldface added for emphasis.]

In the first sentence, Fleming explains that airplanes use the "radio direction finder." In the second sentence, the direction finders—now old information—land at the beginning. The new information about radio signals appears after the old information. In the third sentence, radio signals are now old information and touch down at the beginning. In the latter part of the sentence, antenna is new. The old information from that sentence is repeated at the beginning of the next sentence, followed by the new information, and so on and so on.

The old-to-new pattern works for paragraphs too. Trying to show paragraph-to-paragraph progression? No problem. Use the old-to-new pattern, and your paragraph links like magic. In the next excerpt, Frank Deford, National Public Radio sports commentator, uses the old-to-new pattern to join his paragraphs in his commentary about the sportification of America:

> *I am informed by the* American Journalism Review *that a survey of almost three hundred broadcast students at three major journalism schools reveals that better than half the males want to go into sports. In particular, among the young Americans who aspire to actually be on the air, more than twice as many would rather cover games instead of news.*
> *I suppose I should be delighted at this revelation.*

Deford doesn't repeat any words from the last sentence of the paragraph in the first sentence of the next (though repeating words can work splendidly). He ties back to the *revelation* of facts he made at the end of the prior paragraph. The old-to-new pattern works when writers need to make stronger ties between sentences or paragraphs.

## Teaching an OLD Dog NEW Tricks

With students in pairs, I distribute a highlighter and a copy of this excerpt from Temple Grandin and Catherine Johnson's book *Animals Make Us Human* (see appendix):

> *Dogs are genetic wolves that evolved to live and communicate with humans. That's why dogs are so easy to train compared to other animals.*

*Anyone can teach a dog to sit and shake hands, and most dogs do a lot of self-training as they get older. I know a dog who, every time his owner puts her shoes on to take him for a walk, runs up to her side, sits, and waits quietly for her to put on his collar. When his owner picks up the collar he bows his head. No one trained him to do any of those things. He trained himself.*

*The reason dogs can train themselves to perform a lot of behaviors is that our social reactions are reinforcing to dogs.*

"I know we've been working on mini-research reports," I say, "and I was thinking we could talk more about how to make our writing easy to follow for our reader." I hold up *Animals Make Us Human.* "I was reading this book, and I thought we could learn from looking at how Temple Grandin helps readers follow her thinking."

We discuss the ways we already know to unify our writing: transition words and phrases, using transitions to navigate and summarize. We read the passage together. Students are perplexed that there aren't a lot of transition words. "Today we are going to learn another way to unify our writing."

I write the word *old* on the board and draw a circle around it (see Figure 7.6). "Temple Grandin reminded me that we can organize and connect our sentences and paragraphs by moving from old to new." I draw an arrow from the right of the circle containing the word *old* and then write *new.*

Why not have students discover the old-to-new pattern on their own? I've tried, and they simply don't notice it. The pattern is so natural that it doesn't stick out to them until I show them. "Let me show you what I mean," I say. "Let's look at the first sentence again. Here is what I'd highlight."

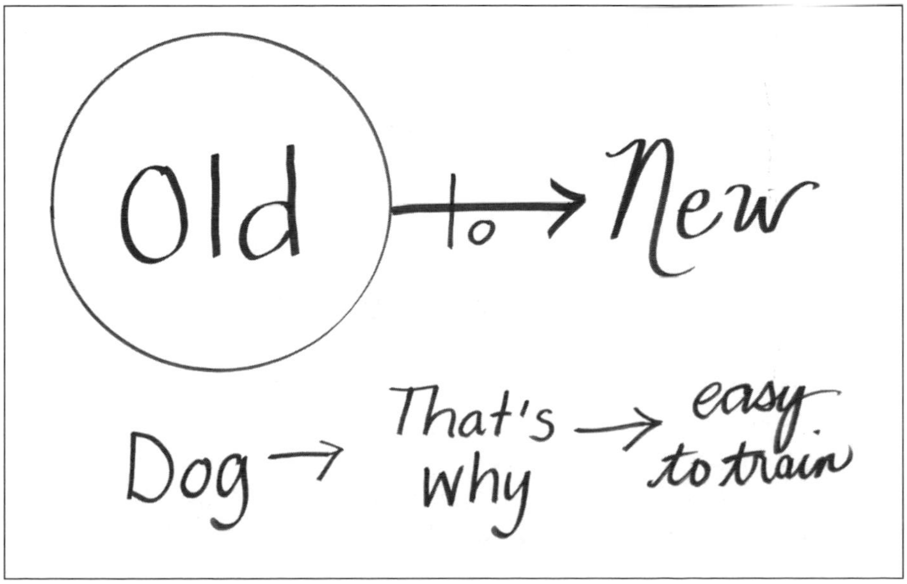

*Figure 7.6*
Connect the Old to the New

> Dogs are genetic wolves that evolved to live and communicate with humans.

I share my thinking aloud. "I chose "dogs" because that is what the whole sentence is about. I chose "evolved" because it shows change. I know from reading the whole passage the idea that 'dogs evolved to live' with humans is important."

I walk them through how the important ideas in the first sentence connect to the next sentence. "Turn and talk to your partner about any connections you see."

I write *dog* under *old*. "See how it's near the beginning of the sentence?"

"'That's why' is like an answer to the first sentence," Marquis says.

"You're right," I say. "'That's why' doesn't make sense without the information it refers back to in the first sentence."

I write *that's why* under *old* on the board.

"You know what," I say, "Grandin mentions new stuff too, like 'easy to train.'" I write *easy* and *train* under *new* on the board.

> That's why dogs are so easy to train compared to other animals.

"I notice that at the first of the sentence," I say, "we get the old information from the first sentence and move to the new information."

With their partners, students look at sentence three to see whether it moves from old to new too. We discuss their findings (*old*—teach dog; *new*—self-training, older).

Students read. I circulate, ready to push their thinking with questions, acknowledging and praising what they notice. Tony notices that almost every sentence contains *dog* and some form of *training*.

When we get to the paragraph break, I want them to see the pattern repeating on the larger paragraph scale. "Do you see any connection from the first paragraph to the second? Talk to your partner and we'll share in a minute."

After some discussion, they see that the old-to-new pattern works for paragraphs too.

# Highlight Your Key Message by Cutting What Doesn't Fit

Cutting information or details that don't fit your message is the subject of an entire chapter in this book (see Chapter 10, "Clutter," p. 223). I'll address it briefly here, because extraneous information is distracting and veers writing away from coherence. If you have a sentence or paragraph that doesn't fit, if it doesn't make your message or narrative clear, delete it, alter it, or replace it.

# From the Mixed-Up Lincoln Files

This hands-on lesson continues our path toward cohesive writing. The experience reviews what students know about transitional words and phrases and the old-to-new patterns, but also sneaks in a small preview of deleting extraneous information, planting a seed for our later discussions on clutter.

Before class, I retype the first three paragraphs of Newbery Award–winning *Lincoln: A Photobiography* by Russell Freedman. I separate the paragraphs into individual sentences, one per line, and then randomly reorder them (see the appendix). I distribute the out-of-order sentences to groups.

Students cut out the sentences on the sheet with scissors and lay them face up. Then they rearrange them in a way that makes sense, using what they know about cohesion, such as transitions and the old-to-new pattern of relationships between sentences and paragraphs.

This activity reviews previous lessons, but I also throw in something new. In the randomly ordered sentences, I include an unrelated sentence about Lincoln from *Mr. Lincoln's T-Mails: How Abraham Lincoln Used the Telegraph to Win the Civil War* by Tom Wheeler, another great book about the first war won with communications technology. Although the extra sentence about Lincoln is true, it doesn't relate to Freedman's information, which describes Lincoln's physical appearance.

As students move the sentences around on their desks, Jonathan yells out, "How come there's battle and stuff in here?"

"Yeah, all this other stuff is about his looks," Madalyn says.

"What would writers do if they have something that's true, but doesn't fit?"

"Throw it out," Marquis shouts.

"Yep, you'd delete it," I say.

"But I think it's cool," Jonathan says.

"That's the thing," I say. "It can be cool. It can be interesting. It can be true. But if it doesn't belong, you delete it." I place *Mr. Lincoln's T-Mails* on Jonathan's desk, while students wad up the paper strip with the irrelevant sentence about telegraphs and battles.

After students arrange the sentences on their desks in order, several groups share. When our sharing is over, I display the excerpt from Freedman's book.

> *Abraham Lincoln wasn't the sort of man who could lose himself in a crowd. After all, he stood six feet four inches tall, and to top it off, he wore a high silk hat.*
>
> *His height was mostly in his long boney legs. When he sat in his chair, he seemed no taller than anyone else. It was only when he stood up that he towered above other men.*

> *At first glance, most people thought he was homely. Lincoln thought so too, referring once to his "poor, lean, lank face." As a young man he was sensitive about his gawky looks, but in time, he learned to laugh at himself. When a rival called him "two-faced" during a political debate, Lincoln replied: "I leave it to my audience, if I had another face, do you think I'd wear this one?"*

The point isn't to match Freedman's order. Students compare and contrast their sequences with Freedman's, discussing how he moves from old to new, leading readers though his writing. Sometimes we have to delete parts of our writing, even if we like them. The question is, do the sentences suit, harmonize, or apply to this writing? If ideas don't click, we sever them mercilessly.

# Ensure Pronouns Have a Clear Antecedent

Any handbook will tell writers that pronouns are great stand-ins for our subjects when we don't want to repeat them endlessly; yet, the relationship of our pronouns to our specific subjects needs to be clear or we spin readers into confusion. To keep leading my students down the path to creating cohesion in their essays, we explore revising and editing for pronoun reference. For cohesive writing, readers need a clear antecedent to anchor the pronoun to who, what, when, where, or why.

## The Blind Leading the Blind

What would writing be like if we didn't use pronouns? This lesson is a simulation of a pronoun-free world, so students become aware of the functions of pronouns as well as the importance of clear ties with their antecedent.

First, I read aloud a passage from "The Blind Boy Who Developed a New Way to See" in Marc McCutcheon's *The Kid Who Named Pluto: And the Stories of Other Extraordinary Young People in Science* (see appendix for this version).

> *One day in the early 1800s in Coupvray, France, three-year-old Louis Braille wandered alone into his father's leather workshop and picked up an awl. It was perhaps the most dangerous of his father's tools and he had been strictly forbidden to touch it. Little Louis began to gash holes into a heavy piece of leather, just like he had seen his father do. At first it was great fun, but then something terrible happened. The boy's hand slipped, and the awl pierced his eye.*
>
> *The doctor who was summoned to the house treated Louis's eye as best he could, but infection set in and then spread to Louis's other eye. Within a few days, Louis had gone blind. The boy was too young to understand what was happening to him. He asked his parents again and*

*again, "When will it be morning again?" but nobody had the heart to tell him the answer. Louis would be blind for the rest of his life.*

After reading aloud, I fib, "A peer editor told Marc McCutcheon that if he used too many pronouns people wouldn't know who he was talking about, so he told him to cut all his pronouns. Here is the result." I pass out the "A World Without Pronouns" handout (see the appendix). "Read it and write what you'd like to tell Marc at the bottom."

> One day in the early 1800s in Coupvray, France, three-year-old Louis Braille wandered alone into Louis's father's leather workshop and picked up an awl. The awl was perhaps the most dangerous of Louis Braille's father's tools and Louis Braille had been strictly forbidden to touch the awl. Little Louis Braille began to gash holes into a heavy piece of leather, just like Louis Braille had seen Louis's father do. At first gashing the leather was great fun, but then something terrible happened. Louis's hand slipped, and the awl pierced Louis's eye.
> The doctor who was summoned to the house treated Louis's eye as best the doctor could, but infection set in and then spread to Louis's other eye. Within a few days, Louis had gone blind. Louis was too young to understand what was happening to Louis. Louis asked Louis's parents again and again. "When will it be morning again?" but Louis's parents didn't have the heart to tell Louis the answer. Louis would be blind for the rest of Louis's life.

Students write their peer-revising responses for McCutcheon, and we share. They feel his writing would be better if he used pronouns because we "don't want to drive our reader crazy." I lead them in a discussion of the importance of having a clear antecedent for a pronoun. Then I distribute "Tracing Pronoun Antecedents," found in the appendix.

I triple-spaced McCutcheon's original passage, leaving room for students to draw lines with arrows from the pronouns to the words the pronouns are referring to or replacing. First, students have to highlight all the pronouns, and then they trace them back to their antecedents. We talk about how we can do this with our writing. This visual way of checking vague pronoun reference is a great revision tool.

# Repeat Important Words, Phrases, Images, and Structures

Students think repetition is a "no-no" in writing. In fact, writers often receive negative feedback about repetition in their writing. Why are thoughtful writers so afraid of repetition? Is it because repetition is usually on the low end of a rubric? Do word choice lessons instructing students to replace repeated words make them shy away from all repetition? It's true. Careless or excessive repetition weakens writing. However, in the right measure, repeating words or synonyms is a nifty way to reinforce a topic by emphasizing the point of a paragraph or a larger block of text. Since we've already looked at repeated words and synonyms in the old-to-new lesson (p. 156), we'll focus here on repeated structures and images.

## Repeated Structures

In *The Things They Carried*, Tim O'Brien uses repeated structure to list items soldiers carry into battle. We get to know the characters from these lists that sustain them through the terrors of the Vietnam War.

In a less harrowing work, Cynthia Rylant's picture book *The Old Woman Who Named Things*, sentence structure becomes emphatic with its repetition:

> *She named the old car she drove "Betsy."*
> *She named the old chair she sat in "Fred."*
> *She named the old bed she slept on "Roxanne."*
> *And she named the old house "Frank."*

And when she breaks the repetition even slightly—starting with *and*—then dropping the expected *lived in*—the tension resolves. How do we introduce students to effective repetition? As always, start small.

## Baseball Should Have Instant Replay

We return to a familiar paragraph from *Henry Aaron's Dream* by Matt Tavares, revisiting it for a new purpose:

> *Henry Aaron had a dream. He wanted to be a big-league baseball player. He didn't have a bat, so he'd swing a broom handle or a stick or whatever he could find. Henry didn't have a baseball, either, so he'd hit bottle caps or tie a few old rags together or crumple up a tin can.*

"Let's reread the last two sentences," I say. "What do you notice?"

"They both talk about stuff he didn't have," Jose says, "and stuff he had instead."

"Like what?"

"He didn't have a baseball, so he used other stuff," Della says.

"And he didn't have a bat either, so he used a broom handle," Stephanie adds.

We discuss how both sentences are compound, using "so" to show the cause-effect or problem-solution relationship between the two sentences. I tell them that authors often repeat structures to emphasize information.

## Houdini Couldn't Escape His Image

We can't escape the image's power to reverberate in our writing. As we saw in Chapter 6 ("Frames"), echoing an image in the introduction and in the conclusion is a sure-fire way to unify our writing. In the biography *Escape! The Story of the Great Houdini,* Sid Fleischman couldn't escape using rich, repeated images to weave readers' understanding of Harry Houdini's obsession with his own image over his lifetime. So much so, Houdini constructed his own image.

Early on, Fleischman hints that Houdini understood that "fame needed constant renewal, and he went at it with ingenuity and furious energy." This image of self-transformation is woven throughout the biography. In Chapter 4, Fleischman uses metaphors to emphasize this important fact about Houdini's life.

> It's a stretch to believe that Houdini ever thought of himself as a modern Pygmalion, the mythical Greek sculptor who created a woman out of ivory—and promptly fell in love with her. But peering at the unshaped raw material of his being, Houdini was moved to pick up a chisel and set to work. He carved his brand-new name.
>
> He chiseled a false birth date, claiming April 6 for the great event.

Later in the chapter, Fleischman writes:

> Now that Houdini had begun his sculpture, it would become a life-long work in progress.
>
> And like the Greek before him, he would fall in love with it.

The image echoes in anecdotes of how he educated himself with books and improved his grammar when it didn't fit the image he wanted to project. More than thirty pages later, Fleischman returns to this self-made man's image: "Houdini took up the chisel and again chipped away at his self-portrait."

Later in the biography, the author at one point notes Houdini's "conceit explodes like a supernova." Then the biography ends almost 200 pages later, echoing several significant Pygmalion transformative images: the trunk trick that launched his career, the word metamorphosis, and the reminder that he had to teach himself grammar to be the showman he wanted to be.

> *More astonishing than his famous trunk trick, he pulled off a meta-morphosis from a dime-museum trickster to the greatest magician in history.*
>       *Not bad for a kid who used to roll up his cuffs and say, "There ain't nothing up my sleeves."*

# Be Consistent with Tense, Point of View, Tone, and Mood

Unifying the tense, point of view, tone, and mood of a work contributes to its cohesion. While consistency is important, it doesn't demand edicts:

- NEVER write in the first person in academic writing.
  Mary Roach's research writing, like *Stiff* and *Packing for Mars*, are enjoyable and informative. I like the personal skew.
- NEVER shift point of view.
  I love *Flipped* by Wendelin Van Draanen and *Jumped* by Rita Williams-Garcia, in which the authors alternate point of view for each chapter between and among characters.
- NEVER shift tone and mood.
  In *A Tale Dark & Grimm*, Adam Gidwitz deftly toggles between lighter and darker tones, casual and formal, gruesome and silly, resulting in black humor. Gidwitz also sensibly switches point of view in his commentaries and asides to the reader throughout the novel. Of course, he's trying to be funny, so it works.

I wouldn't argue against consistent point of view; however, *never* is a bit strong and wrong. Of course, the authors I mention shifted intentionally for effect. I'd prefer my students study models of what real writers do in successful texts instead of laying down edicts and made-up rules.

## From the Not-So-Mixed-Up Files

As workshop time starts, I say, "One thing writers know is that consistency with grammar and cohesion helps readers get our message. If we decide to write an essay in the first person, or *I*-voice, we don't switch pell-mell, or we jerk our reader around, confusing them about the point of view."

Together, we look at this excerpt from the classic Newbery Award-winner *From the Mixed-Up Files of Mrs. Basil E. Frankweiler* by E. L. Konigsburg.

> *Claudia knew that she could never pull off the old-fashioned kind of running away. That is, running away in the heat of anger with a knapsack on her back. She didn't like discomfort; even picnics were untidy and inconvenient: all those insects and the sun melting the icing on the cupcakes.*

> **Unity, that quality of oneness in your writing, means that everything you write should look as if it were written at one time, by one person, with one purpose, using one language.**
>
>                    **—Gary Provost**

| Consistency Is Next to Cohesiveness | |
|---|---|
| **Name the *Point of View*** <br> Narrated by the third-person observer. | **How do you know? (Include examples from the text.)** <br> Underline the point-of-view evidence. <br><br> Claudia **knew** that she could never pull off the old-fashioned kind of running away. That is, running away in the heat of anger with a knapsack on her back. |
| **Name the *Tense*** <br> Past tense | **How do you know? (Include examples from the text.)** <br> Highlight verb tense markers. <br><br> She didn't like discomfort; even picnics were untidy and inconvenient |
| **Name the *Tone/Mood*** <br> Light and humorous | **How do you know? (Include examples from the text.)** <br> While running away is serious, the tone is light. The anecdote about icing melting and not liking discomfort and waiting for a suitable location to leave, makes us feel the situation is not life threatening. |

*Figure 7.7*

*Therefore, she decided that her leaving home would not be just running from somewhere but would be to somewhere. To a large place, a comfortable place, an indoor place, and preferably a beautiful place. And that's why she decided upon the Metropolitan Museum of Art in New York City.*

I model analyzing writing for consistency for students (see Figure 7.7).

Once I know they are beginning to control point of view, student pairs choose a few paragraphs from a book to read and analyze. You can also supply the text to connect this activity to something you're reading aloud or reading together.

After they read, students analyze their passage using the handout (see the appendix). If you prefer, use colored index cards and have students take notes on individual cards—yellow for tense, blue for point of view, and so forth.

# Use Punctuation and Grammar Intentionally to Improve Connections

As I pointed out in this chapter's opening quote, punctuation and grammatical structures are the most basic ways writers show relationships between and among their ideas. These relationships help our ideas combine cohesively. The chart in Figure 7.8 can be used as a guideline for a mini-lesson of discovery with any text.

All punctuation separates, but each little mark has distinct functions. To raise my students' awareness of punctuation's basic functions, we construct a comparative matrix chart (see Figure 8.5, "Five Basic Punctuation Effects"). As both *Writing Next* (Graham and Perin 2007) and the National Council of Teachers of English's (2008) *Writing Now* recommend, these skills are best

*Figure 7.8*

| What's Connecting Your Ideas? | |
|---|---|
| **Mentor Text** | **Punctuation Function** |
| *What's Eating You? The Inside Story of Parasites* by Nicola Davies | *What's Connecting Your Ideas? The Between Story of Punctuation* |
| Humans probably don't have more parasites than other animals, but scientists have studied us the most and have found lots**: head lice, body lice, fleas . . . .** | *Colons*<br>• Introduce lists or sentences with emphasis<br>• Show connection between what comes before and what comes after<br>*Ellipses*<br>• Show information that trails off, either continuing or petering out<br>• Indicate removed information<br>• Are *always* three dots (Sometimes it appears there are four when, as in this case, a period follows an ellipsis to indicate an ending.) |
| Most vertebrates**—birds, mammals, reptiles, amphibians, and fish—** can't be parasites; they're just too big. | *Dashes*<br>• Set off information that is connected<br>• Add information<br>• Show a break in thought<br>*Semicolons*<br>• Connect two sentences<br>• Show separations in lists in which some items in the list contain a comma |
| Human hair mites . . . are tiny relatives of spiders, about one-tenth of a millimeter long **(smaller than a grain of salt)**, with bodies like miniature salamis and four pairs of stumpy legs. | *Parenthesis*<br>• Indicate an aside or nonessential information (parenthetical)<br>• Act like an appositive, renaming or elaborating on what came before |
| *What's Eating You? creatively uses paragraphs, sections, subheadings (**You Are a Habitat, What Makes a Good Parasite?**), graphics, and speech bubbles to communicate information to readers.* | *Paragraphs or Sections*<br>• Show what information goes together<br>• Separate what information is new or different<br>*Subheadings*<br>• Tell the reader what to expect<br>• Name the focus of what follows |

## Grammatical Patterns That Enhance Connection

| Pattern | Function | Mentor Text |
|---------|----------|-------------|
| Subordinate Clauses | • Make causal connections<br>• May show simultaneous action | **When the adult fleas hatch**, they rely on warmth and movement to tell them there is a body nearby . . . |
| Prepositions | • Show relationships<br>• Connect nouns to other nouns<br>• Show location in time and space | One way to avoid getting **on** the wrong host is to never get **off** the right one. |
| Parallel Structures | • Repeat grammatical patterns like lists and balanced pairs<br>• Repeat larger structures | **Balanced Pair**: Polar bears need thick coats to beat the cold, and giraffes need long necks to reach their food. |
| Coordinating Conjunctions | • Connect ideas<br>• Show kinds of relationships between and among ideas | **But** parasites need to be much smaller than ordinary animals to survive in their body habitats. |

*Figure 7.9*

learned in a meaningful context, while focusing on function. Thus, it's important that young writers see examples of each of these punctuation marks in real texts as they are revealed.

Display sentences. Students observe how the punctuation functions in the model sentences—how it supports or directs the reader, how it emphasizes or demonstrates connection—with your facilitation, naming and extending on student observations.

In addition, there are some grammatical patterns that lend themselves to transitions between and among ideas (Figure 7.9). These may also be used as mini-lessons or revision tips.

The sentences and ideas found in Figures 7.8 and 7.9 can be used, one sentence at a time, as mini-lessons to kick off writing workshop or as revision tips to show relationships between and among ideas. The pattern in the chart may also be used as a model for creating a class-specific chart with your students as they read any high-interest nonfiction text, or as a higher-level activity for some students who are in need of extension or differentiation.

## Pulling It All Together

As our discussion of cohesion comes full circle, it's important to see all the strategies work together in a longer excerpt. Let's look at an excerpt from Russ Parsons's *How to Read a French Fry: And Other Stories of Intriguing Kitchen Science*. As you read, note ways Parsons helps his writing hang together.

> The semicolon tells you that there is still some question about the preceding full sentence; something needs to be added . . . you get a pleasant little feeling of expectancy; there is more to come; to read on; it will get clearer.
>
> —Lewis Thomas

*Have you ever noticed that a whole onion smells different from one that's been cut? Have you ever wondered why? Here's the answer: Physically, an onion is 90 percent water, trapped in a fairly flimsy network of cellulose. Within that network is a subnetwork of smaller cells, called vacuoles. These vacuoles separate a variety of chemical components suspended in the water. It's only when the vacuoles are ruptured, either by cutting or by smashing, that these chemical components combine and then recombine again and again in a cascade of chemical reactions, creating the smell and taste we associate with raw onions. Most simply put, what happens is that the contents of these separate vacuoles combine to form a variety of sulfur-rich compounds called sulfonic acids. These acids in turn combine to form still more compounds that provide most of the fresh-cut onion character. What's more, this chain of reaction happens in a flash. It's a little miracle. In fact, not until the 1970s had science advanced to the point that it could begin to decipher what happens in that fleeting instant between the time your knife touches the onion and the fumes reach your nose.*

*Think about it: the chopping of an onion is one of the most common acts in all of cooking. Any good cook has done it thousands, probably millions of times. Yet how many have ever stopped to think about what is really going on? All of this is neither trivial nor purely technical. For example, it's important to realize that these sulfonic acids are extremely unstable, meaning they go away quickly. One of the places they go, of course, is right up your nose, which triggers the crying response we associate with chopping onions (for this reason, these chemicals are called lachrymators, from the Latin word for tears). More critically, they are both water-soluble and heat-sensitive, which means that the chemicals will dissolve in water and will vaporize when heated. In short: soak an onion or cook it and those acrid flavor characteristics go away. By the same token, and perhaps just as useful, chill an onion or rinse it under cold water and you won't cry as much when chopping it. Also, a sharper knife will damage far few cells than a dull one.*

What did Parson's do to make his writing hang together? Take a look at the definitions and examples in the "How Writers Weave Cohesion" chart in Figure 7.10.

## Come Together

Cohesion isn't always automatic. To make sure writing hangs together as one, we reread and revise it. We scour for places where connection breaks down and shore up our guidance system, making everything fit in a harmonious whole. Transitions, clear pronoun reference, punctuation, and grammar are

**And he makes his whole poem one. What's true, what's invented, beginning, middle, and end, all fit together.**

—Horace
(translated by David Ferry)

## How Writers Weave Cohesion

| Cohesion Strategy | How This Writer Does It |
|---|---|
| *Transitional Words and Phrases* <ul><li>Emphasize details.</li><li>Reveal logic.</li><li>Parse details.</li></ul> | It would be irritating, of course, if Parsons started every sentence with a transition. Logical flow and repeated words (sentence hooks) do most of the work, but he certainly uses transitions as well, mostly of the automatic variety: *either, most simply put, what's more, in fact, and, yet, for example, one of the places they go, for this reason, which, in short, by the same token.* |
| *The Old-to-New Pattern: Sentence and Paragraph Hooks* <ul><li>Link one sentence or paragraph to the next sentence or paragraph.</li><li>Repeat a word (or form of a word) in the preceding and following sentence or paragraph.</li></ul> Note: I first encountered this nifty device in Lucille Vaughn Payne's *The Lively Art of Writing* (1969), but have since seen it everywhere, from advice on how to write about science to Colomb and Williams's *Style.* Smith argues that part of coherence is how we end one sentence and begin the next—there must be a connection. | *Sentence Hooks* <br> . . . flimsy **network** of cellulose. Within that **network** . . . <br> . . . smaller cells called **vacuoles**. These **vacuoles** separate . . . <br> . . . compound called sulfonic **acid**. These **acids** . . . <br> . . . all of **cooking**. Any good **cook** . . . <br> . . . meaning they **go** away quickly, One of the places they **go** . . . <br><br> *Paragraph Hooks* <br> **Think about it** is the first line of the second paragraph, which refers back to the last sentence of paragraph one, and then adds new information that expands on the previous paragraph. This follows the old-to-new pattern. |
| *Point of View (POV)* <ul><li>First-person participant (I, we)</li><li>Third-person observer (He, she, it, they)</li><li>Second-person address (You)</li></ul> Note: In this day and age, it's forgivable and common for second-person point of view to sneak into our questions or prose. The rule should always be this: Does it work? Is it noticeable by someone other than a crazed, bloodthirsty grammar maven? | Parsons uses the third-person observer (*What's more, this chain reaction happens in a flash. It's a little miracle*), although, in several sentences, he shifts to the second-person address, which is forgivable. Would we really want Parsons to begin: *Has one ever noticed that a whole onion smells different from one that's been cut? . . . Has one ever stopped to think about?* Or state . . . *fumes reach one's nose?* He also throws in a fair amount of understood second-person address: *think about it, here's the answer.* |
| *Verb Tense* <ul><li>Principal tense (usually past or present)</li><li>Variance in time may be necessary to show something happened in the past or will happen in the future.</li></ul> Note: When writers ask readers a question, it may be appropriate to shift tense as well. Tense is not always static or as easy to explain as we'd like. The point is, don't shift tense unintentionally. | The principal tense is present (*an onion **is**; these vacuoles **separate**; **combine**; chain of reaction **happens***). <br><br> Parsons chooses to shift tense in his questions because he is asking about what happened before you read this piece (*Have you ever noticed?*). When he references the past (*any good cook has done it thousands . . . of times*) or the future (*a sharper knife will damage*), he shifts tenses—intentionally. |

*Figure 7.10 (continued on next page)*

## How Writers Weave Cohesion *(continued)*

| | |
|---|---|
| *Mood/Tone*<br>• Casual versus formal<br>• Humorous versus somber<br>• Removed versus involved<br>Tone is the attitude the writer has toward the work. The pacing, sentence length, and content all contribute to tone. | Parsons chooses a light and casual tone, involving the reader by asking questions and phrases like *think about it.* In a friendly, helpful tone, he defines terms with phrases that start with *meaning* or signaling us when he's going to give us a useful tidbit (putting onions in water or refrigerator). The word choice is straightforward, but he doesn't shy away from more complex terms—he just explains them. |
| *Highlight Key Message by Cutting What Doesn't Fit*<br>• Select your slant.<br>• Reread and cut anything that veers from your purpose.<br>When writing fiction or nonfiction, you can't tell everything. You select a slice or focus and the sentences—details, facts, and scenes—need to be about that slice or focus. If irrelevant facts do sneak in, it's our job to revise them out, giving our piece an impression of unity or oneness in purpose. | Parsons's slant is the essential and practical facts about the onion and what you can do to combat its odiferousness. He stays on topic, or purpose, if you prefer. Whether asking questions or explaining exactly what causes the smell, he lets us know that *all of this is neither trivial nor purely technical.* Following this information is how to douse out the offensive odor. He doesn't tell everything about the cells—or vacuoles—just enough to let us in on the secret. Each sentence talks about the onion, its smell, and what to do about it. He doesn't call to mind irrelevant onion discussion such as onion soup or chopped onions on your hotdogs. Instead, Parsons sticks to onion smells—where it comes from and what you can do about it. |
| *Pronouns*<br>• Clear antecedent and pronoun use (it's easy to tell what each pronoun refers to) gives a piece a connective unity.<br>• Sexist language (consistently using masculine pronouns) isn't necessarily preferable to alternating. I like pluralizing or rewording because using *he or she* repeatedly clunks on the page. | Frankly, in this excerpt, Parsons uses only a few pronouns, choosing instead to specifically name or rename his references. We can learn from that. Sometimes we use too many vague pronouns, but repeating a name is tiresome as well. Here, we can always tell what *it, this,* or *they* are referencing (**chopping of an onion** *is one of the most commons acts in all of cooking. Any good cook has done* **it**). |

Remember, cohesion, like all writing techniques, is about making choices. There isn't a right or wrong choice, but choose a principal one and stick with it. However subtle, shifting around jolts your reader.

*Figure 7.10 (continued)*

all ways to manually improve any writing's unity. Consistency of tense, point of view, mood, and tone all feed the cohesion of a piece, making it a whole, rather than a directionless, incoherent hodgepodge.

# *Energy*
## Creating Rhythm and Style

*Words set up atmospheres, electrical fields, charges. I've felt them doing it. Words conjure.*

—Toni Cade Bambara

As I conferred with my students one afternoon, I realized that, even with all my lessons on the things good writers do, their research writing remained stilted and limp. You know, the lifeless, encyclopedic prose that makes you want to plunge through the nearest window. But instead of diving though the glass, I decided to change my approach.

When I was in high school plays, the director constantly pled with us to exaggerate our movements. "The person in the last row should be able to see them. If you don't feel like you're overdoing them," she said, "you're not doing enough."

To help us understand the problem, she videotaped a scene. When our performances were played back, it was clear that what felt like overdoing movement was hardly noticeable. When we overdid gestures for a later video, it looked just right.

I decided to take a similar approach with students' research writing. I challenged them: "Write with too much personality in your research report. Take it over the top," I said. "Go too far. In fact, I'll give you extra credit for each time you overdo personality. Be bold. Be confident. Entertain me!"

> One must be drenched in words, literally soaked in them, to have the right ones form themselves into the proper pattern at the right moment.
>
> —Hart Crane

To show them what I meant, I read aloud a few models of lively nonfiction by Steven Jenkins, Mary Roach, Bill Bryson, and Nicola Davies. "They are great," I said, "but I want you to stretch even more." We looked at excerpts to see how the writers made their subjects sizzle with metaphor, powerful verbs, varied sentences, alliteration, passion, life, and, yes, research. Unsure, one student asked: "We can write like this for school?"

"Yes," I said. "We can."

Despite my daring them to go too far, interestingly, my young writers rarely did. In fact, much of what they wrote bulged with brilliance. With a few exceptions, going for broke helped two eighth graders create a lively research report on Abraham Lincoln. Here's an excerpt:

> Besides being honest, Abe was also patient like nobody's business. He believed it was wrong to force an issue. He believed events should not be rushed, but "would unfold in due time." But his patience must have really been stretched like a rubber band when he had to deal with his nutso wife, Mary Todd Lincoln. Not to make fun of her mental illness, but Mrs. Lincoln was more than a few bricks shy of a full load. Lincoln had to be patient to wake up to that every day. And he still loved her dearly. No one understood her but her man. I'll bet you a sock full of pennies no one else has ever been that patient ever since.

Their reports acted as a great discussion starter to talk about what worked and what we had to tone down a bit. As the other students reflected on their own reports, we highlighted in different colors what worked and what we'd cut. Writers evaluated the effectiveness of their writing. We problem-solved how to cut parts that didn't work but also learned to relax, to think less about sounding smart, and to think more about reaching an audience. Amazingly, after cutting a few lines and replacing a few words, much of the over-the-top writing was just right. Students were shocked at how much actually worked. And I was shocked at how much fun we had with these papers.

As my theater teacher said, "It's easier to tell you to back off of a gesture instead of repeating: More! More!! More!!!" By attempting to impress their readers with personality, students finally broke the lively research-writing barrier. Since then, I have collected concrete ways to show students how to give their writing energy.

## Energy Is the Thing

Writers choose the path for their writing.

Is the writing going to be humorous? Solemn? Stern? Slow? Who is your audience? What's your purpose? The energy or pulse of our writing depends on knowing the answers to these questions and making choices based on them. Is it appropriate to write a fast-paced, humorous funeral elegy? It depends on who the funeral is for (purpose) and who's attending (audience).

Although in today's world writing is often temporary, we should still consider the energy of everything we write. An e-mail is deleted; social networking posts are hidden or reposted. What gets writing read or ignored? What makes writing stick around long after a thought was put forth? Is it care for each word? Is it thought? What makes writing last?

Why use the word *energy* to describe what every writer needs to know about style, rhythm, sentence variety, purpose, and connecting with an audience? Why not *style, voice,* or *flavor*? I wanted a word that captured the current of life that surges through sentences.

Sentences live—they reach out, they move and breathe. As writers we choose whether our writing surges or retreats with sentence length, phrases, clauses, and words. Energy is the movement of our words, the cadence, the rhythm, the music, the beat, the syntax, the electricity. Energy is what moves the reader through the text, creating mood and bringing variety to the eye and ear.

What makes writing last is the energy that drives the reader forth, deeper into the text.

Is energy in writing new?

Nope.

In *Poetics*, arguably the seminal book on style, Aristotle referred to energy as a "force of expression." The Elizabethans considered energy to mean "the vigor of an utterance, the force of an expression" and "the quality of a personal presence" (Martinás 2005, 45). Energy is personal and forceful and must be molded to address the writing's purpose and audience.

How do we achieve appropriate energy in our writing? Whether it's a manual explaining how to operate a pedometer or a novel designed to entertain, writing should never be dead. Liveliness does lie on a spectrum. Some writing needs subtlety, some needs formality, some needs casualness. No matter the genre or purpose, all writing needs energy to pull the reader through. For instance, consider all the For Dummies and Complete Idiot's Guides that crowd bookstore shelves. Why on earth would we prefer a book for idiots or dummies? It's simple: These books have energy. The authors explain in lively, practical, and straightforward ways. To most readers, the energy of technical or manual writing is deadly. Readers long for someone to explain needed information like a friend—without lulling them to sleep or drowning them in terminology. When an author uses energy well, the subject comes to life.

Let's say you had to write about our body's defense system. Yep, nonfiction. Can you still have energy? Check out how Trudee Romanek starts her book *Achoo! The Most Interesting Book You'll Ever Read About Germs*:

> Tone and personality are once again central to writing, not something to be smoothed and scrubbed.
> —Alexis Madrigal

> She was listening contentedly to the torrent of words spilling from his mouth. His sentences glowed in the light.
> —Mark Zusak

> *Everybody sneezes. But no one sneezes like Donna Griffiths of Worchester, England. She began sneezing on January 13, 1981, when she was twelve and just kept going. Donna sneezed once every minute for days and days. A year later, she'd sneezed about a million times.*
>
> *Eventually, Donna's sneezes slowed down to every five minutes or so. And then, finally, on September 16, 1983, she celebrated her first day without a single sneeze. By then she'd been sneezing for 978 days, almost three years.*
>
> *Why Donna sneezed for so long is a mystery her doctors couldn't explain. Usually sneezes are a sign that there's something in your nose and your body wants to get rid of it. Without even thinking, you take in a big breath and blast it through your nose and mouth, spraying out whatever germs, dust, or other particles tickled your nose in the first place.*
>
> *Sneezing's just one part of your body's defense system—a system working to protect you from germs that can make you mildly sick or dangerously ill. But sneezing isn't the only way your body can clean up its act. Did you know you have a whole army of defenders fighting off germs?*
>
> *Without them, your life would be just one sickness after another.*

What kind of energy does this writing have? Compare it to this definition from *The American Heritage Dictionary of the English Language*:

sneeze— *v.* To expel air forcibly from the mouth and nose in an explosive, involuntary spasm resulting chiefly from irritation of the nasal mucous membrane.

What's the difference? If you say it's a matter of purpose and audience, I'd agree. A book or essay on our body's defenses should look and sound different from a dictionary entry in energy, in scope, and in length. But Romanek's goal is, as her subtitle promises, to write "the most interesting book you'll ever read about germs." She personalizes her writing in a way that we probably wouldn't want our dictionary definitions to do, and yet the connection she made to germs and my body's reaction make her definition clear.

In our expository writing, do we want dictionary energy or something closer to Romanek's? Something in between? Completely different? Much of Romanek's energy comes from the beyond-the-obvious detail she selects. Her sentences are long and short; her transitions move us through the text. For example, this fresh transition links us back to the prior information without being stilted: "Without them, your life would just be one sickness after another." Her focus, her words, her detail, her coherence—all invite us to ride along with her text.

Everything we need to know about writing comes together when we start considering writing's energy. Much of what infuses writing with energy are the ten things every writer needs to know. The way I connect ideas to the reader, the details I select, the words I choose, the way I spill my words on the page even—all these things come together to create energy in writing, moving the reader forward. Each thing every writer needs to know can stoke or extinguish the energy of our writing.

How do you stoke lively writing? Strunk and White (1999) advise, "Vigorous writing is concise." Is it always? Writing can't and shouldn't only have one energy. Discussing the possibilities, seeing and hearing them, trying them on—that's what writers need to make energy work (see Figure 8.1).

Note: While word choice or diction greatly contribute to writing's energy, the next chapter is devoted entirely to the power of words, so it is discussed minimally in this chapter.

*Figure 8.1*

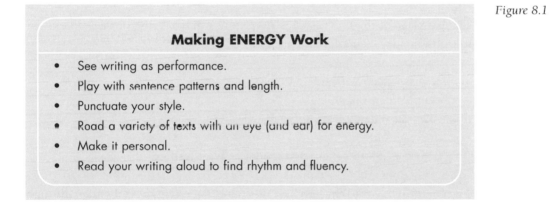

**Making ENERGY Work**

- See writing as performance.
- Play with sentence patterns and length.
- Punctuate your style.
- Read a variety of texts with an eye (and ear) for energy.
- Make it personal.
- Read your writing aloud to find rhythm and fluency.

# See Writing as Performance

How do we get students to understand what energy can do for their writing? Part of what we want them to see is that writing is performance. I've discussed audience in almost every one of the ten things so far, and again, audience comes into play with energy. Strong writers keep the audience in mind—reaching out to them by electrifying their prose with pacing—surging, ebbing, flowing, getting louder, softer, faster, slower.

> **Nothing great was ever accomplished without enthusiasm.**
> —Ralph Waldo Emerson

If we want our students to craft writing that begs to be read aloud, one of the most important things we can do as teachers is read beautiful texts to them. Mostly, I read aloud snippets and sections, but every once in a while when its energy jumps off the page, representing another voice, another personality, another time, another style, I might read an entire book.

> Good writing knows it's performance. Good writers are hams on the page. They feel the presence of the audience the way a stage actor does. The only difference is that the writer's audience must be imagined. People who read aloud well are usually good writers, and a simple way to write well is to *write something you'd love to read aloud.*
>
> —Jack Rawlins and Stephen Metzger

## Wanted: Writing, Dead or Alive

To this end, I choose pieces that teem with energy. One book that begs to be read as performance is a nonfiction picture book, *Bad News for Outlaws: The Remarkable Life of Bass Reeves, Deputy U.S. Marshal* by Vaunda Micheaux Nelson.

The energy jumps off the page in the lead: "Jim Webb's luck was running muddy when Bass Reeves rode into town." The energy continues:

> *Bass hollered from the saddle of his stallion, warning Webb to give up. The outlaw bolted.*
>
> *Bass shook his head. He hated bloodshed, but Webb might need killing. As a deputy U.S. marshal, it was Bass's job to bring Webb in. Alive or dead. Bass had put Webb behind bars before, but the outlaw was back on the run. That would end today.*

The language of the book is consistent in its energy, using phrases like these to bring literary elements into an informational piece:

"area swarmed with horse thieves"
"people liked his pluck"
"Bass was blazing fast on the draw"
"tuckered out"
"Belle was about as far from tender as boot leather"

The energy persists to the conclusion: consistent energy reverberates through every page.

> *Over the years, the name of Bass Reeves faded, like one of those heroes they call unsung. But this story has folks talking again. Talking about the big man who helped bring peace to a big country—Deputy U.S. Marshal Bass Reeves, a true champion of the American West.*

"Did the writer make this information interesting to us?" I ask. "How?" We reread examples and figure out what strategies the author uses. However, my students don't have a lot to say. As my friend Vicki Spandel taught me, if you want to teach an abstract concept to students, show them contrasting examples. After reading *Bad News for Outlaws*, I read aloud the opening paragraph from Art Burton's *Black Gun, Silver Star*, another book about Bass Reeves:

> *Much of what we know today about Bass Reeves persisted in oral stories told by individuals and families whose origins are in frontier Oklahoma. I was able to collect a few of these stories from persons who*

*currently reside in Oklahoma or have lived there in the past. This chapter will focus on these folktales.*

"What makes this writing different?" I ask. "Which would be more fun to perform? Why?"

Students offer many things as they look at the excerpts side by side: The words the author uses are different. The writer uses more of a story structure to give information in *Bad News for Outlaws*.

"What does the writer do?" I ask. We analyze how it was written and what strategies the writer used. Only then can we borrow those for crafting our own prose. In identifying the commonalities and differences, while discussing real texts, students come to know and understand what energy can plug into their writing—pace, rhythm, sentence variety.

Inquiry is a powerful way to get kids inside writing. Students share that the excerpt from *Black Gun, Silver Star* sounds more like a teacher telling you something, whereas *Bad News for Outlaws* entertains while it informs. From there, we look closer at Burton's excerpt and see that words and phrases like "persisted," "whose origins," and "currently reside" distance the writer from the reader. However, in *Bad News for Outlaws*, the old-fashioned metaphoric language and phrases make it seem more authentic. *Bad News for Outlaws* tries to connect the reader to the time and to the drama, not just a string of facts. One piece isn't necessarily better than the other, but each one has a different energy.

I continue reading aloud various pieces. Joyce Sidman, a winner of both the Newbery and Caldecott awards, pairs poetry with expository text on the same pages of her picture books *Dark Emperor and Other Poems of the Night* and *Song of the Water Boatman and Other Pond Poems*. The similar content approached in two styles sparks conversation about energy.

Similarly in the Newbery winner *Good Masters! Sweet Ladies! Voices from a Medieval Village*, Laura Amy Schlitz writes in various structures—poetry, monologue, informational—which helps students discover what gives energy to performance. Of course, the classic *Joyful Noise: Poems for Two Voices* by Paul Fleischman always bring out the performative nature of writing. This choral reading is always a hit, and instructive on the energy of writing.

# Play with Sentence Patterns and Length

We know young writers will do what feels comfortable. They don't play with their writing. They don't try a sentence three different ways when it's not working. They don't explore what a varied sentence pattern or length can do for their writing's rhythm and fluency. Maybe it's because we haven't shown them how important it is. Maybe they are unsure of *how* to do it. Either way, it's our job to get them comfortable playing with sentences.

Playing with sentences begins with witnessing writing as performance. It's a concrete way to reach out and engage our audience's eyes and ears.

## The Buzz Kill Five

Besides finding similar pieces to compare, I can also zap the energy out of a piece of writing, making it fizzle. I simply drain all the life that supports its energy. In Frances O'Roark Dowell's *Falling In*, the energy happens to be a literal part of the story line in the form of a buzz. Here is my energy-drained version:

It was in the morning. Isabelle Bean was very worried. She felt funny this morning. She didn't do her work. Her ear was on her desk. Something buzzed along her fingers. It buzzed up her pencil. Then, spelling period came around. The buzz came from the floor. It came though the desk's legs. It buzzed up the desktop.

She closed both her eyes. She listened to the buzzing. It was like a refrigerator hum.

"What do you notice?" I ask.

"Well," said Ralphie, the sixth-grade critic, leaning his head back, "It makes sense, I guess, but it seems a little . . . "

"Yeah it's . . ."

I wait.

"Let's look at it again," I say.

We reread.

"Did anybody else feel that something's off, like Ralphie?" I ask.

"It's boring," Alicia says.

"What makes it boring?" I ask.

She reads aloud the passage in a singsong manner but doesn't yet have the word to describe it.

"Ah, so it's sounds *singsong*?"

"I guess."

"You know," Alberto says. "Maybe she's saying different stuff, but it all sounds the same."

"Does anyone else see that?" I ask. "What makes it that way?"

When nobody can name it, I change my approach. "Here's something I do when I feel like part of what I am writing is 'blah,' 'singsong,' or 'boring.'" I grab a piece of paper. "I'm going to be like a doctor and give this writing a checkup."

"The first thing I do is fold the paper in half." After folding a paper lengthwise and opening it back up, I place my finger on the left side. "On the left-hand side, I'm going to write all the sentence beginnings down the page. What is the first word of each sentence?"

*Figure 8.2*

| Sentence Checkup | |
|---|---|
| **First Word** | **Word Count** |
| It | 5 |
| Isabelle | 5 |
| She | 5 |
| She | 5 |
| Her | 5 |
| Something | 5 |
| It | 5 |
| Then | 5 |
| Then | 5 |
| The | 6 |
| It | 5 |
| It | 5 |
| She | 5 |
| She | 5 |
| It | 6 |

Together, we make the list. While I write on my paper, another student records it on the board vertically (see Figure 8.2).

"What do you see? Turn and talk to your partner."

After a few minutes of discussion, we come back together and discuss what they see: pointless repetition (too many *its* and *shes*), boring words, no specifics, usually a noun or pronoun.

"They all start the same, so that makes it boring?" Felicia asks.

We decide that one thing that zaps energy out of writing is little or no variety of sentence beginnings.

"This whole variety thing in writing is big. We can't always start every sentence the same way. We need to use sentence variety, but beginnings aren't the only place you need variety. You also need to think about another thing with sentence variety. Do you remember some other ways we need to write with variety?"

If I wait long enough, usually someone can come up with something like variety of length.

"And we can test that on this same sheet of paper. On the right-hand side, write how many words are in each sentence," I say. I list the number of words vertically on my paper and another student records the numbers to the right of the first words on the board.

I explain that the energy of our writing is more than just how long our sentences are and how we start them, but beginnings and lengths of sentences shape the rhythm and pace of whatever we write. "We will look at a revision of this piece of writing tomorrow and see what else we can figure out about energy, but we have a start. Now we are going to give a writing checkup to our own writing."

Students take out a piece that they are currently writing in writing workshop and find a place that has an energy problem or a place that needs a checkup. Students could also use a notebook entry or a past piece from their writing portfolio.

Once students find their piece, they can complete the analysis the same way we did in Figure 8.2, and then put it away until the next day. Awareness today, revision tomorrow. My goal is to create the need for revision, so we can tap back into it over the next few days, expanding on what gives writing energy, how successful authors achieve it, and ways we might try to spice up our sentence variety.

The next day, I show them the "revised" piece, which is actually the original excerpt from Frances O'Roark Dowell's *Falling In*. This time I distribute a photocopy of both versions:

> *On the morning this story begins, Isabelle Bean was convinced she was teetering on the edge of the universe. Which is why, instead of copying the spelling words off the board as instructed by Mrs. Sharpe, she had her ear pressed to her desk. All morning a strange sensation had buzzed along her fingers every time she'd put her pencil to a piece of paper, and by the time spelling period had come around, she had determined that the buzzing was coming up from the floor, through the desk's legs, and up to the desktop.*
>
> *She closed her eyes in order to concentrate more fully on the buzzing. It was like the buzz that a house makes when it thinks no one's home—the refrigerator humming a little tune, the computer purring in the corner, cable lines wheezing softly as they snake through the walls and underneath the floorboards.*

"What do you notice?"

Once we establish that this piece has a lively energy, we reread and attempt to decide why. Grappling with ideas is good for students; this is how they build connections and neural pathways. It's not automatic, and if their answers are thin, they know it, and they will engage in discussion because now they see the need for the information.

When we do the sentence checkup of O'Roark's version, we see that this piece looks different (Figure 8.3). Even though they are of similar content, the sentence beginnings and lengths vary to a greater degree: fewer sentences with more words—as many as fifty-one.

Even though O'Roark's sentences are long, I have to convince students these are not run-on sentences. When we look at how the author breaks up

*Figure 8.3*

| Sentence Checkup for *Falling In* | |
|---|---|
| **First Word** | **Word Count** |
| On | 16 |
| Which | 24 |
| All | 51 |
| She | 13 |
| It | 41 |

phrases and beats, we see they are more connected as she joins sentences together. I am not expecting them to write exactly like O'Roark, but they are at the point where they are ready to start thinking about and trying out new writing techniques and possibilities.

We don't revise passages from their own writing because I don't think they are ready. While some of my most prolific readers and writers might take this information and apply it immediately to their writing, most of my students need to see and discuss more models. I am planting seeds. They don't have enough options yet. Revising for style is sophisticated and difficult. They need to consider more, hear others' and their own writing read aloud, hear contrasting energies, and discover how authors achieve mood, tone, and style that works for their purposes and their audiences.

When the time comes that students are ready for some more options for writing sentences, we explore writer Wendy Mass's *11 Birthdays*. I distribute the 11 Sentence Pattern Options sheet (Figure 8.4; also see the appendix), which shows not only a variety of beginnings, but some other hints writers might keep in mind as they craft their sentences. Students use the models to revise a few sentences in their own writing.

# Punctuate Your Style

Punctuation does more than merely provide separation between and among our thoughts. Punctuation shows relationships. It corrals ideas together; it connects, announces, ellipses, and inflects. Punctuating our style tells our reader how our writing is meant to sound—when the pace quickens, when it slows or pauses, and when the next idea or subject is coming.

## Where Does the Sentence End?

To further explain punctuation's effect on writing's energy, I share a passage from Esmé Raji Codell's *Sahara Special*. Before I read it aloud, I explain that

> **Punctuation marks are the road signs placed along the highways of our communication—to control speeds, provide directions, and prevent head-on collisions.**
>
> —Pico Iyer

### 11 Sentence Pattern Options from *11 Birthdays* by Wendy Mass

**Start with something new (Introductory Elements)**

| | |
|---|---|
| *Prepositional Phrase* Opener | **In a panic**, I try to remember what Stephanie taught me. |
| | **From across the room**, I swear I can feel Leo's eyes on me. |
| *Participial Phrase or Participle* Opener | **Pressing her hands against the cool glass**, she searched the faces of the newborn babies until she found the two she was looking for. |
| | **Grumbling**, I pick up my backpack and run to class. |
| *Adjective* Opener | **Dazed**, I stare up at the dusky sky. |
| *Subordinate Clause* Opener | **As Leo crawled toward Amanda**, he dragged his bear on the ground. (*Although, as, when, while, until, before, if, since*) |

**Combine ideas in new ways (Sentence Patterns)**

| | |
|---|---|
| *Appositives* | The oldest man in town, **Buck Whitehead,** swears Angelina was an old lady when HE was a boy. |
| | Ruby, **the best friend stealer**, follows. |
| *Appositive Adjectives* | Angelina, **small and swift**, was moving even faster than usual because today was the day she had been waiting for. |
| Dash Setting Off an *Appositive* | Dad's inside making his usual mom-working-late dinner—**macaroni and cheese with salami melted on top**. |
| *Serial Comma* | Four parents and many bemused party guests watched as the two babies ***took*** **their very first steps,** ***crashed*** **into each other, and** ***fell*** **to the floor laughing**. |
| | I'm now staring at the **blue-and-white dress, red sparkly shoes, and a wicker picnic basket**. |
| End with *Participial Phrase* or *Participle(s)* | Stephanie shakes her head, ***unwilling*** **to even answer**. |
| | I'm next to him, ***clapping*** **and** ***staring***. |
| | I shake my head, ***frowning***. |
| End with *Adjective* | Amanda watched, **curious**. |
| *Short Sentences* | **Dad chuckles**. |
| | **The air smelled like cake**. |

*Figure 8.4*

Sahara, the narrator, is in a meeting with her mom and a school counselor. They are discussing trouble with Sahara's schoolwork, and they've just finished reading some letters she had written to her dad after he abandoned the family.

> *Mom looked at the file and her face went gray again, and again I felt gravity give out. Look at that, a pile of messy work, of unfinished work, a sloppy diary of me since Daddy left. Why didn't I write more carefully in third grade? Why didn't I finish that assignment in fourth grade? I watched as Mr. Stinger fed my letters back into the long file cabinet. The cabinet closed with a metal sound, a safe full of evidence against me. Waiting there for when they need to pull it out and call me dumb.*
>
> *When we got out of the office, my mom talked in a low voice. "What do you want me to do, Sahara? Say I'm sorry that I couldn't keep him? Fine. I'm sorry. I tried my best. Can't a woman get a divorce without her kid going all special ed on her?"*
>
> *I wanted to say, Don't be sorry, Mom, I couldn't keep Daddy either, but I was wise now. I kept my mouth shut. . . .*
>
> *I stared her in the eye, but I didn't answer her. I knew I was being fresh and bad, but I couldn't lie and say yes. Do it for what? Do it for who? They took what I gave them, took what I didn't give them, they used it all the same way, to feed the file. I was through with giving them evidence. They wouldn't get anything more out of me.*
>
> *Mom looked at me, furious. I thought she would slap me for the first time in my life. She didn't. She stomped away. I stood there, wishing she had slapped me. You're supposed to put an exclamation point at the end of strong feelings. A slap would have felt like that. But instead, her heels clicked out her punctuation, dot dot dot. . . .*
>
> *I couldn't see where my sentence would end.*

After the second reading, I ask what students notice or what sticks with them.

"The file cabinet being full of evidence against her," Victoria offers.

"The comparison gives it energy," I say.

"Yeah," Lisa says, "and then she says her messy work is a sloppy diary of her since her daddy left."

"That was bad," Ramon says. "I like that."

"So," I say, "readers respond to comparisons, even when we don't use the word *like* or *as* to do it. She is speaking metaphorically."

We zoom in on the two sentences and see what the author did. "Let's see how she caught our attention or made these two sentences stand out," I say. "We are looking for evidence of why these sentences stood out." I write one of the sentences on the board:

> Punctuation directs you how to read, in the way musical notation directs a musician how to play.
>
> —Lynne Truss

*Look at that, a pile of messy work, of unfinished work, a sloppy diary of me since Daddy left.*

"You know what I see," I say. "She could have written the same information like this."

Look at that. It is a messy pile of my work. It is my unfinished work. It is a sloppy diary of me since Daddy left.

"What's the difference?" I ask. Students note that we have more sentences now.

"There are a lot of *it ises*," Ruby says.

In contrast, Codell's original sentence uses commas to set off appositives, which helps Codell combine more ideas into one sentence and not repeat words like *it is* over and over: "Look at that, *a pile of messy work, of unfinished work, a sloppy diary of me since Daddy left.*" I explain that Codell is using an appositive (italics), which renames or expands on the *that* to which she refers. Appositives can rhythmically punctuate our style. "Commas set off an appositive that renames a noun in the sentence," I sum up. "Commas also help us combine and cut unneeded words."

"What about the *dot dot dot* thingy?" Yvette asks.

"Yes," I say, looking at Yvette. "What about that?"

"That's a comparison, too. Her mom was all acting like punctuation. And she did it without *like* too. 'Her heels clicked out . . .'"

"That's the senses!" Ramon interrupts.

"Wow," I say. "You've really got me thinking. I agree it's a comparison, it's sensory, but this reminds me of the way punctuation shapes energy. Each punctuation mark means something, telling us how something should be read aloud or in our heads. That *dot dot dot* you mention is called an ellipsis. It gives us a way to tell our reader this isn't over."

"Like her last sentence," Carmen says.

"Exactly!" I say.

Later, I reread the section where the narrator asks questions and the mom asks questions and we discuss how it tells my voice to go up, and changes the way we say words, or the inflection from sentence after sentence.

Codell's excerpt causes kids to talk a lot about how punctuation contributes to meaning and energy. So much so that the next day, we start a chart on the five basic functions of punctuation. We chart different punctuation marks on a comparative matrix like the one in Figure 8.5, discussing the five functions of punctuation. Reviewing the *Sahara Special* excerpt, we find all three terminating marks as well as commas and ellipses. As we put them in the matrix, we focus on how they function for a writer and name the commonalities and differences. We continue adding to the chart over the

## Five Basic Punctuation Effects

| Terminate | Combine | Introduce | Enclose | Remove |
|-----------|---------|-----------|---------|--------|
| Period | Comma , | | Comma , ———— , | |
| Question Mark ? | | Ellipsis . . . | | Ellipsis . . . |
| Exclamation Point ! | Colon : | Colon : | | |
| | Semicolon ; | | | |
| | | | | Apostrophe ' |
| | | | Quotation Marks " " | |
| | Dash — | Dash — | Dash — | Dash — |
| | | | Parenthesis and Brackets ( ) [ ] | |
| | Hyphen - | | | |

Many wonder whether ellipses can terminate a sentence. Ellipses communicate an open-ended, still unfolding message when used correctly as three dots. An ellipsis is always three dots. Sometimes writers add a fourth dot, which is not part of the ellipsis. It's a period. The ellipsis needs the period to terminate.

*Figure 8.5*

next few days until the chart is full. Many of them can't believe there are so few functions and punctuation marks to choose from to punctuate their style. They seem relieved.

# Read a Variety of Texts with an Eye (and Ear) for Energy

Harvey and Goudvis said it (2007). Marie Clay said it (1993). Teachers need to be selectors and collectors of effective texts, which can be used to target instruction. Richard Allington says that one thing struggling readers need

The idea is to write it so that
people hear it and it slides
through the brain and goes
straight to the heart.
—Maya Angelou

most is access to good texts (2011). These experts were talking about reading instruction, but selecting and collecting the right texts is just as important for writing instruction. If we want students to write with appropriate energy for various texts and situations, then they need to be exposed to a variety of texts, written for different purposes and audiences, in different genres, with varying passion, pace, and style. Young writers need to stew in these pieces of literature, discussing, noticing, analyzing, comparing, contrasting, imitating, and experimenting.

Every text's energy won't appeal to us; however, we can note a text's effects, what makes it distinctive, how the author creates the energy, so we can intentionally emulate or avoid it. Once you get to know the energy of a book or author, it's recognizable. Look at the following excerpts from a 2009 Newbery Honor book. Do they have a certain energy or style?

> *Fish wanted the full hokeypokey on my savvy.*

> *I stared at the fuzzy images on the small TV screen across the room; there was so much static it was like trying to watch television through soda pop bubbles.*

> *. . . his breath a wild mix of bluster and Buffalo wings.*

This author goes on to use words such as *scumble, splump, higgledy-piggledy*, and *flimflamming*. These words, these details, these rhythms from Ingrid Law's *Savvy* create an energy—a personality, a tone, a voice. She has a definitive style, whether you like it or not. Perhaps it made you all higgledy-piggledy, but it's not ours to judge as much as give students access to different texts and support their discovery of the exact energy they want for their own writings.

## Did You Do That on Purpose?

There is no right or wrong when it comes to a writing's energy. The question is whether it's an appropriate energy for the purpose and audience. I use the following two texts to demonstrate that the kinds of energy we use can be modified, depending on our audience and our purpose for writing. An author's purpose gets a lot of play in the reading arena, but it is an essential energy shaper of writing as well. What is your purpose for writing? Usually we fall back to the standard acronym for purposes: PIE.

**P**ersuade
**I**nform
**E**ntertain

Is a writer's purpose one or all of the above? It depends. If I write about the life cycle of a dragonfly for the *Encyclopedia Britannica*, my primary purpose is to inform. For whom am I writing? Readers, including children, refer to the encyclopedia when they want quick information. That's a consideration too. Here is an *Encyclopedia Britannica* excerpt on the dragonfly's life cycle:

> *After mating, the female usually lays eggs immediately . . . Eggs are laid in several ways. Species with a well-formed ovipositor place them either within or on plant tissue, above or in the water. Some climb beneath the water's surface to lay and may remain submerged for an hour or more. Species without an ovipositor dip the abdomen in water (sometimes while in flight) and wash the eggs off or stick them onto leaves of plants close to the water's surface. Others drop them through the air onto the water's surface. Eggs that are laid in running water usually possess adhesive or tangling devices that prevent their being swept downstream.*

This just-the-facts energy is an encyclopedic one. I suppose that's appropriate.

On the other hand, if I write these same facts for a picture book, I might approach the subject as Heather Lynn Miller did in *This Is Your Life Cycle (With Special Guest Dahlia the Dragonfly)*. In this excerpt, Dalia has just emerged from a pond and is now a guest on every insect's favorite show, *This Is Your Life Cycle*. Her mother is the first mystery guest on the show:

**Mother:** *I'm so glad you made it to the surface without being eaten by some nasty bass. I remember the day I deposited you and your brothers and sisters. You were all such sweet, tiny eggs.*
**Dahlia:** *Mom, is that you?*
**Announcer:** *That's right Dalia. It's your mother! Audience, take a look at this photo of young Dahlia. Have you ever seen such a cute egg?*
**Mother:** *I found a perfect patch of swamp grass with tall, tender shoots . . . I whipped out my ovipositor and went to work poking tiny holes in the blades of grass. I knew that laying my eggs inside would help keep you safe from hungry fish. By the end of the day, I had laid over 800 eggs. I was so exhausted when I finished, I just sat down and died.*
**Announcer:** *We all know how that goes—right, audience? It's the story of an insect's life. We hatch, we grow, we mate, we die!*

Neither text is right or wrong. They are just for different purposes and audiences. Using these juxtaposing examples gives us opportunities for richer conversations. How do you want to sound? Is there one way? Is there an in-between? What's your purpose? Who's your audience? What appeals to them? What's the best form for a particular piece? When we discuss students' answers to these questions, with access to well-chosen contrasting texts to reference, we deepen students' sense of purpose and audience and their necessary effects on a text's energy.

## Shop Around for Your Point of View

Since energy is affected by point of view, I flood my students with numerous examples. By exploring point of view with contrasting texts, students delve deeply into them, processing how they are alike and how they are different. Most important, the conversation comes back to experimenting with these different approaches to point of view to find their own unique style.

Here is a set of two fiction excerpts that discuss shopping from particular points of view. They vary in energy, pace, and style. Looking at them cements many discussion points we've had about energy. I start with this excerpt from Matt de la Peña's *Ball Don't Lie*:

> *Third Street Promenade is blowing up. A hundred shopping bags swinging in rhythm. Marching, marching, marching. Plastic people with plastic hair, pushing and shoving. Plastic world. Stop in the middle of traffic on a cell phone.* Dana, I'm like already here. I'm just outside Crate & Barrel. *A near pileup outside Gap Kids.*
>
> *There are stairs and elevators in Santa Monica Place. There are open doors and red sale signs. This-is-who-we-are music oozing out of every mall shop.*
>
> Can I help you?
>
> Is there something in particular you're looking for?

Briefly, students describe what they notice. The line about "this-is-who-we-are music oozing" from the shops connects with them. They also point out how de la Peña's description reminds them of shopping, with quick cuts and lots of action to see. Then, we highlight which words and phrases make us feel that way. They note the short sentences, many of which we identify as fragments. Then we suppose why de la Peña chose to use sentence fragments—perhaps to create a staccato style.

"He, like, wants to get you into the way shopping is; it's this and that, real quick," Ramon says, "and you feel that way when you read his writing."

The next day, I share another piece about shopping from Kate Klise's *Deliver Us from Normal*. You may want to read the first several pages, which include even more reflection than excerpted here:

> *When you pulled though the gates of Bargain Bonanza (YER DADGUM DISCOUNT LEADER!), if you were like me, you'd try to*

*avoid eye contact with the waving rodeo clowns standing under the HOWDY, PARDNERS! sign.*

*So you'd look to your left (if you were coming from town) and see the green sign next to the highway: THANKS FOR VISITING NORMAL!*

*Years ago some high school kids spray-painted the word BEING in black letters over visiting. So the sign read: THANKS FOR BEING NORMAL! No one ever replaced the sign or removed the graffiti.*

*I grew up thinking it was our city motto; Thanks for BEING normal! It was a polite way of expressing our town's only commandment: Be Normal! They made it sound so easy.*

*For my family, being normal wasn't easy. Looking back, I don't even know if it was possible. . . .*

*To appreciate Bargain Bonanza, you should know enormous round hay bales were scattered throughout the store. You should also know that the Bargain Bonanza jingle ("Roundin' up bargains, drivin' down prices, woo hoo woo hoo, it's all for YOU!") was my favorite song until I was ten and knew better.*

*Somebody in upper management must have thought hay bales were a cheap way of adding atmosphere to a 750,000-square-foot discount store.*

*A cardboard cutout of Cowboy Cal, the fictional founder of Bargain Bonanza, twirled from the ceiling, directly over my head.*

"How is this like Matt de la Peña's shopping experience, and how is it different?" I ask. Students discuss point of view: Klise's first-person narrator is in the writing, feeling and reflecting, while de la Peña's third-person narrator is removed, observing and reporting. Different details reveal far different shopping experiences. Sentence fragments make de la Peña's mall more fragmented, helping us visualize many things, while Klise's description is a single focus, one place to describe, but she also takes on a more reflective energy, thinking about much more than the shopping.

We pull out our writer's notebooks and talk about where we shop and what it's like. Partners have a few minutes to brainstorm and discuss, and then we freewrite about our experiences. "Write about back-to-school shopping for supplies or clothes like Klise," I say, "or mall shopping like de la Peña if you prefer."

## Passion, Pace, and Parallel Structure

I share this excerpt from *Gunpowder: Alchemy, Bombards, & Pyrotechnics* by Jack Kelly. On its own, this text models a great deal of what we can do when we care about and know our subject. That's why choice with topics is so important for writers. With choice often comes passion, authority, and force.

> Your own winning literary style must begin with interesting ideas in your head. Find a subject you care about and which you in your heart feel others should care about. It is this genuine caring, and not your games with language, which will be the most compelling and seductive elements in your style.
>
> —Kurt Vonnegut

This conviction gives writing energy. To appreciate the excerpt, we reread it a few times. This way students will have a chance to notice the power in the piece, all the things that charge its energy.

> *Fire ignites our dreams and our anxieties. It speaks to us in a language more basic than thought. Our instincts respond to the flicker of flame, to the wavering colors of the coals, to the roar of conflagration.*
>
> *Fire needs fuel, oxygen, heat. It needs an initiator—a tiny bit of metal struck to white heat by friction against flint, a spark. The heat of the spark rips apart molecules of fuel. Carbon and hydrogen atoms combine with oxygen. The reactions are exothermic—they give off heat to ignite more fuel, a chain reaction. The complex process remains something of a mystery to science even today. We understand roughly what is happening, but the flame appears to have a life of its own. Its energy bursts out as heat, which makes particles of soot incandescent.*
>
> *Mankind has lived with natural fire for eons—the hearth, the campfire, the candle flame have been our intimates. Like human lungs, the flames are nourished by oxygen from the air. As convection carries away the hot spent gases, fresh air reaches the fuel. But oxygen makes up only 20 percent of the atmosphere. The thirst for oxygen puts a perpetual brake on natural flames.*

Besides being a gold mine of examples on balance and parallel structures, Kelly's text crackles with energy. But its pace and flow are created with structures of three and balance that create a clean, white-hot energy.

"How do you think Kelly feels about the subject of gunpowder?" I ask. "How can you tell?"

We discuss how enthusiastic Kelly is, noting his word and detail selection. We also zoom in on the repeating parallel structures of three:

> *Our instincts respond* ***to the flicker of flame, to the wavering colors of the coals, to the roar of conflagration.***
>
> *Fire needs* ***fuel, oxygen, heat.***
>
> *Mankind has lived with natural fire for eons—**the hearth, the campfire, the candle flame have been our intimates**.*

In the last excerpt, we notice how prepositional phrases are together, nouns are together, and Kelly leaves out the coordinating conjunction before the last item in the series. This little trick is hard to beat, giving the text energy as well as cohesion.

After we looked more closely at that, students notice the pairs Kelly uses as well. "We call that balancing," I say.

*Fire ignites **our dreams and our anxieties**.*

***Carbon and hydrogen atoms** combine with oxygen.*

We also look at the way he uses stacked appositives and the present tense:

*It needs an initiator—**a tiny bit of metal struck to white heat by friction against flint, a spark**.*

I explain how his use of the present tense helps as its "energy bursts out as heat." We talk about one thing we've learned from this piece that we'll try in our freewriting later that day.

> For I know that the energy of the creative impulse comes from love, and so too all its manifestations: admiration, compassion, glowing respect, gratitude, praise, tenderness, adoration, enthusiasm.
>
> —Brenda Ueland

# Make It Personal

Energy surges between writers and readers. For this to occur, readers want to actively participate in making meaning with words. To support this, we can make our writing personal. If you have something new to say or explain, link it to something familiar to your reader. Anytime you're writing outside your audience's experience, it behooves you to connect your experience to a common one. Writers hunt for what will make their writing clear to their audience. Good history, science, and math writers know this. They make their subject personal in several ways:

- Connect to the present and familiar.
- Place the reader in the situation.
- Share events through the eyes of those who experienced them.
- Show your energy.

As usual, we return to successful models to show students the various ways they can make their writing personal.

## Connecting to the Present and Familiar

"Would you be surprised if Abraham Lincoln used e-mail to win the Civil War?" I ask. Students discuss the reasons they would be surprised, and then I read aloud an excerpt from Tom Wheeler's *Mr. Lincoln's T-Mails*:

> *The evening news video from the Iraq War showed a huge head-quarters tent filled with soldiers and airmen sitting at computer terminals. They were sending electronic messages—some to the front line to position troops and deliver intelligence, some to the rear to bring up the*

*supplies necessary to keep the army advancing. "My goodness," I thought, "it's war by e-mail."*

*Shortly thereafter I was standing . . . amidst the miles of files in the vaults of the National Archives in Washington. Among the documents . . . was a book of glassine pages, each of which contained a handwritten telegram in the precise, forward-leaning cursive of Abraham Lincoln. As I turned the pages in awe, my vocation as a telecommunications executive and my avocation as an amateur historian collided; I was holding in my hands the physical record of the first time a national leader had ever used telecommunications as a regular part of his leadership. Remarking on the similarities between Lincoln's telegrams and the e-mails so common to us all, I . . . said, "These are Mr. Lincoln's T-Mails."*

*Abraham Lincoln was the first national leader to project himself electronically. The command and control by e-mail that the evening news showed being employed in the 21st-century war traces its roots to the 19th-century American Civil War.*

"How does the author draw us into the text?" I ask.

Blank stares.

"Look back at the text," I say. "What things does the author do to try to get us to understand what he's explaining? How did he reach out to us, try to involve us?

"He talked about some stuff we know," Brian offers.

"Like?"

"E-mails. We all know those," Brian says, "But maybe they used to have something like them way back then."

"But there was a lot of stuff I've never heard of, though . . . like gasoline sheets?" Patrice says.

As we continue the discussion, we reread and notice how Wheeler

- compares e-mails to telegraphs;
- connects with readers by using something familiar like e-mail to help us understand something less familiar like telegraphs (T-mail);
- coins (I helped with that word) the term *T-mail* so it sounds like something familiar;
- and explains how he stumbled upon the information, inviting us to think and discover along with him.

## Placing the Reader in the Situation

To demonstrate how we can place a reader in a situation, I share an excerpt from the heavily lauded (National Book Award, Newbery Honor, Robert F. Siebert Honor) *Claudette Colvin: Twice Toward Justice* by Phillip Hoose.

*If, like Claudette Colvin, you grew up black in central Alabama during the 1940s and 1950s, Jim Crow controlled your life from womb to tomb. Black and white babies were born in separate hospitals, lived their adult lives apart from one another, and were buried in separate cemeteries. The races were segregated by a dense, carefully woven web of laws, signs, partitions, arrows, ordinances, unequal opportunities, rules, insults, threats, and customs—often backed by violence. Together, the whole system of racial segregation was known as "Jim Crow."*

This device of putting us back in time as if we were Claudette's peer gives this excerpt energy. We talk about how we might use this strategy of putting readers in the shoes of our subjects. In fiction or nonfiction, we can use the second-person point of view (*you*-voice) to make the reader experience it as Claudette did.

Students also comment on the way "womb to tomb" is fun to say, and how Hoose's rhythm and repetition of pattern in "born in separate hospitals, lived their adult lives apart from one another, and were buried in separate cemeteries" adds to the energy. We look deeper at the serial comma, and I show them how the author uses consistent tense for each action in the series (boldface) and followed each verb with a prepositional phrase (italics).

Black and white babies **were born** *in separate hospitals*, **lived** their adult lives *apart from one another*, and **were buried** *in separate cemeteries*.

Hoose gives us plentiful information using parallel structures, which keep the energy flowing.

"Do the items in this list have anything else in common?" I ask.

After some thinking on the students' part and wait time on my part, they see each phrase also shows separation: *separate, apart, separate*. Olivia says the *were* verbs and the *separates* are at the beginning and ending of the list.

"We hear the balance because Phillip Hoose structured it," I explain. "We can do this with our serial commas too." I pose another question: "Why do you think Phillip Hoose used more than three items in a list with 'laws, signs, partitions, arrows, ordinances, unequal opportunities, rules, insults, threats, and customs'?"

Students note how the writer makes the reader experience everything being stacked against you—law after law after law. He purposely overwhelms us with a too-long list to show cumulatively how wrong it was. I extend on their answers and show how the author bookended this long list with a "carefully woven web of laws" and balances the end of the list with the weight of knowing the web of laws were "often backed by violence."

## Sharing Events Through the Eyes of Those Who Experienced Them

Whether it's yellow fever in *An American Plague* or World War I in *Truce*, author Jim Murphy masters the art of making history interesting. By making plagues, wars, fires, and blizzards about people, he shares the stories of those affected by and struggling with the events—living, breathing, deciding, worrying human beings like me—or not like me. Murphy infuses energy into history, allowing us to be transported.

Another lauded nonfiction writer, Russell Freedman, author of *Immigrant Kids* and *Kids at Work*, knows children are his audience, so he makes sure history is seen through their eyes when possible. In *Children of the Great Depression*, Freedman places us in the past by weaving in a quotation from a young girl's letter to the First Lady:

> *Kids who could not tune in to the popular shows of the 1920s often felt isolated and lonely. "We are just poor renters on a farm and there is no money for a radio or the books I like so much," a fourteen-year-old Texas girl wrote to Eleanor Roosevelt. "Dear First Lady, I have read of your kindheartedness and the cheer you have brought so many. Can't you suggest some way I can get a radio so I can hear the music and talk and news from outside my very small little world?"*

The actual words of a real child suffering in the Depression show us how different their lives were and how isolated they often felt.

Even the nonfiction writers found on the *New York Times* best-seller list employ this strategy, recording history or science through the lens of those people who experienced it or its effects. This strategy hooks and involves any reader. In Rebecca Skloot's *The Immortal Life of Henrietta Lacks*, the author writes about the person whose cells were used to create the HeLa cell. Today, her cells are in almost every lab in the world. I probably wouldn't read a science book about the HeLa cell, but Skloot hooked me by making it personal. She gave science human energy. We get to know Henrietta Lacks.

> *There's a photo on my wall of a woman I've never met, its left corner torn and patched together with tape. She looks straight into the camera and smiles, hands on hips, dress suit neatly pressed, lips painted deep red. It's the late 1940s and she hasn't yet reached the age of thirty. Her light brown skin is smooth, her eyes still young and playful, oblivious to the tumor growing inside her—a tumor that would leave her five children motherless and change the future of medicine. Beneath the photo, a caption says her name is "Henrietta Lacks, Helen Lane, or Helen Larson."*

I am starting to care about Henrietta, and then I learn she was never paid for her cells. She never gave her permission to have them taken, and her family lives in abject poverty. Skloot made a book about a gene and its scientific revolution personal. That's an energy a reader can relate to.

All the pieces discussed in the section are nonfiction, and all the authors use the very things that make fiction buzz and reverberate with energy. So can our students—if we let texts like these show them how. If we encourage them as they write by honoring and celebrating all the moments of energy that break through, they will.

## Show Your Energy

One sure-fire way to bring the energy down in your writing is to tell rather than show. But we have to keep looking for fresh ways to show while knowing when it's necessary to simply tell. You can, in fact, extinguish the energy of your writing by showing everything (see Chapter 4, "Detail," p. 61).

Since I live in Texas, students always write sentences like, "It was hot." Finding fresh ways to say the same old thing is one way we begin to craft energy and life in our prose. For fun, I share that we can *show* it is hot rather than tell. Dialogue and description are ways we can show with energy. I pick two excerpts from award-winning novels that do just that.

### How Hot Was It?

First, I share a passage from Sherman Alexie's National Book Award winner, *The Absolutely True Diary of a Part-Time Indian*.

> It was July. Crazy hot and dry. It hadn't rained in, like, sixty days. Drought hot. Scorpion hot. Vultures flying in the sky hot.
>
> Mostly Rowdy and I just sat in my basement room, which was maybe five degrees cooler than the rest of the house, and read books and watched TV and played video games.
>
> Mostly Rowdy and I just dreamed about air-conditioning.
>
> "When I get rich and famous," Rowdy said, "I'm going to have a house that has an air conditioner in every room."
>
> "Sears has those big air conditioners that can cool a whole house," I said.
>
> "Just one machine?" Rowdy asked.
>
> "Yeah, you put it on the outside and you connect it through air vents and stuff."
>
> "Wow, how much does that cost?"
>
> "Like a few thousand bucks, I think."
>
> "I'll never have that much money."
>
> "You will when you play for the NBA."

*"Yeah, but I will probably have to play pro basketball in, like, Sweden or Norway or Russia or something, and I won't need air-conditioning. I'll probably live in, like, an igloo and own reindeer or something."*

*"You're going to play for Seattle, man."*

*"Yeah, right."*

*Rowdy didn't believe in himself. Not much. So I tried to pump him up.*

*"You're the toughest kid on the rez."*

*"I know," he said.*

*"You're the fastest, and strongest."*

*"And the most handsome, too."*

*"If I had a dog with a face like yours, I'd shave its ass and teach it to walk backwards."*

*"I once had a zit and it looked like you. Then I popped it. And then it looked even more like you."*

*"This one time, I ate, like, three hot dogs and a bowl of clam chowder, and then I got diarrhea all over the floor, and it looked like you."*

*"And then you ate it," Rowdy said.*

*We laughed ourselves silly. We laughed ourselves sweaty.*

*"Don't make me laugh," I said. "It's too hot to laugh."*

After reading the passage, I ask students what they notice and, specifically, what energizes the selection. I lead students to focus on the dialogue and its effect.

"It tells you stuff without *telling* you stuff," Ramon offers.

We discuss how the dialogue highlights the back and forth of friendship, realistically reflecting the way friends support each other and lightheartedly tear each other down. We feel the heat in the boys' idle conversation, the dreaming of air-conditioning.

We light on how Alexie achieves his energy with natural-sounding dialogue. It's always clear who is speaking, even though identifiers are rarely used. If it were too cluttered with dialogue tags, that would snag the back-and-forth energy of the piece. Equally important, if it weren't evident who was speaking, it would kill the energy too.

Dialogue is one way to show it's hot, but it's not the only way.

Since writing's energy can be cranked up with flavorful description, I share another example, *The Evolution of Calpurnia Tate* by Jacqueline Kelly. This book illustrates the heat differently. I read aloud the passage twice, and then ask students how the author shows the heat.

*By 1899, we had learned to tame the darkness but not the Texas heat. We arose in the dark, hours before sunrise, when there was barely a smudge of indigo along the eastern sky and the rest of the horizon was still pure pitch. We lit our kerosene lamps and carried them before us in the dark like our own tiny wavering suns. There was a full day's work to be done before noon, when the deadly heat drove everyone back into our big shuttered house and we lay down in the dim high-ceilinged rooms like sweating victims. Mother's usual summer remedy of sprinkling the sheets with refreshing cologne lasted only a minute. At three o'clock in the afternoon, when it was time to get up again, the temperature was still killing.*

> Style is a very simple matter; it is all rhythm. Once you get that, you can't use the wrong words.
>
> —Virginia Woolf

Students note the contrast in setting between the two excerpts and how each author reveals it. Description primarily moves the energy in *Calpurnia Tate*. Words like *taming* the heat personify it, and other words like *wavering*, *deadly, dim, victims,* and *killing* give the writing a heavy, humid tone. Phrases like *pure pitch* stun us visually.

Without the interactions between characters shown in *The Absolutely True Diary of a Part-Time Indian*, this piece's personality differs significantly. Comparing and contrasting, hearing and discussing various texts and approaches allow young writers to build their stores with all the possibilities of what writing can do.

# Read Your Writing Aloud to Find Rhythm and Fluency

Writers need to know the effect of their words, the pulse of their writing. One of the best ways to achieve this is for writers to read their work aloud. We need to hear our writing "sing out its melody" (Benedict 2001, 14). Something transpires when we read aloud our own writing: As a reader, clumsy words or phrases jolt us in ways they didn't when we wrote them. Reading aloud uncovers what works and what doesn't, what's missing and what's out of place, and, most important, what doesn't make sense or reach the reader. All these issues have the potential to stoke or drain our writing's energy.

When we realize our words aren't saying what we intended, we are given a gift. Writers can revise. When we realize our words crash against one another, we can change their order, we can cut, we can add, we can alter until it flows.

As they read their writing aloud students will uncover issues. A few guiding questions help them think specifically about possible issues:

- Where do you stumble?
- Where does your writing sing?
- Can you rewrite your sentence so your reader won't stumble?
- Is something missing or out of place?
- Do you need transitions to bring your ideas together?
- Can you repeat a structure or create balance?

> The right word may be effective, but no word is ever as effective as a rightly timed pause.
>
> —Mark Twain

After they read their pieces aloud, encourage writers to mark any problem areas and reflect for a minute on what worked and what didn't.

As writers advance, they hunger for new ways to target and tweak energy in their writing. I guide students to consider their writing's music. If it doesn't sing, students need strategies to revise and to add music to their prose (Figure 8.6). Of course, we use the music makers with caution. We consider our audience and purpose. Music makers are used sparingly and subtly. When they are overdone, they seem flowery and insincere.

These models help readers consider other ways to ensure their sentences sing, but we also need to consider what responses our writers will get as they read aloud. These need to be modeled.

*Figure 8.6*

| The Music Makers | |
|---|---|
| **The Music Makers** | **Models** |
| *Alliteration* (repeated beginning sounds) | Wind picks up dust and **s**wirls it in whirlwinds—dust **s**torms that **s**weep the **s**avanna. |
| *Assonance* (repeated vowel sounds) | Dust **i**s l**i**ttle b**i**ts of th**i**ngs. |
| *Balanced and Repeated Structures (Parallelism)* | **A flower drops pollen. A dog shakes dirt** *from its fur.* **A butterfly flutters**, and scales *fall off its wings.* |
| *Onomatopoeia* (words imitate actual sounds) | An ocean wave breaks. **Slap!** It splashes salt into the air. |

All examples excerpted from *Stars Beneath Your Bed: The Surprising Story of Dust* by April Pulley Sayre. Bold and italics are added.

## Models of Peer and Class Response

If we want students to keep their passion and energy, we have to give students guidelines for the kind of feedback they give when responding to peers' writing. Often, the response models they've seen in the past have been harsh.

To prevent energy-squelching harshness, I share with them the "two stars and a wish" method, a concrete strategy for responding to others' writing. This common format is helpful in giving feedback for almost anything. It works particularly well for writers, for we know that what's celebrated gets repeated.

> I always tell my students to listen to the music in their writing when they read aloud. If they are paying attention, and if they have any sort of ear for tune and rhythm, they will hear that too many sentences of the same length create a monotonous beat; that forced transitions are like the wrong bridge between riffs; that overlong, breathless sentences can be the same as music without rests, those essential silences that are as important for emphasis as the notes themselves.
>
> —Helen Benedict

First, I model the process in a fishbowl conference with a volunteer writer. Once a volunteer comes to the front of the class, the writer reads a section of his or her writing. I explain that the most important feedback we can give a writer is what is strong, what is working in his or her writing. "One thing I really liked was your opening sentence. Can you reread that? I like the way you grab my attention with a quote. It drives me on to listen to the rest of your writing." After modeling a star, I look to the class, "What's something else that you think worked in this writing?"

Students share what they notice. We name what the writer did, and why it works for us as an audience.

"While it's important to tell writers at least two things that work in their writing," I say, "we all want to grow too. It's important if there was a breakdown in the writing or a confusing part or a question you are left with that we let the writer know after we tell them what works well in their writing." Our wish can be a question or statement. I show them a frame like this on the board as I model it:

You know, when you said _____, I was left wondering about

_____.

Now students pull out a piece of an in-process writing and bring them to a group of three. One writer reads aloud his or her writing, word for word. Writers may make marks on their own papers as they read them aloud but should only read the words on the page. Students must read their own writing aloud. They read aloud their own words to hear the rhythm of their voices, where it falters, where it needs work. I teach them to circle problem areas they discover, so they can return to them later.

An additional benefit of writers reading their pieces aloud, aside from identifying problem areas, is that other writers don't jump on mere mechanics. Peer response is more than the missing comma or the ending quotation mark. It's about how our words reach our readers. While mechanics are a part of this, we also want to consider all the other components that make writing sizzle with energy.

After listening to the reader read his or her writing aloud, responders share two things that work well. Here are a few examples:

- I like the way you used the word _____.
- The verb _____ was really powerful.
- The _____ (dialogue, lead, conclusion, detail, transition) really works.

I reinforce that we have to point to something specific in the writing, naming the word, the sentence, or the section, then explain why it affected us.

After sharing what works, responders share one thing that could be made better or clarified:

- The part at the end gets choppy, like you were in a hurry. I think you could make those sentences smoother.
- What did you mean when you said _____?
- Could you break up the part about _____ more?
- I didn't follow the part where _____.

Our goal is to be specific and kind, and to give them one thing they can improve on. As writers, our goal isn't to argue. Our goal is to take in listeners' responses and consider them. Even if we don't like them, we consider them. These lessons in kindness and thoughtful, text-based feedback are valuable for writers of any age. Responders need reminding periodically, so our responses never squelch a writer's or writing's energy.

## Finding the Energy

Your eyes and your ears help you find where energy needs to be tweaked, but going back over our writing one more time is often the last thing we want to do. Remember that reading your writing aloud—performing it—helps you discover the energy you need. Play with sentence length, punctuation, rhythm, and style. Don't forget, when choosing your subject, find an angle you care about. If you have passion about your subject, if you care about it, that's always telegraphed to your reader through the life in your prose.

# Words

## Crafting Precise Diction

*When you say a word—negative or positive—you release powerful forces. Every word you say has power. There is no such thing as a power-less word.*

—Marianne Williamson

I can't remember how old I was when I finally figured out the best words don't always cascade automatically from my lips or fingertips. The best words, the truest words, the most chock-full-of-communication words come when I revise. While freewriting, I may scratch down *he ran hurriedly*. Later when I revise, I ask myself questions: Are my words accurate, concise, clear, and concrete? I try *he raced*. Who is *he* by the way? As the writer, I know, but does my reader? Is he a shoplifter, an overweight child, an energetic waiter?

Nouns, verbs, adjectives, and adverbs—all the parts of speech give writers a chance to enhance their diction. Young writers need to know a choice exists and have a notion of how to decide which words will have the best rhetorical effect on a case-by-case, text-by-text, paragraph-by-paragraph basis.

# Accuracy

When choosing the right word, the first thing to consider is its accuracy. Will the word say what I want it to? In this passage from *Do the Math: Secrets, Lies, and Algebra*, Wendy Lichtman's narrator wonders about her history teacher's accuracy concerning a mathematical term:

> The very first thing that Mr. Wright talked about in history class was the U.S. Constitution test. "This is a test of infinite importance" is what he said, which is, of course, ridiculous. Infinite *means that there's no end to something—that it's immeasurable. You can never get to the end of the number line, for example, because you can always add one more number, so that is infinite. But give me a break, no test is close to being of "infinite importance."*

# Concreteness and Specificity

Accuracy is crucial, but specific, concrete words are the best of all. In the picture book *El Barrio*, Debbi Chocolate explores the Spanish word *barrio*, which the glossary defines as neighborhood. But the glossary isn't needed. Page after page, illustration after illustration, the author concretely defines *el barrio*, bringing it alive by describing all the narrator sees: bodegas, storefront churches, sparkling graffiti, holiday celebrations, a quinceañera, and rain-washed murals.

Writing advice books are packed with admonitions to avoid jargon, clichés, slang, and lingo. What kinds of words should we use? Long ones? Short ones? Old ones? New ones? We can follow Winston Churchill's maxim, "Broadly speaking, the short words are the best, and the old words best of all," but even Churchill says, "broadly speaking." It's not black or white. However, clarity is preferred, and writing to impress usually has the opposite effect. It's a balancing act to consider both audience and purpose while crafting words that will transmit our message to the reader most effectively.

# Words Gone Wild

Often, teaching diction strategies to young writers leads them to believe they need adjective strings, adverbs to modify every verb, and scads of hard-to-pronounce words. The more obscure, the better. We know that's not true, but students don't. Students think overwritten texts must be genius: If they can't understand it, it must be good.

We must smash this belief. If students don't have any notion of how to choose words wisely, how will they ever find the right words? Words need not be complicated to be strong. Simple can be brilliant. In the nonfiction picture book *Stars Beneath Your Bed: The Surprising Story of Dust*, April Pulley Sayre demonstrates how well-chosen nouns and verbs prove our language doesn't have to be complicated to be compelling.

> *Dust is made everywhere, everyday. A flower drops pollen. A dog shakes dirt from its fur. A butterfly flutters, and scales fall off its wings. That's dust. Dust is little bits of things.*

The language is direct and simple and radiant—*flower drops, dog shakes, butterfly flutters.*

# Precision, Music, and Life

Words amaze us, baffle us, name our world and our experience. While vocabulary is definitely part of choosing the just-right word, we need to move the study of words beyond traditional vocabulary exercises. Diction is not memorizing vocabulary, not memorizing word lists, not overusing the thesaurus, not replacing all the short words with long ones. When it becomes these things, we risk killing curiosity like fictional third grader Clementine's principal in *The Talented Clementine* by Sara Pennypacker:

> *"I've been wondering. What's the difference between smashed and crashed?"*
> *Mrs. Rice handed me her dictionary.*
> *And then suddenly I didn't want to know anymore. That's the miracle about dictionaries.*

Words help us make meaning. As we refine students' understanding of the power of words, let's ensure we don't make words about looking up definitions like Mrs. Rice. I want my students to know words' magic, like the narrator in Sharon Draper's *Out of My Mind*:

> *Words.*
> *I am surrounded by thousands of words. Maybe millions.*
> Cathedral. Mayonnaise. Pomegranate.
> Mississippi. Neapolitan. Hippopotamus.
> Silky. Terrifying. Iridescent.
> Tickle. Sneeze. Wish. Worry.
> *Words have always swirled around me like snowflakes—each one delicate and different, each one melting untouched in my hands.*

> *Deep within me, words pile up in huge drifts. Mountains of phrases and sentences and connected ideas. Clever expressions. Jokes. Love songs.*
>
> *From the time I was really little—maybe just a few months old—words were like sweet, liquid gifts, and I drank them like lemonade. I could almost taste them.*

The right words communicate; the wrong words obfuscate. How do we help students find those just-right words? What revision options make words work (Figure 9.1)?

*Figure 9.1*

### Making WORDS Work

- Know the difference between first thoughts and thoughtful revision.
- Enhance your writing with accurate, specific, and concrete words.
- Punch up your prose with vivid verbs.
- Consider connotation and denotation.
- Finesse fresh figurative language.

# Know the Difference Between First Thoughts and Thoughtful Revision

I want students to know that unlimited choices exist when it comes to the words they use in their writing. When revising, students rarely see the possibilities for change. Perhaps we haven't done enough to help them see the contrast between strong diction and whatever comes to their mind first. Certainly, it is important for students to understand (as discussed with the concept of motion in Chapter 1) that our first words are an essential, valuable part of the writing process. But they must also learn there comes a time when writers pause, revise, and look back. Writers ensure they have selected the best possible words that say exactly what they want, communicating the exact tone or attitude they desire. All without making writing feel overwritten or heavy-handed. More isn't always better; in fact, it's often worse.

To begin our discussion of the difference between first thoughts and thoughtful revision, I display the following sentence:

> Words become sapped by overuse.
> —Arthur Plotnick

The water is really, really cold. It hurts a lot. It's very hard to swim in really cold water. Really, *really* hard.

"What is this writer describing?" I ask.

"She's saying it's cold," Brittany says.

"How's she doing?" I ask.

"Well, I can tell it's cold," Brittany continues.

"Is she showing or telling?"

"She's really only telling," Ramon offers.

"Let's compare it to another excerpt from the award-winning *Swimming to Antarctica* by Lynne Cox."

"No way. She didn't really swim there. It's all ice," Jarvis says.

I smile. "Let's read and see."

"Wait, is it true?" Jeanette asks.

"Yep, it's a memoir—nonfiction."

I display the introductory paragraphs of Cox's book.

> *The water stings. It's icy cold. My face feels as if it's been shot full of novocaine and it's separating from my skull. It's as if I'm swimming naked into a blizzard. My hands are numb, and they ache deep down through the bone. I can't tell if they are pulling any water. They feel as though they are becoming detached from my body. I look down at them through the ash-colored water: they are splotchy and bluish white; they are the hands of a dead person. I take a tight, nervous breath. Suddenly it occurs to me that my life is escaping through my hands.*
>
> *This frigid and ominous sea is behaving like an enormous vampire slowly sucking the warmth, the life from my body. . . .*

"What do you notice?" I ask.

"I can feel the cold," Dora rubs her arms.

"What words or phrases make you feel the cold?"

"*Stings!*" she says.

"Yeah, *stings* is a powerful verb, isn't it?" I say. "Even though it's *telling* in one way, it's also *showing*. I feel *stings* more than *it's really, really cold*. How about you? Sometimes we use words like *really*, trying to prove it's cold. But in *the water stings*, the verb *stings* does the work of *really, really cold*, doesn't it?" I pause and give the students a chance to process this. "What else makes it cold?"

"My hands are like a dead person's," shares Marcus.

"Ah, comparisons. Comparing her hands to a dead person's does help us imagine how cold it is."

"And it's like she got a shot in her face," offers Ruby, touching her cheek. I explain what novocaine is and when it's used.

"Ouch," says Priscilla.

"Yeah, and it's like her face is peeling off," Alberto says.

"Lots of comparisons," I say. "Comparisons seem to really capture us as readers. What's that tell us?"

"We should use comparisons?" Pricilla asks.

They share what they think, and we continue to suppose how we might try some of these things that work in Cox's piece in our own writing. We end up creating a list of a few things we learned from Lynne Cox.

- Be careful of words like *really* and *very*.
- Let verbs do some of your work.
- Pick words that show rather than tell.
- Use comparisons to make your ideas come across.

Students take out a piece of their writing. They reread and look for a place to play with the ideas and thoughts that emerged from our discussion. We attempt, reach, reflect, and refine.

# Enhance Your Writing with Accurate, Specific, and Concrete Words

To target diction at the word level, I've found revising for the most effective words works best when I am concrete with my teaching. What is more concrete than naming a person, place, or thing? Our names, our friends' names, Reese's Peanut Butter Cups, recliners, and roaches all evoke a reaction. So I set out trying to teach my students how, in their writing, to do as Natalie Goldberg advises: "Give things the dignity of their names" (2010, 90).

## Name Names with Showing Nouns

Fiction writer David Long (2002) argues, "Concrete words are exact words; writing saturated with them orients us in time and space" (23). For example, we could write *They met on a corner*, but we paint a clearer picture when we write: *Jacob and Priscilla met on the corner of Pickwell and Dollarhide*. Your reader doesn't have to know where Pickwell and Dollarhide intersect, but making the location exact tells your reader that you know what you're talking about. Long put it this way:

> *If you tell me you saw "a bird," you haven't told me much; I may even have reason to distrust you. Bird is an idea, a category. Maybe you were lazy, maybe you didn't think I was worthy of the details, maybe, in fact, you weren't there. But say, "Late morning a pair of juncos landed on the feeder by the north window," and you've let me see something.* (2002, 24)

> She rediscovers the purpose of her life: to grasp the meaning of the earth's wild enchantment, to call each thing by its right name . . .
> —Boris Pasternak

Name names and your writing will stick with readers. Not car, but Cadillac; not flower, but daisy; not dog, but collie. We all have connections to things, and those relationships come to life when we name names. Compare reactions to the following two sentences: *The bug ran up my leg* might make you flinch; *The cockroach ran up my leg* will make you cringe and shudder. Naming names in our writing is a must if we want our words to stick with readers and if we want to take advantage of all the shades of meaning that specific nouns have.

To demonstrate the specific noun concept, I begin by reading aloud the following passage from Cynthia Rylant's *Missing May*. The main character, orphaned Summer, has been passed around from relative to relative, treated "like a homework assignment." Summer has just come to live with her Aunt May and sees May has a lot of stuff, but Cynthia Rylant doesn't write *May had a lot of stuff*, or even more specifically, *May had a lot of food*. Rylant names names:

> *My eyes went over May's wildly colorful cabinets, and I was free again. I saw Oreos and Ruffles and big bags of Snickers. Those little cardboard boxes of juice that I had always, just once, wanted to try. I saw fat bags of marshmallows and cans of Spaghetti-Os and a little plastic bear full of honey. There were real glass bottles of Coke looking cold as ice in the refrigerator and a great big half of a watermelon taking up space. And, best of all, a carton of real chocolate milk that said Hershey's . . . glistening Coke bottles and chocolate milk cartons to greet me. I was six years old and I had come home.*

I read the excerpt again, telling students, "When I am finished, I will ask for nouns that stick with you. Close your eyes and listen for nouns as I read again." Students' ability to analyze texts increases when I read short excerpts more than once. If students need more prompting, I add, "Cynthia Rylant didn't write 'She had stuff to drink.' What did she write?" Then, I make a lopsided T-chart with the right side larger than the left. As students offer nouns, I record them in the wider right-hand side of the chart. If they say, "juice boxes," I fill in the blanks for the student by writing the phrase from the excerpt, "Cardboard boxes of juice I always, just once, wanted to try." After the right-hand column is filled, I rewrite each specific noun's less specific counterpart on the left side.

"What would be a boring way to say 'juice box'?"

"Liquid," Johnny offers.

"Stuff to drink," Crystal suggests.

"Yes, that is truly dreadful, Crystal." We have fun by celebrating the most boring answers. In particular, I try to use nouns like *stuff* and *things* on purpose. Seeing what is wrong will help them get it right later. Besides, students relish being wrong on purpose!

> What we have to learn, we learn by doing.
>
> —Aristotle

After analyzing the excerpt, students are ready to write. I get them working with a freewrite prompt that asks them to describe the specifics of a place they know well, such as the contents of their pantry, refrigerator, room, or locker. As students share their freewrites, I ask, "What nouns were named?" Shawn wrote about his room, and students quickly identify his naming nouns: "As Gerald walked into my room, he noticed food from ages ago: moldy sandwiches. He noticed the floor was stained with Big Red and grape Kool-Aid. What he didn't notice were the cockroaches running around on the dusty furniture."

"What works here?" I query.

"Grape Kool-Aid," Amanda offers.

"Yes, we all have a relationship with grape Kool-Aid. Have you ever spilled it in your mom's white kitchen?"

Ray writes:

> I opened the stubborn door, peering through the glassless window. I slowly looked around, noticing the cans of corn and green beans. Looking lower, I discovered red cans of tomato and blue cans of cream of mushroom soup. Even lower on the shelf was a pile of potatoes, covered in sprouting heads. Up above the corn and green beans, I spotted a blue box of macaroni. I had found the pantry.

Students quickly notice Ray's naming nouns and how he moved what he had found to the end of the description. In addition, students see that Ray didn't have to use name brands to get a response from readers. Students gain a lot from seeing, hearing, and analyzing models.

Next we move to looking for models in the novels students read. I want students to find examples of naming names in their independent reading. I have them copy into their reading journals sentences or passages that name names. As students share their examples, they see that this isn't just something English teachers make students do; "real" writers do this when they want to create images in their readers' minds.

Once my students have analyzed a model, tried this in some freewriting, and found examples in their reading, they are ready to refocus on their own writing and revise for specific nouns. Students select a piece of writing they want to revise and read through it, highlighting any unspecific nouns. They choose one sentence to revise. After choosing their sentence, students take an unlined sheet of paper and make a "hot dog" fold. Opening the paper in landscape position, they label the top half *Before* and the bottom half *After*. They record their original sentence in the top section in pen or pencil with no embellishments. Then, on the bottom half, they write their revision using bright colors to highlight the nouns they make over or add, embellishing with all the extras they want. In appearance, the bottom half should be flashy and "better than" the top section. Students then post their changes on the Noun Makeover bulletin board.

## Give a Reader a Clue

If you choose a noun not known by everyone—a foreign word or a science-fiction term—you can still use the precise word without losing your reader. Give your reader a context clue.

For example, in science fiction, future settings often require new vocabulary. In *The Hunger Games*, Suzanne Collins defines the world of *Panem* using the grammatical pattern of the appositive, renaming and expanding on the noun that precedes it.

> *He tells of the history of Panem*, the country that rose up out of the ashes of a place that was once called North America.
>
> *The result was Panem,* a shining Capital ringed by thirteen districts, *which brought peace and prosperity to its citizens.* (Emphasis added.)

If Collins didn't supply context clues, the reader wouldn't be transported to the constructed world. Appositives come in handy for more than science fiction.

Often students want to use Spanish or other foreign or specialized words. Periodic use of this kind of specific diction adds flavor to writing. However, writers need to define the word or phrase, so they don't lose their reader. Tony Johnston peppers Spanish brilliantly in her picture book *Day of the Dead*, using appositives to rename the italicized Spanish words and phrases:

> *Mama is making* empanadas, *little pastries fat with meat.*
> *For days* las tias, *the aunts, have been grinding dry chiles to powder.*
> *For days Mama had baked* pan de muertos, *bread of the dead.*

Go ahead and use an unfamiliar word, but let the reader in on the secret. Consider your audience, and if the word needs to be defined, give the reader a context clue.

> Every world has its own vocabulary, even those worlds that might seem simple or mundane, and precise naming takes us deeper into the world being described.
>
> —Rebecca McClanahan

# Punch Up Your Prose with Vivid Verbs

While specific nouns are important for making writing concrete, it's the verbs that provide action. Without verbs, writing wouldn't get anything accomplished. Vivid verbs give writing zip. Look how Paulo Bacigupi drives us through the opening paragraph to his Printz Award–winning novel, *Ship Breaker*:

> *Nailer **clambered** through a service duct, **tugging** at copper wire and **yanking** it free. Ancient asbestos fibers and mouse grit **puffed** up around him as the wire **tore** loose. He **scrambled** deeper into the duct, **jerking** more wire from its aluminum staples. The staples **pinged** about the cramped metal passage like coins **offered** to the Scavenge God, and Nailer **felt** after them eagerly, **hunting** for their dull gleam and **collecting** them in a leather bag he **kept** at his waist. He **yanked** again at the wiring. A meter's worth of precious copper **tore** loose in his hands and dust clouds **enveloped** him. (Boldface added.)*

Sixteen meaning-packed verbs (or verbals) are in this one paragraph. No wonder we keep moving. When rereading a passage like this, observe the care the author put into finding accurate, exact verbs that appeal to the senses.

## Revising Verbs Is for Squirrels

To get students to focus on the power of verbs, I found the following vivid-verb-packed passage about squirrels from *Ubiquitous: Celebrating Nature's Survivors* by Joyce Sidman.

> *One of the oldest groups of mammals, squirrels first evolved in North America and spread to other continents during periods of great continental shifts and climate change—when other, less successful mammals disappeared. One of the reasons squirrels thrived is that many of them adapted to life in the trees, where few predators could follow them. To this day, speed, climbing ability, and the world's most versatile tail enable them to evade midlevel predators such as coyotes or foxes. They are also omnivores, eating anything handy: seeds, nuts, fruits, insects, mushrooms, small mammals, and frogs. Most squirrels live very happily alongside humans, raiding food sources at will and gnawing with ease through wood, plastic, even metal. Squirrels survive cold northern winters by "scatter-hoarding": burying nuts and seeds, then digging them up later. Some of these nuts are forgotten and sprout into saplings—thus it is said that industrious squirrels plant more trees than humans do.*

While I could share the excerpt as it is, instead I distribute one in which I have changed some of the strong verbs to weaker ones. Here is the alternate version with weaker verbs in boldface type (see the appendix):

> One of the oldest groups of mammals, squirrels first **started appearing** in North America and **moved** to other continents during

periods of great continental shifts and climate change—when other, less successful mammals **went away**. One of the reasons squirrels **lived** is that many of them **adjusted** to life in the trees, where few predators could **come after** them. To this day, speed, climbing ability, and the world's most versatile tail **help** them to **get away from** midlevel predators such as coyotes or foxes. They are also omnivores, eating anything handy: seeds, nuts, fruits, insects, mushrooms, small mammals, and frogs. Most squirrels live very happily alongside humans, **finding** food sources at will and **chewing** with ease through wood, plastic, even metal. Squirrels **live through** cold northern winters by "scatter-hoarding": burying nuts and seeds, then digging them up later. Some of these nuts are forgotten and **grow** into saplings—thus it is said that industrious squirrels **start** more trees than humans do.

I display the paragraph and students brainstorm possibilities to replace bold-faced verbs and phrases. I explain that even though some boldfaced verbs or phrases are more than one word, single verbs can replace them.

After students brainstorm, we compare their choices with Sidman's. No right answer exists. We generate verbs and decide which ones reflect the desired meaning. Then students return to their own writing to revise a few verbs, searching for repeated or weak verbs to replace with more concrete or showing ones.

## Sorting Showing Verbs

Instead of merely distributing a list of verbs that appeal to the senses, I shuffle words in a list randomly (see the appendix). I distribute the scrambled list of sensory verbs of movement (Figure 9.2) to groups of three or four students. Next, students cut the list up, so that one word is on each strip of paper. Students read through the words and do an open sort, deciding how to categorize them on their own.

They look for patterns: How are the words alike, and how are they different? What categories do they find? What groups do they make? After sorting the verbs into categories, students label their categories and share them. Each group has a dictionary if they need it. Later the process can be repeated with sensory verbs of sound (Figure 9.3 and the appendix), following the same procedure.

Writing is made up primarily of specific concrete nouns and powerful verbs. However, we can't leave the topic of verbs without touching on what energizes verbs and what can steal the power from verbs. Figure 9.4 reminds us to use active verbs and adverbs in moderation, which cleans up writing immensely. These ideas are looked at in more depth in Chapter 10.

*Figure 9.2*

## Sensory Verbs of MOVEMENT

| Quick | | Slow | |
|---|---|---|---|
| Hurry | Chase | Creep | Stalk |
| Scamper | Hurl | Crawl | Edge |
| Scramble | Swat | Plod | Sneak |
| Dart | Flick | Lumber | Stagger |
| Spring | Whisk | Tiptoe | Waddle |
| Spin | Rip | Bend | Drag |
| Stride | Shove | Amble | Sway |
| Streak | Swerve | Saunter | Lift |
| Trot | Smash | Loiter | Drift |
| Gallop | Plummet | Stray | Droop |
| Dash | Bounce | Slink | Heave |
| Bolt | Dive | | |
| Careen | Swoop | | |
| Rush | Plunge | | |
| Race | Swing | | |
| Zoom | Fly | | |
| Zip | | | |

See the appendix for a mixed-up sensory verbs of movement list for students to cut apart, sort, and label the categories.

*Figure 9.3*

## Sensory Verbs of SOUND

| Loud Sounds | | Soft Sounds | |
|---|---|---|---|
| Crash | Screech | Sigh | Crackle |
| Thunder | Whistle | Murmur | Peep |
| Blare | Grate | Snap | Buzz |
| Thud | Slam | Patter | Gurgle |
| Boom | Clap | Swish | Chime |
| Smash | Stomp | Whir | Tinkle |
| Explode | Jangle | Rustle | Clink |
| Roar | | Hiss | |

See the appendix for a mixed-up sensory sound verb list for students to cut apart, sort, and label the categories.

| Modifiers in Moderation | | |
|---|---|---|
| **Additional Strategies** | **What It Does for Your Writing** | **When It Works vs. When It Doesn't** |
| Active Verbs | Active verbs make writing trim, clear, and bursting with energy. They electrify our prose and keep it moving. | **Miles off, thunder echoed.** vs. Miles off, there was the sound of thunder. |
| Adverb Moderation | Used in moderation adverbs can add dimension to writing. However, if a better verb could do the work, replace the verb rather than adding on to a dull verb. | **Elphaba scowled.** vs. Elphaba angrily scrunched her face. |

"When It Works" mentor sentences excerpted from Gregory Maguire's *Wicked*.

*Figure 9.4*

# Consider Connotation and Denotation

All words have shades of meaning, and writers need to attend to these subtle differences so they paint the right picture. Does the music of the word we chose match the tone or mood we want to create? If I describe a setting and I mention the brown shag carpeting, is it enough to call it brown shag carpeting? If we are going for accuracy, that's accurate. However, is brown shag carpeting an intentional sign pointing us to something about the setting or the character who lives there? Maybe it's supposed to be the 1970s or maybe we need to show that the carpet hasn't been changed in a while. Should the carpeting be chocolate brown or cow patty brown? Does it matter?

Although directness, clarity, and aesthetics are important, to make the right choice, we must consider the perception of the words we use. Will the negative or charged perception of a word smudge our meaning? Will it enhance it?

Effective writers consider connotation and denotation. *Connotation* is the perceived meaning of a word, a range of positive or negative reactions, and *denotation* is the dictionary definition of a word. Connotation is all about tone or mood. I can use various words to say the same thing on the surface, but because of a word's connotation, I may send a different message to my reader. For example, I might write:

Bill helped Tim.
Bill enabled Tim.

> Sensitize yourself to denotation and connotation.
>
> —Constance Hale

Le mot juste (The right word)

—Gustave Flaubert

*Helped* has a positive connotation. The definition of *enabled*—or denotation—implies help in "providing a means," but it also has a negative connotation. *Enabled* may mean making it possible for a drug addict to keep taking drugs. Loaning them money or bailing them out of trouble is seen as enabling—or helping them—to destroy themselves. The words have similar denotations but different connotations. Every word has power. Every word.

Choices communicate.

## Words Color My World with Tone and Mood

Colors connote feelings and can act as a vehicle of tone and mood. To introduce this concept, I use the picture book *Yesterday I Had the Blues* by Jeron Ashford Frame. When students enter, "Colour My World" by Petula Clark blasts from my iPod. After lowering the volume, I ask, "What color is your world today?"

The students stare at me as if I've lost my mind.

"Have you ever thought of describing your day or your mood with a color? Jeron Ashford Frame did, and she wrote a book about it." I read aloud from the book in which the narrator has the blues one day and the next day has the greens. His sister has the pinks, Mom has the reds, and Dad has the grays.

> *Daddy says he got the grays. The straight shoelaces, coffee in the car grays. The lines between his eyes, lookin' at his watch grays.*

After reading, I give groups of three the text for one color and mood. Groups reread their page and discuss these questions:

1. Is this writer showing or telling? How do you know?
2. What mood is described? How do you know?
3. How can we use something Jeron Ashford Frame does in our own writing?

We discuss

- connotations and denotations of the color words;
- how the author coins names for feelings (the cumulative list, or a-bunch-of-things-that-show-the-mood technique, such as "straight shoelaces," "coffee in the car grays," etc.);
- shades of color and the subtle difference in feelings they may evoke; and
- how that connotation creates a tone that sets and reflects a mood.

In pairs or individually, students write about a mood using a color and naming technique found in Frame's *Yesterday I Had the Blues*. Manuel works on his own, and suddenly we know why Manuel is extra quiet.

Today I have the blacks.
The school bus came three minutes early and I missed it blacks.
The wake my mom when she worked all night blacks.
The never hear the end of it can't wait to get to school blacks.
The but I'm late and have detention anyways blacks.
Today I have the get off my back blacks.

His mood lifted after he shared. Writing is expression, and the right mood and tone speak volumes.

# Finesse Fresh Figurative Language

Students are learning about dust in their science class, and we think about how a writer can describe something that can't be seen.

"I've got a connection," Shivaun says.

I'm nervous. What follows this statement is not always illuminating, but I'm game. "What are you thinking, Shivaun?"

"Well, when we talked about nonfiction reading the other day, you said writers give you a comparison so you can see it. It was a text feature like a whale is the size of three school buses, so we can get an idea."

Later that evening I read National Book Award winner *The Worst Hard Time* by Timothy Egan and come across a comparison of how small dust is and why it could get into the lungs of people and livestock during the 1930s, giving them dust pneumonia.

The next day, I share the sentence—the comparison—and we talk about how useful they are to readers.

> Even with Vaseline in their noses and respiratory masks over their faces, people could not help from inhaling grit. Dust particles are extremely fine, sixty-three microns or smaller. By contrast, a period at the end of a typewritten sentence is three hundred microns.

Then I share a passage from Kenneth Davis's *Don't Know Much About Space*. Davis effortlessly uses comparison to help the reader understand the size of the universe:

> The galaxies of outer space are filled with stars. Does ten trillion million stars mean anything to you? It sounds like one of those phrases that little kids make up when they want to think of the absolutely hugest possible number there is. But that is how many stars astronomers say there are in the universe. If everybody on Earth—all six billion people—counted

> Metaphors have a way of holding the most truth in the least space.
>
> —Orson Scott Card

*1,000 stars per second for twenty-four hours a day, it would take fifty
years to count all those stars. You could get tired just thinking about it.*

In some cases, writing *the absolutely hugest possible number there is* would be
frowned on for its overuse of adjectives and reliance on an adverb, but can't
you just see the kid who is trying to come up with the big number using that
adjective list? Davis deftly uses his words to help us understand the vastness
of space. Comparisons and contrasts are exactly what a writer of fiction or
nonfiction needs to paint a picture with words.

## Metaphors Be With You

In a literature circle, a group was reading the Newbery Honor book *Savvy* by
Ingrid Law. They were noting comparisons and asking whether they could
start a list of them. This is the perfect time to discuss similes as another form
of comparisons that writers use.

### Similes

*The Lincoln Sleepy 10 had only a few cars in the parking lot, and
its vacancy sign was buzzing and blinking like a bug light.*

*Lester poked his head out the door of the bus, his combed-over hair
flapping madly like a grocery sack on a barbed wire fence.*

Of course, once one group begins, others join in. We start with similes. I
don't immediately bring up metaphors yet—I let that concept arise. They see
the difference once they know similes well. It's not really about identifying
metaphors and similes as much as understanding another option for making
words more concrete for readers. One student, who had her very own literature circle (don't ask!) found a metaphor in dialogue in Jacqueline Kelly's *The
Evolution of Calpurnia Tate*:

*. . . That boy needs piano like a snake needs a hoopskirt.*

We discuss how similes reveal information about the father's character and
his expectations for his son and the 1800s Texas setting. Another group of
students reading Adam Gidwitz's *A Tale Dark and Grimm* shares these similes:

*Her eyes flashed like the ocean on a sunny day.*
*Her guilt burned her like the scouring wind.*

A group of boys reading *Bad News for Outlaws* by Vaunda Micheaux Nelson
shares:

> *This was near as risky as a grasshopper landing on an anthill.*

I had to join in on the meta-thon, and I shared this excerpt from *Woe Is I Jr.: The Younger Grammarphobe's Guide to Better English in Plain English* by Patricia O'Conner:

> Quotation marks are like road signs you see when you enter and leave a city. Just as the signs define the city limits, quotation marks show where speech begins and ends.
>
> The quotation marks at the beginning (") look like a tiny 66 with the holes filled in. The quotation marks at the end look like a tiny 99 with the holes filled in. It helps to remember that 66 comes before 99.

## Comparisons and Contrasts Help Writers and Readers Understand

As always, we bring the conversation around to how we can use comparisons and contrasts in our own writing. Here are some of the students' answers:

- Comparisons help readers see.
- Comparisons help writers show rather than tell.
- Comparing unfamiliar stuff to objects most people know helps people understand.
- Using *like* and *as* links comparisons in similies.
- Sometimes showing what something is not is a way to describe.
- You can reveal things about character and setting with your comparisons.
- The words you use can give your writing a tone or energy.

At some point, writers know that metaphors and similes are figurative language. We can define metaphors for them, but they really learn by seeing examples. A simile is metaphoric language, but it is not interchangeable with the word *metaphor*. A simile compares two unlike things to create a connection that helps the reader see how they are alike. For example, David Lubar's *Dunk* begins, "His voice ripped the air like a chainsaw." That's a simile. The next sentence is metaphoric: "The harsh cry sliced straight though my guts the first time I heard it."

The figurative language options chart (Figure 9.5) defines other figurative language that can add pizzazz to students' prose.

## That's So Cliché

Students are advised to avoid clichés since they are so overused they make writing stale; however, to avoid clichés, students have to know what they are.

> Poetry is the establishment of a metaphorical link between white butterfly wings and the scraps of torn-up love letters.
>
> —Carl Sandburg

## A Few Figurative Language Options

| Figurative Language | | Describes something by comparing it with something else |
|---|---|---|
| Simile | Use of *like* or *as* in a comparison | In Sandra Cisneros's *Caramelo,* the narrator describes her father's skin: "pale as the belly side of a shark." The simile works especially well because the family is at the beach at the time of comparison. |
| Metaphor | A comparison made without the words *like* or *as* | I lie in bed looking out at the night's piñata-spill of stars.<br><br>    Still, a worm of doubt squirms in my mind.<br>—Tony Johnston, *Any Small Goodness: A Novel of the Barrio* |
| Hyperbole | Dramatic exaggeration | It would have taken a lumberjack ten minutes to cut down all the trees in Kansas. —Truman Capote, *In Cold Blood* |
| Alliteration | Repetition of beginning sounds | The women wore dark dresses, and big black hats trimmed with black lace, like fabulous flowers. The men wore suits without sweat stains. —Neil Gaiman, *Anansi Boys* |
| Onomatopoeia | When words imitate the sound they make | *Mwaam, mwaam, mwaam.* Is it conceited to want to kiss your own work? —Rita Williams-Garcia, *Jumped* |
| Personification | Description of nonhuman thing as if it is doing things a person would do | A seed is sleepy. —Dianna Aston, *A Seed Is Sleepy* |

Figure 9.5

Though not often considered figurative language, clichés often began that way. To help students realize the problem with clichés, I read and display a self-penned, cliché-filled passage with the clichés in bold.

### What Goes Around Comes Around

    My mom always said, **"It's better to be safe than sorry."** But I guess I couldn't resist **my fifteen minutes of fame**, and went ahead and **stood my ground**. Let me **cut to the chase** and take you on **a trip down memory lane**, which is **easier said than done**. **To the best of my knowledge**, I was doing a **good deed for the day** when I told off some **Johnny Come Lately** who was bullying my **one true friend**. I yelled, **"Watch your tongue!"**

Then **it hit me like a ton of bricks**. Johnny Come Lately's fist, that is. **When push comes to shove**, I thought I could fight him. **Every dog has its day**, right? I didn't worry about putting myself **in harm's way**. I tried to **knock the daylights** out of Johnny. If I had **flattened him like a pancake**, it would have been a real **feather in my cap**. **At the end of the day**, **it goes without saying**, he gave me a **knuckle sandwich**. **To save face**, I thanked him and **headed on my way**.

Students giggle as I read.

When I finish, I ask, "What made you laugh?"

"That's lame," Jordan says.

"What made it lame?" I ask.

"Those things that sound all old people-y, like a guy on TV," Jordan says. "It sounds fake."

"Yeah, like old people," Eliza says, "on PBS or something."

"Let's look at all the bolded phrases." After a minute, I ask, "Does anybody know what those are called?"

"Phrases," Chris says.

"That's a good guess, Chris. A phrase is a group of words that aren't a sentence by themselves. These are called clichés. Have you ever heard of them?"

"Yeah, you're not supposed to use them."

"Yes, or—like Jordan said—you might sound lame."

I explain that *cliché* is a French word from when printing was done with metal plates with words placed on them. In *The Word Snoop*, Ursula Dubosarsky explains:

> *A particular kind of fixed metal plate, called a* stereotype, *was invented as a quick, cheap way to print something over and over again, instead of making up a new plate each time. Cliché (meaning "clicked") was a word for the sound the plate made in the press, and was often used for the name of the plate itself.*

According to Dubosarsky, the first time clichés are used they often are considered a good, fresh way to describe something. Then, everybody uses them until they lose their power through repetition. Over time, they become trite or, should I say, shopworn? Figure 9.6 lists some fun examples of clichés.

This is not to whip up fear of scrawling a cliché when students are getting their thoughts on paper. It is merely one other thing they can revise or hone their message with. No one ever died from using a cliché. See? I'm still breathing.

*Figure 9.6*

> ## Clichés on Display: Having Fun at Clichés' Expense
>
> *Agree to disagree.* People never really agree to disagree. They just get tired of arguing.
>
> *Can of worms.* Don't open this one too often. And don't unnecessarily disturb its cousins, *nest of vipers* and *hornet's nest.*
>
> *Come to a head.* Sometimes seen as bring to a head, this phrase has its humble beginnings in dermatology. Need I say more?
>
> *Draw a blank.* This is what you do when you run out of clichés.
>
> *Fools rush in.* And when they get there, they use clichés.
>
> *Head over heels.* I've never understood this one. Wouldn't heels overhead make more sense?

Excerpted from Patricia O'Conner's *Woe Is I Jr.: The Younger Grammarphobe's Guide to Better English in Plain English.*

## What a Wonderful Word

Writers discover all sorts of interesting things when we trace a word's origin. Every English classroom needs a few word origin books. Check formatting and ease of use before you buy. The ultimate resource is the *Oxford English Dictionary*. It is extraordinary for word origin.

When I was writing my books on grammar, I found out that the word *grammar* actually comes from *glamour*. At one time, correct grammar was considered almost magical and certainly something for only the upper crust of society. Over time, it lost its glossy image and became drudgery for schoolchildren.

Sometimes understanding a word's origin adds a dimension to a term, providing a link that helps readers and writers comprehend the word at a deeper level, expanding thought.

## Adjectives Have Their Place

> When you catch an adjective, kill it.
>
> —Mark Twain

Adjectives have gotten a bad rap. An adjective in and of itself isn't bad. Like everything else, moderation is key. We have all experienced adjectives filling in the gaps for us while reading or writing. For example, in *A Tale Dark and*

*Grimm*, Adam Gidwitz uses adjectives deftly to help describe a character's appearance—adjectives are describing words, after all:

> *Johannes tottered in on* **bowed** *legs, heaving his* **crooked** *back step by step and leering with his* **one good** *eye. His* **long** *nose sniffed at the air. His mouth puckered around* **two rotten** *teeth. But despite his* **grotesque** *appearance, when he came within view, the* **old** *king smiled and said, "Ah, Johannes!" and drew him near.*

Adjectives modify or enhance nouns, but if a specific noun can do the work, let it. Although adjectives can grow tiresome, they are not to be ignored. If we use adjectives, they should do some work. The more we appeal to the senses, the more concrete our writing. The sensory adjectives list (Figure 9.7) illuminates possibilities, cuts to the chase, and fills in the blanks for what showing adjectives can do.

## Sorting Is Processing

Before I distribute the list shown in Figure 9.7 to students for the first time, I shuffle the words out of order, mixing categories (see appendix). Then student groups take the scrambled lists and cut them into strips, so there is one word on each strip. They read through the words, scrounging for patterns. I place a dictionary at each table for reference. I circulate among the groups, prompting, questioning, and directing if necessary.

Once groups finish their sort, they label each category with a sticky note. We share our categories, and then if it's beneficial, we do a closed sort for each of the senses.

At the end of the activity, students choose two or three words that appeal to them and paste them in their writer's notebooks, with the intention of using these words in the next few days. If they use them, they share with the class. Later, I give them a sorted list like the one in Figure 9.7 to glue in their writer's notebooks.

> It is with words, by words, and through words that we make sense of ourselves.
>
> —Aidan Chambers

# The Last Word

Words can thrill, chill, and spill across the page. It's up to writers to care enough to pause and revise their words, ensuring accuracy, specificity, and concreteness. We can even play with the music of our words. Students need to know it's okay to start small—with a sentence or two or a verb or noun or two. In these playful attempts, they come to know their own power to select the best words, creating both clarity and beauty while making meaning.

## Sensory Adjectives

| Touch | Taste | Smell | Sight | |
|---|---|---|---|---|
| Balmy | Appetizing | Sweet | Dismal | Stretched |
| Cool | Oily | Scented | Rotted | Lean |
| Coarse | Buttery | Fragrant | Used | Slender |
| Icy | Salty | Aromatic | Worn | Muscular |
| Lukewarm | Bitter | Perfumed | Untidy | Sturdy |
| Warm | Bittersweet | Heady | Shabby | Robust |
| Sticky | Sweet | Fresh | Messy | Hardy |
| Damp | Hearty | Balmy | Cheap | Strong |
| Slippery | Mellow | Earthy | Ramshackle | Healthy |
| Mushy | Sugary | Piney | Tired | Frail |
| Oily | Ripe | Odorous | Exhausted | Fragile |
| Waxy | Bland | Pungent | Crooked | Pale |
| Rubbery | Tasteless | Tempting | Loose | Sickly |
| Tough | Sour | Spicy | Curved | Tiny |
| Crisp | Vinegary | Savory | Straight | Imposing |
| Leathery | Fruity | Fishy | Orderly | Regal |
| Silky | Tangy | Acidy | Formal | Stately |
| Satiny | Unripe | Burnt | Crisp | Elegant |
| Velvety | Raw | Gaseous | Flat | Immense |
| Smooth | Medicinal | Reeking | Rigid | Massive |
| Furry | Fishy | Putrid | Narrow | Gigantic |
| Feathery | Spicy | Rotten | Overloaded | Dazzling |
| Fuzzy | Peppery | Spoiled | Cluttered | Opulent |
| Hairy | Hot | Sour | Crowded | Lavish |
| Prickly | Burnt | Rancid | Bruised | Exotic |
| Gritty | Overripe | Sickly | Blurry | Serene |
| Sandy | Spoiled | Stagnant | Bleary | Miniature |
| Rough | Rotten | Moldy | Colorless | Timid |
| Sharp | Refreshing | Musty | Glistening | Nervous |
| Thick | Zesty | Mildewed | Misty | Frightened |
| Dry | | Damp | Smudged | Bold |
| Dull | | Dank | Streaked | Dramatic |
| Fragile | | | Tarnished | Irresistible |
| Tender | | | Animated | Energetic |

Words like *silky, velvety, leathery* (noun + *y*) can also be used without the *y*, if used to modify a noun or another verb: *He threw his **acid**-washed jeans on the **fur** rug and put on his **silk** pajamas and **rubber** sandals before heading to Wal-Mart.* Find a shuffled list of these words in the appendix for students to cut, sort, and use to label their categories.

*Figure 9.7*

# Clutter
## Deleting the Extraneous

*Out of clutter, find simplicity.*
*From discord, find harmony.*
*In the middle of difficulty lies opportunity.*

—Albert Einstein

One summer, after teaching full time, writing a book, and training around the United States, boxes of resources and paperwork cluttered my home office. I added piles and never took anything away. Eventually, the piles got closer and closer to the door until I could hardly walk in the room. Since I couldn't find what I needed in the mess, I'd buy more, over and over, until so many useful things filled the room, I couldn't find any of them.

I called in Helene, a professional organizer like the ones on TV. Together, we tackled the mess, so I could once again use my office and resources. First, we pulled everything out, putting it into piles, like items with like. We moved things, getting rid of duplicates and triplicates. We figured out what I really needed, and so I could access those items, we got rid of everything else. I purged good stuff, but it was in the way of what I needed right then.

"You only have so much space," Helene explained. "If you want to be able to use it, purge the clutter—the piles and stacks of things choke out any possibility of getting things done."

> Whatever you do . . . avoid piles.
>
> —T. S. Eliot

A few months later, Helene returned for another session. I asked her, "What is the opposite of clutter?"

"Space."

Helene's antonym works for writing too. Getting rid of clutter gives writing its due space: space for thought, space for readers to soak in what's important, space for what matters most. When we clear out the clutter, our best thoughts surface and shine.

Clutter is in part about space, but it's also about compression. Abraham Lincoln said of a rival: "He can compress the most words into the smallest ideas of any man I ever met." My high school English teacher attempted to give me the same message: "You say so much, yet say so little." She was saying I wasn't crafting words. Instead, I was merely flinging them, repeating them, saying anything to fill the page. She wanted me to think about what I had to say, and send that message well. That's the whole point of writing, isn't it? I missed her message though. It was too abstract. I needed to see a contrast.

Why should we even care if our writing is clutter free? Why does our writing need be tight and to the point? For starters, in the twenty-first century, our lives are overwhelmed with technology, input, and data. People demand information in the quickest possible format. If we want to reach readers, we clear out a space, find a focus, and zero in on the detail and words that give our writing the energy it needs. For example, which of these sentences would you prefer to read?

> There are different kinds of writing, but the kind people are most likely to like is the kind that is extremely effortless and a pleasant experience to read.

> Clean writing is an effortless pleasure to read.

Readers appreciate writers getting to the point quickly. Fiction writer Elmore Leonard advises writers to "leave out the parts that readers will skip." With all the choices readers have today, writers must worry about their writing being skipped altogether. Readers literally have too much information at their fingertips. To make writing stand out, it must be clear of clutter and say only what is essential (Figure 10.1).

# Stop Thinking That *More* Is Always *Better*

One consequence of always showing children ways to add to and enhance their writing is that they come to believe more is better. More is not always better. In fact, it's often worse. But how do you show students uncluttered writing?

*Figure 10.1*

## Making CLUTTER REMOVAL Work

- Stop thinking that *more* is always *better*.
- Delete unneeded repetition.
- Cut meaningless qualifiers and other deadbeat words.
- Sever sentences that don't belong.
- Combine your sentences to clean up clutter.

Writing without clutter, in general, demonstrates all the things that make writing strong: appropriate focus, selective detail, cohesive message, ample energy, and just-right words. A strong piece of writing is clutter free. Its strength lies in what it lacks. This is challenging to demonstrate, but the principles remain the same. We return to the research-based method of comparing and contrasting strong and weak models (Marzano, Pickering, and Pollack 2004).

I read aloud a passage from the Newbery winner *When You Reach Me* by Rebecca Stead. In this excerpt (Version 1 in the appendix), the narrator describes her mom's boyfriend:

> *Richard looks the way I picture guys on sailboats—tall, blond, and very tucked-in, even on weekends. Or maybe I picture guys on sailboats that way because Richard loves to sail. His legs are very long, and they don't really fit under our kitchen table, so he has to sit kind of sideways with his knees pointing out toward the hall. He looks especially big next to Mom, who's short and so tiny she has to buy her belts in the kids' department and make an extra hole in her watchband so it won't fall off her arm.*
>
> *Mom calls Richard Mr. Perfect because of how he looks and how he knows everything. And every time she calls him Mr. Perfect, Richard taps his right knee. He does that because his right leg is shorter than his left one. All his right shoes have two-inch platforms nailed to the bottom so his legs match. In his bare feet, he limps a little.*
>
> *"You should be grateful for that leg," Mom tells him. "It's the only reason we let you come around."*

After we read Version 1 aloud, I ask, "What words or phrases stick with you?"

"Well, her mom's boyfriend is stuck up," Patrice scrunches her nose.

"What in the text tells you that, Patrice?"

"He's Mr. Perfect. Rich people are the only people who sail on boats, like somebody on a commercial or something, all wearing sweaters and stuff."

[F]or any writer, the ability to look at a sentence and see what's superfluous, what can be altered, revised and expanded, or especially cut, is essential.

—Francine Prose

> One line of dialogue that rings true reveals character in a way that pages of description can't.
>
> —Anne Lamott

"So, the part about his nickname and sailing is important," I say, "helping us get to know Richard. What else sticks with you?"

"He's got a funny leg," says Philip.

"Why do you think the author includes that information?"

"It's the only reason they can like him, because nobody likes to be around perfect people," Patrice says.

"Yeah, Mom says that in some dialogue at the end, doesn't she?" I reread the sentence. "Writers make decisions about what information they include and what they don't. They follow the Goldilocks rule: Not too much and not too little."

Ralph laughs.

"Sometimes we write with so much detail, our story gets lost or crowded out." I hand out copies of Version 1, and students reread silently. "Let's take a closer look."

After they read, I ask, "What works in this writing?"

"It gives you pictures," Victoria says.

"Where does it do that, Victoria?" I ask.

Victoria points to lines in the excerpt, and other students say detail, description, and energy, always backing up their comments with lines from the text.

I grab Version 2 (see the appendix), an altered excerpt of Stead's text, which I've photocopied on colored paper. "Here's a second version," I continue as I distribute them. "I want you to read it and think about whether it's stronger or weaker. Compare it with Version 1, line to line, paragraph to paragraph." Students place the two versions beside each other. "Decide which one you like better and why."

**Version 2**

Richard looks the way I envision guys on sailboats—tall, blond, and very tucked-in, even on Saturdays and Sundays. His white shirt is carefully tucked into his dark jeans. Or maybe I picture guys on sailboats that way because Richard loves to sail sailboats on the ocean or lake water. His legs are very long, and they don't really fit under our kitchen table my mom got at Macy's, so he has to sit kind of sideways with his knees pointing out toward the hall, angular like a bird's long legs. He looks especially enormous next to Mom, who's short and so tiny she has to buy her belts in the kids' department at the department store and make an extra hole in her watchband with an ice pick so it won't fall off her arm.

Mom calls Richard Mr. Perfect because of how he looks and how he knows everything. And every time she calls him Mr. Perfect, Richard taps his right knee, like he is playing a bongo drum extra lightly so no one can hear. He does that because his right leg is exactly two inches shorter than his left one. All his right shoes have two-inch platforms made of wood nailed to the bottom of his shoe so his legs match each other. In his bare feet, he limps a little like his foot is hurt a little.

"You should be grateful for that leg," Mom warns him, looking very serious. "It's the only reason we let you come around."

Much of the year, we have compared and contrasted weak and strong models, but usually the stronger is longer. This time the second piece is longer but not necessarily better. I want to see what they say.

Students read and then begin talking with their partners. While students discuss their reactions, I circulate, listening, encouraging them to compare line to line. After a few minutes, the discussion has peaked. "What do you think of this second version?"

"Version 2 has more details," Brittany says.

During the next few minutes of discussion, several students insist Version 2 is better because it has more detail. Adding detail is part of the puzzle, but every time writers include more, they reread their writing to ensure those additions actually enhance it. This step is often skipped.

I ask Jose, who I overhead during partner talk say that he wasn't sure all of the detail was good.

"What do you think, Jose?" I ask. "Is more detail always better?"

He shrugs.

"So you like all the detail?"

"No."

"Let's reread Version 2," I say. "The focus is on describing Richard. Search for any words or phrases that might not be needed to get to know Richard."

"But I thought that was the point: More detail is always better," Alicia says.

"Let's reread them side by side, line by line, and see what you think."

I read aloud the first sentence and pause.

"Well," Jose speaks up, more confident now. "*Weekend* is the same thing as *Saturday and Sunday*, but it only takes one word." See Figure 10.2 for more comparisons.

"Yeah, but you have to make your writing longer," Raymond jumps in.

"You know guys, it seems like we're always supposed to make writing longer, but that's not always the best thing. Jose makes a good point. If using the word *weekend* says the same thing in fewer words, that's better." I scan their faces. "Let's read on."

"I see the part about what he's wearing is added, but I like that because I can see it," says Tiffany. "But then that whole part about *sailing on ocean and lake water . . .*" Tiffany shakes her head no.

"Yeah, you don't need *water*," Ramon says.

"Or really *ocean* or *lake* either," I add. "I mean, we know he's not sailing on parking lots. If he were, that would be worth explaining, but he's not, so those words are unneeded."

*Figure 10.2*

| | Comparing and Contrasting Clutter | |
|---|---|---|
| **Version 1** | **Version 2 Extras** | |
| *Weekends* | Saturdays and Sundays | |
| | Repetition of "tucked-in" | |
| *Sailboats* | Sailboats on the ocean and lake water | |
| *Kitchen table* | Kitchen table my mom got at Macy's | |
| | Angular like a bird's long legs | |
| | Like he is playing a bongo drum no one else can hear. | |
| | Exactly two inches | |
| *Match* | Match each other | |
| *Limps a little* | Limps a little like his foot is hurt a little | |
| *Mom tells him* | Mom warns him, looking very serious | |

I pull out my backpack. "It's good to have a lot of stuff with you so you can use it when you need it. But what happens if you never clean out your backpack?"

"It gets too heavy," Jonathon says.

"Right, and what happens when it gets too heavy?"

"You have to clean it out."

We continue discussing the value of cleaning things out, and I explain that William Zinsser says we should cut words that don't do any work. "If I put a banana in here," I keep pulling things out of my backpack, "it might be useful for a day or two, but after it gets smushed on the bottom, it's only going to make a mess."

"Gross!" Casey grimaces.

"It can't serve me anymore, because I can't eat it. It's useless. I have to get it out." Looking at all the stuff from my backpack strewn across the desk, I say, "If my backpack is stuffed too full, I can't pull anything out or find what I need. Those extra words weigh down your writing just like too much junk weighs down your backpack."

> **Once you have some words looking back at you, you can take two or three and throw them away.**
>
> —Bernard Malamud

# Delete Unneeded Repetition

To remove the clutter, writers pore over their writing, searching for words or phrases that don't move the work forward. Once found, they delete or compress them. If one word can do the work of three, use one. Cutting clutter is breaking away from loved words and phrases, divorcing ourselves from something we may still quite like; but nonetheless, if the word is not doing any work, it saps power and energy from our writing.

Removing clutter is your chance to apply—and reapply—what we know makes writing work. Writing that moves and doesn't waste anyone's time. "It's about saying more with less; about making the complex simple . . . making beautiful sense," argues Mark Tredinnick in *Writing Well: The Essential Guide* (2008, 3–4).

Tighten your writing. That's a doable action.

## Double Trouble

Writers watch for double trouble in their writing. The technical word for this phenomenon is *tautology*. Tautologies are redundancies. For example, if I write *I looked at the frozen ice*, that is a tautology. Ice is always frozen, so that's not only a wasted adjective, it's double trouble. *Free gift* is a tautology. If it's a gift, it better be free.

Phrases like *brief summaries, famous celebrities,* and *illegal crimes* needlessly repeat. Double trouble often happens when a foreign word is used in English. I remember a band called The Del Fuegos, which, when translated from Spanish, means "The of the Fires." *Chai* is a Hindi word for tea, so chai tea is "tea tea." Sometimes when we know something by its acronym, we unknowingly repeat. ATM means automated teller machine, but I have more than once heard it called an ATM machine. I still catch myself saying ELL (English language learner) student. Though it's a small thing, we can scour our words, providing the purest prose we can muster.

## Tautology Experiment

Word removal and revision can be like a game. What can I get rid of that isn't communicating? To get students into the flow of searching out and deleting clutter, we zoom in on tautology-filled versus tautology-free sentences. Students can't remove clutter if they don't have concrete approaches. The only way for students to deal with this double trouble is to model finding these problem pairs and showing them how to remove them.

I display this sentence from Marilyn Singer's *What Stinks?*

> *Any wolf or dog can tell you that one of its favorite uses for poop—many kinds of poop, in fact—is to wear it like perfume.*

> It's satisfying to see that sentence shrink, snap into place, and ultimately emerge in a more polished form: clean, economical, sharp.
>
> —Francine Prose

> When rewriting, pretend someone will give you $100 for every word you are able to cut.
>
> —Noah Lukeman

Then I show another version of the sentence, which is now two sentences, and partners compare and contrast the sentences.

> A most favorite use of poop that any wolf or any dog can tell you about—many different kinds of poop, in fact—is for the dog and the wolf to put on poop like it's a sweet-smelling perfume.

I introduce them to the word *tautology*—what we'll call double trouble. I distribute the Tautology 101: Double Trouble chart (Figure 10.3), and we review it. Looking at the sentences again, they start to get it: "You don't need *most* because *favorite* is already the most!" "You don't have to say *any* twice—just *any wolf or dog*," "Yeah, and perfume is already *sweet* and we know it *smells*!"

*Figure 10.3*

### Tautology 101: Double Trouble

| Cluttered | Clean |
|---|---|
| Advance planning (advance warning) | Planning |
| Armed gunman | Gunman |
| Closed fist | Fist |
| Different kinds | Kinds |
| Pair of twins | Twins |
| Past history | Past |
| Unexpected surprise | Surprise |
| Very unique | Unique |
| At the present time | Now |
| Could possibly | Could |
| Reason why | Reason |
| Surrounded on all sides | Surrounded |
| Add up (hurry up, start off) | Add |
| Cancel out (empty out, write out, etc.) | Cancel |
| Fall down (kneel down, write down, etc.) | Fall |
| Lag behind | Lag |
| Refer back | Refer |
| Said loudly | Yelled |
| Connect together (combine together, mix together, etc.) | Connect |

Unneeded words can be *adjectives* that repeat what the noun already says (*past* history), *adverbs* that repeat the verb (smile *happily*), and *prepositions* after verbs (empty *out*).

## From Strange Pairs to Strange Parrots

The next day, students pull out their Double Trouble lists (Figure 10.3), and we review them. Next, I share sentences with added clutter—the altered opening sentences of Sy Montgomery's *Kakapo Rescue: Saving the World's Strangest Parrot.*

> The time is hours past 12 o'clock midnight. You'd think to your-
> self that any self-respecting parrot would be in a peaceful sleep. But
> this would not be true of a parrot that has been given the name of Lisa.

I give them the text, triple spaced, and set a timer for five minutes. "See how many words you can remove that aren't doing any work." I circulate, watching for student's strategies, prompting and thinking about my next instructional moves.

"*Midnight* is already *12 O'clock*, so you don't need both," Gloria yells.

"Thanks for helping the rest of the class," I say. The rest of the discoveries of clutter are hushed. Afterward, we debrief about their changes, discussing when meaning was altered, eliminating redundancies, and exploring strategies we used to delete double trouble.

Now I display Montgomery's original words—not so we can see the right answer, but to see how our individual actions compared with the author's.

> *It's hours past midnight. You'd think any self-respecting parrot
> would be asleep. But not Lisa.*

Ramon wants to count the words. Students discover you don't need to say *the time is* and they notice how *a parrot named Lisa* is better than *a parrot who has been given the name of Lisa.*

"The first one has thirty-nine words, and the other one has fifteen. And that's a lot off."

"But," Dora asks, "how are you going to fill up the whole page?"

"Let's talk about that. Think for a minute. Is the purpose of writing to fill a page?" It's a worthy discussion, and we have to revisit it often.

Extend this lesson by distributing clutter-free passages to students who revise them with clutter. Removing or adding clutter helps them identify it. After they finish adding unnecessary words, groups exchange new versions and the students declutter them.

> The trick is leaving out
> everything but the essential.
> —David Mamet

## Cut Meaningless Qualifiers and Other Deadbeat Words

When writing, our job is to create meaning that communicates with a reader. Meaningless qualifiers, like *very, kind of,* and *sort of,* and other deadbeat

*Figure 10.4*

> ## Deadbeat Words: Words That Don't Do Much Work
>
> | | | |
> |---|---|---|
> | Absolutely | Just | Sort of |
> | All | Kind of | Totally |
> | Completely | Quite | Very |
> | Definitely | Really | Would |

I don't tell students never to use these words. I am sure I have used them in this book at one point or another. But, when we are looking for ways to weed out clutter, these words can be easy marks for cutting. At times, though, they may support rhythm, energy, and style.

words take up space. When students hunger for more cutting options, I share an abbreviated version of Ken Macrorie's (1988) Bad Word List from his classic work on nonfiction writing, *The I-Search Paper* (Figure 10.4).

## The Good, the Bad, and the Barbie

Before distributing the Deadbeat Words list, we look at an altered piece from *The Good, the Bad, and the Barbie* by Tanya Lee Stone:

> Ruth Handler definitely looked absolutely nothing like a Barbie doll toy. And she would not aspire to look a great deal like a Barbie doll. Sort of a tomboy, Ruth was really confident, very self-assured, and kind of ambitious. She came into this world on November 4, 1915, in Colorado's state capital city, Denver, Colorado. Ruth was her parents' tenth and her mom and dad's very last child, and only the third member of her immediate family to be completely born in the United States.

Students clean up this version, ridding it of deadbeat words and any other repeated or unnecessary information. Then, we compare students' clean versions with Tanya Lee Stone's original.

> *Ruth Handler looked absolutely nothing like a Barbie doll. And she did not aspire to. A self-proclaimed tomboy, Ruth was confident, self-assured, and ambitious. She was born Ruth Mosko on November 4, 1915, in Denver, Colorado. Ruth was her parent's tenth and last child, and only the third member of her family to be born in the United States.*

"How come she left in *absolutely*?" Jerome asks.
"Maybe she doesn't always follow the rules," Veronica suggests.

We discuss that deadbeat words are merely possibilities to cut. You rarely use them, but when you do, do so with caution. Besides curse words, no words are really bad words, but some words are unneeded. The more we cut, the more people see our message.

## *There Is* a Better Way

There has to be a better way to start sentences than with *there are* and *there is*—not to mention *there has*. Usually, writers can recast sentences without these empty words. By highlighting this construction and showing how it can be revised away, we demonstrate both what cluttered writing looks like and what can be done about it. Most cluttered writing looks fine to students. With contrasting examples, modeling, and practice, they start to identify clutter like *there are/there is* and cut it. It's a long path. Someday, when students have only forty characters to express themselves, they will be glad to know how to reduce their word count without changing meaning.

## Striking Soil

To show how *there is/there are* add little meaning to sentences, I display a few overdone examples to bolster students' awareness.

> There are many people who think soil is unclean. There is a popular word for soil. It is dirt. There is an Old English word *drit* that the word *dirt* comes from. *Drit* meant manure.

"What do you notice?" I ask.

Students name that the excerpt is about dirt and that most of the sentences start with *there*, and we work our way around to the fact that these two constructions, *there is/there are*, can be removed.

"Let me show you how easy it is to remove *there are* from the first sentence." I write on the board: *Many people think soil is unclean.*

"What did I do?" We discuss that I only dropped the words *there are* and the sentence's meaning did not change. "Let's see how the author, Raymond Bial, expressed these ideas in his book *A Handful of Dirt*:

> *Many people think of soil as unclean. Soil is popularly called "dirt,"*
> *from the Old English word* drit, *meaning manure.*

"What did the author do differently?" I ask.

"He moves stuff around, but it says the same thing faster," says Jordan.

"Yes, he moves the important nouns to the front, getting to the point instead of all this *there is/there are* business, which ends up jumbling sentences."

> We are a society strangling in unnecessary words, circular constructions, pompous frills, and meaningless jargon.
>
> —William Zinsser

*Figure 10.5*

| **Good Riddance,** ***There Is*** **and** ***There Are*** | |
|---|---|
| There are many problems. | Many problems exist. |
| There is a big issue with schools not having enough money. | Schools don't have enough money. |
| There were doughnuts being served in the cafeteria. | Doughnuts were served in the cafeteria. |

I display the Good Riddance, *There Is* and *There Are* chart (Figure 10.5). The list shows how easily sentences can be rearranged to cut these pesky constructions.

Then, students read the following sentences with a partner:

> There are earthworms constantly burrowing through soil. There are vast networks of tunnels that make excellent channels for air and water, as well as other small creatures. There are as many as 1,600 earthworms that may live in a square meter of soil.

Students reformulate the sentences and share. Next, we compare and contrast our responses with Raymond Bial's original:

> *Earthworms constantly burrow through the soil. Their vast networks of tunnels make excellent channels for air and water, as well as other small creatures. As many as 1,600 earthworms may live in a square meter of soil.*

> If it is possible to cut a word out, always cut it out.
> —George Orwell

If students are ready, they reread some of their writing, searching for *there is/there are* constructions—or anything they can trim. This practice builds fluency. Now they have a concrete memory of how to edit and revise clutter.

# Sever Sentences That Don't Belong

Sometimes sentences hit a sour note, not because they need to be rewritten but because they need to be removed. Often revision is adding and clarifying. But refining, truly refining, involves cutting entire sentences that don't belong.

## One of These Things Is Not Like the Other

Instead of showing my students a paragraph with an outlier sentence—one that doesn't fit—I give them a list of sentences first to scaffold the idea of keeping like with like, as we discussed in Chapters 3 and 5, on focus and form. When I give them an entire paragraph first, for some reason, it's harder to see what doesn't belong in the block of text. When I separate them out, students come to know they can separate out each sentence in a paragraph to see which may not belong.

In the sentences, excerpted from *The Tiger: A True Story of Vengeance and Survival*, author John Vaillant describes the Russian Amur tiger. I read through them aloud, one at a time. All of the sentences are from the book, but all of them except one are on the same page. The outlier sentence was found several chapters away.

### The Amur Tiger

*The thickly maned head can be as broad as a man's chest and shoulders, and winter paw prints are described using hats and pot lids for comparison.*

*Picture the grotesquely muscled head of a pit bull and then imagine how it might look if the pit bull weighed a quarter of a ton.*

*Add to this fangs the length of a finger backed up by rows of slicing teeth capable of cutting through the heaviest bone.*

*Between 1992 and 1994, approximately one hundred tigers—roughly one quarter of the country's wild population—were killed.*

*Consider then the claws: a hybrid of meat hook and stiletto that can attain four inches along the outer curve, a length comparable to the talons on a velociraptor.*

"Now look at the sentences all together." Students think the information is cool, and the sentences are all about the Amur tiger. But no one points out that any are different.

"What is the author doing in each sentence?"

Students say the author explains, informs, describes, and gives details.

"Does anyone notice a sentence that is different from the others?" I ask.

"That *between* sentence is different," Alicia says.

We discuss how the sentence beginning with "Between 1992 and 1994" isn't like the others. It's a statistic about how many tigers were killed. I point out that all the other descriptive sentences come from the same page of this book. This statistical one isn't like the others. We link this to focus. Even though we have sentences with cool facts, they may not belong. Like goes with like, just like Helene the professional organizer says. And then sometimes, it's as simple as deleting or moving a sentence that doesn't fit.

Later, we move this finding what doesn't belong to paragraphs and then, of course, back to their own writing, discovering that removing clutter also sharpens focus.

> If you would be pungent, be brief, for it is with words as with sunbeams—the more they are condensed, the deeper they burn.
>
> —Robert Southey

# Combine Your Sentences to Clean Up Clutter

Sentence combining, a proven research-based instructional strategy (Graham and Perin 2007), is one of the best ways to integrate what students have learned about cleaning out clutter. Sentence combining relies on talking and making sense of sentences, helping students to plumb the depths of their syntactic awareness—the flow of the English language.

In *Writing Next*, Graham and Perin (2007) conclude:

> *Sentence combining involves teaching students to construct more complex and sophisticated sentences through exercises in which two or more basic sentences are combined into a single sentence. Teaching adolescents how to write increasingly complex sentences in this way enhances the quality of their writing.* (18)

Everything I know about sentence combining comes from the work of Frank O'Hare and William Strong. I highly recommend Strong's book *Coaching Writing* (2001) for an overview. For students to find sentence combining success, I model how to do it, and then we do it together before they try it on their own.

## Sentence Combining on DRAFT

"I was reading this book," I say as I hold up *If a Tree Falls at Lunch Period*, "and I really like it. I can picture exactly what the author is writing about. I wonder how she does this? Since we've been working on revising and clearing out clutter like unneeded repetition, I thought we'd take some sentences that Gennifer Choldenko may have had in her first draft and revise them."

I display and read aloud the sentences clumped together with numbers like Strong and O'Hare suggest (Figure 10.6). The numbering cues students to which sentences to combine and keeps introductory lessons from going awry. For example, 1.1 and 1.2 can be combined.

"What are you seeing?" I ask.

Silence.

I allow them time to process.

Alfonzo squints his face and says, "We could put some of them together."

"Yeah, it says some stuff twice," Dora says.

"Show us where you see that, Dora?" Dora points at the repetition in 2.1 and 2.2.

I draw a box around the two sentences on the board. "Dora, can you draw one clean editing line through the repeated or unnecessary words?"

Dora draws a line through "The chairs in the dining room are" in the second sentence.

*Figure 10.6*

**Decombined Sentences from**
*If a Tree Falls at Lunch Period*

1.1 I scoot into our breakfast nook.
1.2 We always eat dinner there.

2.1 The chairs in the dining room are white.
2.2 The chairs in the dining room are silk.

3.1 Even my mother is afraid.
3.2 She is afraid to sit on the chairs.

Students combine the two sentences by talking it out, saying possible combinations aloud until they find one that works, and recording it on paper.

"What did you do to join or combine the sentences?" I take several answers. If they articulate that they deleted repeated or unnecessary information, I jump on that. "You're saying you didn't need the words 'the chairs in the dining room are' because that phrase is in both sentences. One way to clean out clutter from our sentences is to delete repeated parts and then combine them."

I write the word *delete* on the whiteboard. I ask students to help me be more exact and add something to *delete*. We end up with: *Delete repeated or unnecessary information.*

"Now I want you and a partner to combine sentences 1.1. and 1.2." I point to the tip we just wrote on the board.

Partners combine sentences 1.1 and 1.2. We share combinations, comparing and contrasting, listening and evaluating whether they carry the same information. Trina's group came up with a sentence students liked best.

I scoot into our breakfast nook: We always eat dinner there.

We compare it to Gennifer Choldenko's sentence.

*I scoot into our breakfast nook, where we always eat dinner.*

They aren't the same, but that's great. We are looking for options that make sense, options that work. Students must learn that writing is about exploration and expression rather than being right or wrong.

Students combine the last two sentences on their own. However, if they still need modeling, we do it together.

*Figure 10.7*

### How to DRAFT New Sentence Combinations

**D**elete unnecessary and repeated words.

**R**earrange sentence parts/chunks.

**A**dd connector words.

**F**orm new verb endings.

**T**alk it out.

Only **D** focuses on deleting clutter. However, to delete clutter, students may need to do things from the rest of the mnemonic. Adding words and forming new verbs occur naturally as we encourage students to "talk out" combination possibilities.

A few years ago, after we'd completed several sentence combining exercises, the students and I designed a mnemonic device, DRAFT, to help us remember the ways to combine sentences. Credit for the thinking that went into creating the list goes to my reading of Strong and O'Hare. My sixth-period English class of 2007 came up with the mnemonic device (Figure 10.7).

## Combining and Uncombining

I take Mike Lupica's sentence from *Long Shot* and decombine it. I then show my students the decombined sentences and ask them whether they can make them into one sentence by talking it out.

> There was this guy named Pedro.
> He was on Ned's team.
> He was on his team today.
> Pedro was a point guard.

I remind them of the acronym DRAFT: What can we do when we DRAFT our new sentence combinations? (See Figure 10.7.) We compare what the students have done, and then we look at and name what the author did.

> *Pedro,* **a point guard**, *was on Ned's team today.*

## Combining Sentences with Velcro

Continuing our quest to rid writing of superfluous words, we practice rearranging sentence parts, emphasizing the power of talking out combinations. I share a paragraph by Ira Flatow (1993), excerpted from *They All Laughed . . . From Light Bulbs to Lasers: The Fascinating Stories Behind the Great*

The simpler you say it, the more eloquent it is.

—August Wilson

*Inventions That Have Changed Our Lives*. I remind students that scientists are always thinking and noticing, like writers. To set up the excerpt, I explain, "One day George de Mestral took a walk and something stuck to his jacket."

> *Upon arriving home, he found his jacket covered with cockleburs. Picking the sticky seed pods off his clothing, de Mestral wondered what act of natural engineering could account for their tenacious sticking ability. Whereas you or I might just curse the darned cockleburs for being such a nuisance, de Mestral pulled out his microscope and took a careful look. Focusing in on the cockleburs' structure, he noticed that they were covered with little hooks that entangled themselves in the loops of fabric of the jacket. Mother Nature had invented an ingenious method for catching a free ride to the next seeding spot by lodging her seed carriers in the fur of passing birds and animals.*
>
> *If nature could be so resourceful, why not take advantage of her design and turn nuisance into necessity?*

After reading aloud, students guess what useful invention Flatow is writing about. We discuss Velcro (a combination of *velvet* and *crochet*). Then I show them the excerpt broken into many choppy, repetitive sentences. I distribute the decombined sentences from Flatow's book on a handout (see the appendix).

1.1  De Mestral arrived home.
1.2  He found his jacket was covered with something.
1.3  It was cockleburs.

With the first section, I model applying DRAFT to the sentences. "We can probably take out this *something* because we can replace it with *cockleburs*, like it says in the third sentence; then we don't need that." I point back to DRAFT on the wall (Figure 10.7). "That's deleting."

I model talking it out. "I have to keep talking out my sentences: *De Mestral arrived home and found his jacket was covered with cockleburs.* No, wait. **When** *De Mestral arrived home, he found his jacket covered with cockleburs.* I deleted several words and rearranged a few parts, but I didn't change the verbs. Let me look again. Should I?" I look back and consider. "Nope. This wasn't too hard because I kept talking it out." I point to the T in DRAFT on the board.

I look out at the class. "Now it's your turn; let's try the next cluster of sentences. See if you can apply DRAFT to reformulate your sentences." (See the appendix for more clusters.) While students combine the sentence clusters, I circulate—assessing and prodding, stopping to reteach or model, if necessary. Then, we compare with Ira Flatow's original.

## For Delete's Sake

Don't delete for delete's sake. After a few experiences removing unneeded information, students are ready to reread their own writing, looking for things to delete. Start small with an activity I like to call Take 5: "Let's see who can surgically remove five words in five minutes. Go!" It's not about cutting content that is doing work. It's about taking out the excess.

Not all detail is excess. This point will, of course, need to be mediated throughout the clutter discussion. If a detail reveals something useful, then it stays. Sometimes one significant detail tells more than pages of description. Don't cut for the sake of cutting. Here is one of my favorite details in Dan Chaon's *Await Your Reply*, a novel I recently read:

> *She put her Diet Coke on a doily on the coffee table, and a bead of sweat ran down the side of the can.*

Often the decision to cut or not comes down to purpose and audience. Dan Chaon was writing a 320-page novel for adults. The detail gave the scene texture. If his word count were limited, he might cut it, but it put us in the setting with the doily, the heat, the Diet Coke. Not everything should be cut.

# Clutter-Free Closing Words

Effective writers stop writing when they've said what they need to say: their message shines through. Extraneous words, phrases, and ideas clutter writing when they don't do work. No wonder clutter has its origins in *clot* and *clatter*. Unneeded writing clots writing's energy flow and keeps your point from rising above the clatter. Delete freely and often, but do it with a surgeon's scalpel, not an explorer's machete.

# Epilogue
## What Stays?

*Well-kept record of trees . . .*

—Kathi Appelt

Much like a cross section of an ancient tree, writers have rings on their insides. These tiny imprints tell the story of writers' experiences and environment. Each ring reveals their history, their deep knowing from their first encounters with words until their most recent writing experiences: the words spoken in their classrooms about writing, the tones, the attitudes, the judgments, the praise, the time spent on writing, the type of writing, and the connections made or not made to reading. All of these experiences leave behind a ring.

The amount of growth made each year shows on a writer's cross section. Will it be a boon year or a lean drought? In Kathi Appelt's poetic novel *The Underneath*, I paused when I read this phrase: "the well-kept record of trees." And all I could think about was the "well-kept record of trees" and what it had to do with writing instruction.

I wondered: What forever rings am I leaving in my students? What attitudes am I etching? What do I emphasize? What do I quite literally co-construct in my students' brains that will forever shape their interactions with the printed word and all that surrounds it?

# Neural Plasticity: The Keeper of Records

We know now more than ever how brains are shaped and how they continue to be shaped throughout our lives. Neural plasticity and its implications on instruction and learning have been explored in several sources (Healy 1999; Jensen 2005; Restak 2004; Willis 2008; Wolf 2008), demonstrating scientifically what the research says are the ways writing teachers make their mark.

Our interactions—the input we receive or don't receive—physically shape our brains, affecting our capacity to think and learn. This is what neuroscientists call *neural plasticity*. This neural networking of the brain, like the memory of trees, imprints feelings or emotions and associations on which future connections are built. The more we learn about the brain, the more we know emotion and brain development are inextricably connected. Author, middle school teacher, and neurosurgeon Judy Willis (2008) explains:

> *Neuroplasticity is the genetically driven overproduction of synapses and the environmentally driven maintenance and pruning of synaptic connections. Once neural networks are formed, it is the brain's plasticity that allows it to reshape and reorganize these networks, at least partly, in response to increased or decreased use of these pathways. After repeated practice, the connections grow stronger, that is, repeated stimulation makes each neuron more likely to trigger the next connected neuron. The most frequently stimulated connections also become thicker with more myelin coating, making them more efficient.*

In other words, neural networks will continue to grow. When we orchestrate experiences, connections are made. The more neural connections students make during their contact with us, the more development occurs. On the other hand, underused neural pathways will wither away. Inaction leaves its mark too.

What we spend our energy and time on creates larger connections in students' brains. And what we aren't doing, what we are leaving out, simply dies on the vine. Am I focusing too much on topics of little enduring value to my students' lives as writers? Am I letting too many valuable experiences be pruned away by whatever flavor-of-the-month interruption or test pushes its way into my classroom?

Teachers shape students' brains for the year or semester we teach them. We facilitate the formation of those rings, and the rings that follow will forever be affected. Knowing this, we realize the great power of our words and actions regarding writing. Since connections will always be made, rings will always form.

That's quite a responsibility, but I prefer to think of it as an opportunity—a real, concrete, doable opportunity to literally shape young minds. We are not powerless. We can't control their environments outside our class—their world, their technology, the threats that loom over them—but we can create an environment that will nurture them as writers while they are with us.

Trees tell the story of floods, droughts, good times, and bad times. What story do you want to leave behind? What words and ideas about writing do you want to ripple through your students, long after they leave your class?

In terms of assessment and feedback, do I say enough of the right things? Are my words kind and constructive? Too often "constructive criticism" may not be constructive at all. I can't think of my feedback in terms of what I intend, only what the feedback actually leaves behind in the student. Does it build up or tear down? Am I building on their strengths, or am I clear-cutting all their faults?

How much of my curriculum is experienced and how much is told? How much is assigned and how much is taught? And, more important, how much is discovered by the student through well-orchestrated experiences and encounters with models and discussions?

Simplicity makes a difference. How long do we dwell in revision? How much time do I spend supporting students' while they are still in process? How much time is spent giving concrete, doable tips on any kind of enduring writing task? How much of that is accessible to and applied by our students?

> Kind words can be short and easy to speak, but their echoes are truly endless.
> —Mother Teresa

# The Rings I Want to Leave

It takes just one act, one saw, one strike of lightning to stop a tree's growth and bare it to the world. Writing exposes our insides, our deepest thoughts, and our loss. Writing springs from the writer, not an outside source that comes into the writer. I want to imprint that. I want to imprint confidence. I want to imprint efficacy, practicality, competence, curiosity, discovery. I want to imprint the joy that can be found in the hard work of the writing process. I want to imprint experiences and encounters that allow children to flourish and achieve but are also grounded in effective practice and research.

To find the right words and actions that echo and reverberate through young writers' minds for a lifetime, we must create a space where our young writers take on the behaviors of writers. We support these writing behaviors by what and how we demonstrate and inspire writing through models, how we set students free to write and to make meaning, how we nudge revision and refinement in accessible ways. We break down the pieces, parts, and wholes that make writing work. We find those right actions and lessons that are true to a writing process that will be applied throughout their writing lives.

As musician Charles Mingus said, "Making the simple complicated is commonplace; making the complicated simple, awesomely simple, that's creativity." That's the art of being a writing teacher. What imprint do you want to leave behind in your writers?

Decide. And then get in motion. Your students are waiting for a place for writing to happen.

# Appendix

# Power-Writing Chart

| Number of Words | Round 1 | Round 2 | Round 3 |
|---|---|---|---|
| 121+ | | | |
| 111–120 | | | |
| 101–110 | | | |
| 91–100 | | | |
| 81–90 | | | |
| 71–80 | | | |
| 61–70 | | | |
| 51–60 | | | |
| 41–50 | | | |
| 31–40 | | | |
| 21–30 | | | |
| 11–20 | | | |
| 0–10 | | | |

Fearn, L. (1980). *Teaching for Thinking*. San Diego: Kabyn Books, p. 124.

# Classical Invention Cards

### Definition

1. How does the dictionary define _____?

2. What earlier words did _____ come from?

3. What parts can _____ be divided into?

4. What other words mean approximately the same thing as _____?

5. What are some examples of _____?

### Circumstance

1. Is _____ desirable? Why?

2. Who has done or experienced _____?

3. If _____ starts, what makes it end?

4. What would it take for _____ to happen now?

5. What would prevent _____ from happening?

### Comparison

1. What is _____ similar to? In what ways?

2. What is _____ different from? In what ways?

3. _____ is superior to what? In what ways?

4. _____ is inferior to what? In what ways?

5. _____ is most unlike what? In what ways?

### Testimony

1. What have you heard people say about _____?

2. Do you know any facts or statistics about _____? If so, what?

3. Do I know any famous or well-known sayings about _____?

4. Have I heard any poems or songs about _____? Any books or articles? TV or movies?

5. What could I research on _____?

### Relationship

1. What is the purpose of _____?

2. Why does _____ happen?

3. What is a consequence of _____?

4. What comes before _____?

5. What comes after _____?

Adapted from classical invention questions found in Neeld (1987).

# Focus Finder Cards

## Focus Finder

1. What's one thing that surprised you?

2. What's one thing that will surprise your reader?

3. If your reader could take away only one thing, what would that be?

4. What kinds of questions will your reader have?

5. What image sticks in my mind?

6. What's the most important quote I heard or read?

7. What's one sentence that says what you want to say?

Based on questions by Don Murray (1993)

## Focus Finder

1. What's one thing that surprised you?

2. What's one thing that will surprise your reader?

3. If your reader could take away only one thing, what would that be?

4. What kinds of questions will your reader have?

5. What image sticks in my mind?

6. What's the most important quote I heard or read?

7. What's one sentence that says what you want to say?

Based on questions by Don Murray (1993)

## Focus Finder

1. What's one thing that surprised you?

2. What's one thing that will surprise your reader?

3. If your reader could take away only one thing, what would that be?

4. What kinds of questions will your reader have?

5. What image sticks in my mind?

6. What's the most important quote I heard or read?

7. What's one sentence that says what you want to say?

Based on questions by Don Murray (1993)

## Focus Finder

1. What's one thing that surprised you?

2. What's one thing that will surprise your reader?

3. If your reader could take away only one thing, what would that be?

4. What kinds of questions will your reader have?

5. What image sticks in my mind?

6. What's the most important quote I heard or read?

7. What's one sentence that says what you want to say?

Based on questions by Don Murray (1993)

# Purpose-Audience Lottery

| **Purpose** | **Audience** |
|---|---|
| Ask for help with class work. | Write to your principal. |
| **Purpose** Ask for help with class work. | **Audience** Write to your best friend. |
| **Purpose** Ask for help with class work. | **Audience** Write to a classmate you don't know well. |
| **Purpose** Ask for help with class work. | **Audience** Write to your teacher. |
| **Purpose** Ask for help with class work. | **Audience** Write to a parent or guardian. |
| **Purpose** Ask for help with a disagreement you have with a friend | **Audience** Write to your principal. |
| **Purpose** Ask for help with a disagreement you have with a friend. | **Audience** Write to your best friend. |
| **Purpose** Ask for help with a disagreement you have with a friend. | **Audience** Write to a classmate you don't know well. |
| **Purpose** Ask for help with a disagreement you have with a friend. | **Audience** Write to your teacher. |
| **Purpose** Ask for help with a disagreement you have with a friend. | **Audience** Write to a parent or guardian. |

# Offramp to Fame Pitted with Potholes *by Leonard Pitt*

"I want to be famous."

My grandson told me that when he was six. I repeat: six.

It has always struck me as a vivid illustration of the way we've been transformed by the omnipresence of media. Time was, little boys dreamt of being cops, cowboys and superheroes. But that was long ago.

Fame itself is the dream now, the lingua franca of the media age, democratized to such a degree that every Tom, Dick and Snooki can be a star. If you're not famous, you're probably not really trying.

Fame, the thinking seems to be, is an end unto itself. It solves all problems, fixes all shortcomings, makes all things OK. Except that fame actually does none of those things. Fame does not change what you are; it only magnifies it.

Here, then, is Ted Williams, who is now famous. And if you think I mean the Hall of Fame baseball player, you've likely been out of the country a few days. That brief time span encompasses the entirety of this Ted Williams' fame.

It began Jan. 3 when a videographer for *The Columbus Dispatch* posted online a startlingly incongruous video. This wild-haired homeless man with a hand-written sign is panhandling at a freeway offramp. But when he speaks, it is in the trained and manicured baritone of a professional announcer. Which, it turns out, he once was, before alcohol, crack, homelessness and petty crime reduced him to what the video captured.

That video went viral and made Williams, 53, a literal overnight sensation. By Jan. 6, he was on *Today*. He's done *The Early Show, Jimmy Fallon, Dr. Phil, Entertainment Tonight* and has job offers from Kraft Foods, the Cleveland Cavaliers and MSNBC.

Then came Jan. 10. Williams was in L.A. to tape an episode of *Dr. Phil* reuniting him with the family he abandoned. He and one of his adult daughters were briefly detained by police following a violent argument at a hotel. Williams has said he was two years clean and sober, but his daughter said he was drinking again. He denied it. Until two days later, when he canceled all his engagements and announced that he was entering rehab.

And was any of this not sadly predictable?

One is reminded of how divers who ascend too quickly from the depths sometimes get the bends. To go from a freeway offramp to the *Today* show in three days is the metaphoric equivalent.

"It's almost choking me," he told the *Dispatch*.

"People in rehab," he told *ET*, "we're fragile. . . . You jump out of this car, there's a camera there, you roll down your window just to flip a cigarette out the window, and there's somebody that points at you. . . . Remember, I, a week ago, was holding a sign where people wouldn't give me the time of day."

Not that it's surprising his story resonated. This is a nation of long shots and second chances; it is in our DNA to root for underdogs.

So Williams has become a sort of national reclamation project. But some of us, I suspect, unconsciously believe that fame—and its frequent companion, fortune—are enough to get the job done.

Williams himself seemed to buy into this. Consider a sequence from *Dr. Phil* where he faced the 29-year-old daughter he later had the argument with. Having left her behind for the joys of coke and booze when she was a child, he now promised to buy her a Louis Vuitton purse.

You don't get to where Ted Williams got in his life unless you have some serious, as they say, issues—questions of character, dependency and emotional health. It is naive to believe those things can be fixed—for Williams or anyone who faces similar challenges—in a single lightning strike of overnight sensation.

Let us be glad Williams now has a second chance. But let also hope his decision to go into rehab means he, at least, now understands better what fame can and cannot do.

It is nice to be famous. It is better to be whole.

# Expository Text Structures

| | |
|---|---|
| **Sequence** | Organize events in a chronological way. |
| **Procedural** | Organize a process so others may follow and either do or understand the process. |
| **Listing** | Organize actions, events, or specific points with bullets, commas, or numbers. |
| **Classification** | Organize a subject into categories or explain the category into which an item falls. |
| **Compare/Contrast** | Organize information by highlighting similarities and differences. |
| **Problem/Solution** | Organize information by defining a problem and then suggesting possible solutions. |
| **Cause-and-Effect** | Trace the results of an event or the reasons an event happened. |
| **Graphics** | Captions, graphs, charts, diagrams, photos, and icons. |

# Lead Collection Sheet 1

_____ **Leads**

**Example from my reading**

**Celebrations from my writing**

# Lead Collection Sheet 2

| |
|---|
| **Lead Pattern** |
| **Example from my READING** |
| **Celebrations from my WRITING** |
| **Lead Pattern** |
| **Example from my READING** |
| **Celebrations from my WRITING** |

## Moving from Old to New

Dogs are genetic wolves that evolved to live and communicate with humans. That's why dogs are so easy to train compared to other animals. Anyone can teach a dog to sit and shake hands, and most dogs do a lot of self-training as they get older. I know a dog who, every time his owner puts her shoes on to take him for a walk, runs up to her side, sits, and waits quietly for her to put on his collar. When his owner picks up the collar he bows his head. No one trained him to do any of those things. He trained himself.

The reason dogs can train themselves to perform a lot of behaviors is that our social reactions are reinforcing to dogs.

—Temple Grandin and Catherine Johnson, *Animals Make Us Human* (2009)

# From the Mixed-Up Lincoln Files

His height was mostly in his long boney legs.

---

After all, he stood six feet four inches tall, and to top it off, he wore a high silk hat.

---

At first glance, most people thought he was homely.

---

When he sat in his chair, he seemed no taller than anyone else.

---

When a rival called him "two-faced" during a political debate, Lincoln replied: "I leave it to my audience, if I had another face, do you think I'd wear this one?"

---

In the slightly more than a year between the first battle and the rematch on the same ground, Abraham Lincoln had discovered the power of the telegraph to project his voice, as well as to extend his eyes and ears.

---

It was only when he stood up that he towered above other men.

---

Lincoln thought so too, referring once to his "poor, lean, lank face."

---

Abraham Lincoln wasn't the sort of man who could lose himself in a crowd.

---

As a young man he was sensitive about his gawky looks, but in time, he learned to laugh at himself.

Sentences from Russell Freedman, *Lincoln: A Photobiography* (1987).

# A World Without Pronouns

One day in the early 1800s in Coupvray, France, three-year-old Louis Braille wandered alone into Louis's father's leather workshop and picked up an awl. The awl was perhaps the most dangerous of Louis Braille's father's tools and Louis Braille had been strictly forbidden to touch the awl. Little Louis Braille began to gash holes into a heavy piece of leather, just like Louis Braille had seen Louis's father do. At first gashing the leather was great fun, but then something terrible happened. Louis's hand slipped, and the awl pierced Louis's eye.

The doctor who was summoned to the house treated Louis's eye as best the doctor could, but an infection set in and then spread to Louis's other eye. Within a few days, Louis had gone blind. Louis was too young to understand what was happening to Louis. Louis asked Louis's parents again and again. "When will it be morning again?" but Louis's parents didn't have the heart to tell Louis the answer. Louis would be blind for the rest of Louis's life.

Comments for Marc:

Marc McCutcheon, *The Kid Who Named Pluto and the Stories of Other Extraordinary Young People in Science* (2008).

# Tracing Pronoun Antecedents

One day in the early 1800s in Coupvray, France, three-year-old Louis Braille wandered alone into his father's leather workshop and picked up an awl. It was perhaps the most dangerous of his father's tools and he had been strictly forbidden to touch it. Little Louis began to gash holes into a heavy piece of leather, just like he had seen his father do. At first it was great fun, but then something terrible happened. The boy's hand slipped, and the awl pierced his eye.

The doctor who was summoned to the house treated Louis's eye as best he could, but infection set in and then spread to Louis's other eye. Within a few days, Louis had gone blind. The boy was too young to understand what was happening to him. He asked his parents again and again, "When will it be morning again?" but nobody had the heart to tell him the answer. Louis would be blind for the rest of his life.

# Consistent Point of View, Tense, Tone, and Mood

| Consistency Is Next to Cohesiveness | |
|---|---|
| **Name the** *Point of View* | How do you know? (Include examples from the text.) |
| **Name the** *Tense* | How do you know? (Include examples from the text.) |
| **Name the** *Tone/Mood* | How do you know? (Include examples from the text.) |

# 11 Sentence Patterns

| 11 Sentence Pattern Options from *11 Birthdays* by Wendy Mass | |
|---|---|
| **Start with something new (Introductory Elements)** | |
| *Prepositional Phrase* Opener | **In a panic**, I try to remember what Stephanie taught me.<br><br>**From across the room**, I swear I can feel Leo's eyes on me. |
| *Participial Phrase or Participle* Opener | **Pressing her hands against the cool glass**, she searched the faces of the newborn babies until she found the two she was looking for.<br><br>**Grumbling**, I pick up my backpack and run to class. |
| *Adjective* Opener | **Dazed**, I stare up at the dusky sky. |
| *Subordinate Clause* Opener | **As Leo crawled toward Amanda**, he dragged his bear on the ground. *(Although, as, when, while, until, before, if, since)* |
| **Combine ideas in new ways (Sentence Patterns)** | |
| *Appositives* | The oldest man in town, **Buck Whitehead,** swears Angelina was an old lady when HE was a boy.<br><br>Ruby, **the best friend stealer**, follows. |
| *Appositive Adjectives* | Angelina, **small and swift**, was moving even faster than usual because today was the day she had been waiting for. |
| Dash Setting Off an *Appositive* | Dad's inside making his usual mom-working-late dinner—**macaroni and cheese with salami melted on top**. |
| *Serial Comma* | Four parents and many bemused party guests watched as the two babies ***took*** **their very first steps,** ***crashed*** **into each other, and** ***fell*** **to the floor laughing**.<br><br>I'm now staring at the **blue-and-white dress, red sparkly shoes, and a wicker picnic basket**. |
| End with *Participial Phrase* or *Participle* | Stephanie shakes her head, ***unwilling*** **to even answer**.<br><br>I'm next to him, ***clapping*** **and** ***staring***.<br><br>I shake my head, ***frowning***. |
| End with an *Adjective* | Amanda watched, **curious**. |
| *Short Sentences* | **Dad chuckles**.<br><br>**The air smelled like cake**. |

# Revising Verbs Is for the Squirrels

One of the oldest groups of mammals, squirrels first **started appearing** in North America and **moved** to other continents during periods of great continental shifts and climate change—when other, less successful mammals **went away**. One of the reasons squirrels **lived** is that many of them **adjusted** to life in the trees, where few predators could **come after** them. To this day, speed, climbing ability, and the world's most versatile tail **help** them to **get away from** midlevel predators such as coyotes or foxes. They are also omnivores, eating anything handy: seeds, nuts, fruits, insects, mushrooms, small mammals, and frogs. Most squirrels live very happily alongside humans, **finding** food sources at will and **chewing** with ease through wood, plastic, even metal. Squirrels **live through** cold northern winters by "scatter-hoarding": burying nuts and seeds, then digging them up later. Some of these nuts are forgotten and **grow** into saplings—thus it is said that industrious squirrels **start** more trees than humans do.

# Sensory Verbs of Movement Sort

- Cut along lines so that each word is separated.
- Sort the words into groups.
- Label the groups or categories.

| Loiter | Swoop | Whisk | Zip | Swing |
|---|---|---|---|---|
| Fly | Lift | Droop | Chase | Rush |
| Drag | Plunge | Drift | Swerve | Careen |
| Bounce | Sway | Heave | Shove | Slink |
| Smash | Dive | Bolt | Stalk | Hurl |
| Waddle | Race | Edge | Saunter | Gallop |
| Rip | Tiptoe | Plummet | Hurry | Sneak |
| Dash | Streak | Scamper | Crawl | Trot |
| Stagger | Flick | Amble | Zoom | Dart |
| Stray | Plod | Spring | Creep | Lumber |
| Bend | Scramble | Stride | Spin | Swat |

# Sensory Verbs of Sounds Sort

Choose from an open or closed sort.

| Sensory Verbs Sort for Sounds—Closed Sort | | | | | |
|---|---|---|---|---|---|
| Loud Sounds | | | Soft Sounds | | |
| Crash | Chime | Rustle | Buzz | Swish | Peep |
| Thunder | Blare | Whir | Boom | Crackle | Tinkle |
| Stomp | Slam | Clap | Clink | Gurgle | Roar |
| Jangle | Hiss | Whistle | Screech | Murmur | Thud |
| Patter | Grate | Explode | Smash | Snap | Sigh |

| Sensory Verbs Sort for Sounds—Open Sort | | | | | |
|---|---|---|---|---|---|
| Crash | Chime | Rustle | Buzz | Swish | Peep |
| Thunder | Blare | Whir | Boom | Crackle | Tinkle |
| Stomp | Slam | Clap | Clink | Gurgle | Roar |
| Jangle | Hiss | Whistle | Screech | Murmur | Thud |
| Patter | Grate | Explode | Smash | Snap | Sigh |

# Sensory Adjectives Sort

| | | | | | |
|---|---|---|---|---|---|
| Fresh | Silky | Rubbery | Bleary | Slippery | Crisp |
| Hearty | Cluttered | Perfumed | Damp | Salty | Spicy |
| Heady | Untidy | Zesty | Fragile | Slender | Fragrant |
| Vinegary | Tarnished | Bittersweet | Robust | Shabby | Serene |
| Fruity | Messy | Mellow | Exhausted | Elegant | Coarse |
| Earthy | Rotted | Used | Imposing | Refreshing | Bland |
| Sturdy | Hardy | Spoiled | Sticky | Lukewarm | Aromatic |
| Stately | Ramshackle | Sweet | Savory | Healthy | Crisp |
| Pungent | Formal | Dull | Gigantic | Lavish | Waxy |
| Leathery | Spicy | Muscular | Fishy | Overloaded | Orderly |
| Sour | Burnt | Spoiled | Immense | Sickly | Oily |
| Rough | Peppery | Feathery | Sickly | Irresistible | Sharp |
| Fragile | Dank | Dry | Burnt | Massive | Balmy |
| Thick | Animated | Reeking | Moldy | Regal | Glistening |
| Tender | Velvety | Rotten | Rigid | Frail | Buttery |
| Rancid | Dismal | Energetic | Smudged | Medicinal | Cheap |
| Musty | Bruised | Tired | Gritty | Fishy | Unripe |

# Got Clutter? Version 1

Richard looks the way I picture guys on sailboats—tall, blond, and very tucked-in, even on weekends. Or maybe I picture guys on sailboats that way because Richard loves to sail. His legs are very long, and they don't really fit under our kitchen table, so he has to sit kind of sideways with his knees pointing out toward the hall. He looks especially big next to Mom, who's short and so tiny she has to buy her belts in the kids' department and make an extra hole in her watchband so it won't fall off her arm.

Mom calls Richard Mr. Perfect because of how he looks and how he knows everything. And every time she calls him Mr. Perfect, Richard taps his right knee. He does that because his right leg is shorter than his left one. All his right shoes have two-inch platforms nailed to the bottom so his legs match. In his bare feet, he limps a little.

"You should be grateful for that leg," Mom tells him. "It's the only reason we let you come around."

From Rebecca Stead, *When You Reach Me* (2009).

# Got Clutter? Version 2

Richard looks the way I envision guys on sailboats—tall, blond, and very tucked-in, even on Saturdays and Sundays. His white shirt is carefully tucked into his dark jeans. Or maybe I picture guys on sailboats that way because Richard loves to sail sailboats on the ocean or lake water. His legs are very long, and they don't really fit under our kitchen table my mom got at Macy's, so he has to sit kind of sideways with his knees pointing out toward the hall, angular like a bird's long legs. He looks especially enormous next to Mom, who's short and so tiny she has to buy her belts in the kids' department at the department store and make an extra hole in her watchband with an ice pick so it won't fall off her arm.

Mom calls Richard Mr. Perfect because of how he looks and how he knows everything. And every time she calls him Mr. Perfect, Richard taps his right knee, like he is playing a bongo drum extra lightly so no one can hear. He does that because his right leg is exactly two and a quarter inches shorter than his left one. All his right shoes have two-inch platforms made of wood nailed to the bottom of his shoe so his legs match each other. In his bare feet, he limps a little like his foot is hurt a little.

"You should be grateful for that leg," Mom warns him, looking very serious. "It's the only reason we let you come around."

Adapted from Rebecca Stead, *When You Reach Me* (2009).

# Combining Sentences with DRAFT

1.1     De Mestral arrived home.

1.2     He found his jacket was covered with something.

1.3     It was cockleburs.


2.1     He picked seed pods off his clothing.

2.2     The seed pods were sticky.

2.3     De Mestral wondered what natural act of engineering could account for their tenacious sticking ability.


3.1     You and I might just curse the darned cockleburs for being such a nuisance.

3.2     De Mestral pulled out his microscope.

3.3     He took a careful look.


4.1     He focused in on the cockleburs' structure.

4.2     He noticed that they were covered with little hooks.

4.3     The hooks entangled themselves in the loops of fabric of the jacket.


5.1     Mother Nature had invented an ingenious method for catching a free ride.

5.2     The ride was to the next seeding spot.

5.3     It did this by lodging her seed carriers in the fur of passing birds and animals.


6.1     Nature can be so resourceful.

6.2     Why not take advantage of her design and turn nuisance into necessity?

Sentences decombined from Ira Flatow's *They All Laughed . . . From Light Bulbs to Lasers: The Fascinating Stories Behind the Great Inventions That Have Changed Our Lives* (1992).

# Bibliography

## Professional Sources

Ackerman, Diane. 1990. *A Natural History of the Senses*. New York: Random House.

Allington, Richard. 2011. *What Really Matters for Struggling Readers: Designing Research-Based Programs*. 3rd ed.Upper Saddle River, NJ: Allyn & Bacon.

Anderson, Carl. 2000. *How's It Going? A Practical Guide to Conferring*. Portsmouth, NH: Heinemann.

Anderson, Jeff. 2005. *Mechanically Inclined: Building Grammar, Usage, and Style into Writer's Workshop*. Portland, ME: Stenhouse.

———. 2007. *Everyday Editing: Inviting Students to Develop Skill and Craft in Writer's Workshop*. Portland, ME: Stenhouse.

Benedict, Helen. 2001. "Tone Deaf: Learning to Listen to Music in Prose." *Poets & Writers*, November/December.

Buehl, Doug. 2001. *Classroom Strategies for Interactive Learning*. 2nd ed. Newark, DE: International Reading Association.

Bradbury, Ray. 1990. *Zen in the Art of Writing: Releasing the Creative Genius Within You*. Santa Barbara, CA: Capra.

Carr, Nicholas. 2010. *The Shallows: What the Internet Is Doing to Our Brains*. New York: W. W. Norton.

Carroll, Joyce Armstrong, and Edward E. Wilson. 2008. *Acts of Teaching*. 2nd ed. Portsmouth, NH: Heinemann.

Clay, Marie M. 1993. *An Observation Survey of Early Literary Achievement.* Portsmouth, NH: Heinemann.

Colomb, Gregory G. and Joseph Williams. 2010. *Style: Lessons in Clarity and Grace.* Boston: Addison Wesley Longman.

Common Core State Standards Initiative. 2010. *Common Core State Standards: English Language Arts.* Washington, D.C.

Dean, Deborah. 2008. *Genre Theory: Teaching, Writing, and Being.* Urbana, IL: National Council of Teachers of English.

Derewianka, Beverly. 1990. *Exploring How Texts Work.* Rozelle, NSW, Australia: Primary English Teaching Association.

Dillard, Annie. 1989. *A Writing Life.* New York: Harper&Row.

Dillon, Sam. 2010. "What Works in the Classroom? Ask Students." *New York Times*, December 10.

Dorfman, Lynne, and Rose Cappelli. 2007. *Mentor Texts.* Portland, ME: Stenhouse.

———. 2009. *Nonfiction Mentor Texts.* Portland, ME: Stenhouse.

Elbow, Peter. 1998. *Writing Without Teachers.* 2nd ed. New York: Oxford University Press.

Fearn, Leif. 1980. *Teaching for Thinking.* San Diego: Kabyn Books.

Fearn, Leif, and Nancy Farnan. 2000. *Interactions: Teaching Writing and the Language Arts.* Boston: Houghton Mifflin.

Fletcher, Ralph, and JoAnn Portalupi. 1998. *Craft Lessons.* Portland, ME: Stenhouse.

Freire, Paulo. 2000. *Pedagogy of the Oppressed.* New York: The Continuum International Publishing Group.

Gallagher, Kelly. 2006. *Teaching Adolescent Writers.* Portland, ME: Stenhouse.

Garner, Betty K. 2007. *Getting to Got It!* Alexandria, VA: Association for Supervision and Curriculum Development.

Gelb, Michael J. 2000. *How to Think Like Leonardo da Vinci: Seven Steps to Genius Every Day.* New York: Bantam Dell.

Goldberg, Natalie. 2010. *Writing Down the Bones: Freeing the Writer Within.* Boston: Shambhala.

Graham, Steve, and Dolores Perin. 2007. *Writing Next: Effective Strategies to Improve Writing of Adolescents in Middle and High Schools.* New York: Carnegie Foundation.

Graves, Donald. 1984. "The Enemy Is Orthodoxy." In *A Researcher Learns to Write.* Portsmouth, NH: Heinemann.

Hart, Jack R. 2006. *A Writer's Coach: An Editor's Guide to Words That Work.* New York: Pantheon Books.

Harvey, Stephanie, and Anne Goudvis. 2007. *Strategies That Work: Teaching Comprehension for Understanding and Engagement.* Portland, ME: Stenhouse.

Hayakawa, S. I. 1990. *Language in Thought and Action.* New York: Harcourt.

Healy, Jane. 1999. *Endangered Minds: Why Children Don't Think—and What We Can Do About It*. New York: Simon & Schuster.

Jensen, Eric. 2005. *Teaching with the Brain in Mind*. 2nd ed. Alexandria, VA: Association for Supervision and Curriculum Development.

Lamott, Anne. 1995. *Bird by Bird: Some Instructions on Writing and Life*. New York: Anchor Books.

Lane, Barry. 1993. *After the End: Teaching and Learning Creative Revision*. Portsmouth, NH: Heinemann.

Langer, Judith, et al. 2000. *Guidelines for Teaching Middle and High School Students to Read and Write Well: Six Features of Effective Instruction*. Albany, NY: National Research Center on English Learning and Achievement.

Long, David. 2002. "Stuff: The Power of the Tangible." *Poets & Writers*, September/October.

Lunsford, Andrea. 2011. *How Students Write Today: Findings from Two Research Studies Sessions at Texas Council of Teachers of English*, January.

Macrorie, Ken. 1988. *The I-Search Paper*. Portsmouth, NH: Boynton/Cook.

Martinás, Katalin. 2005. Energy in Physics and Economy. Unpublished paper presented at the Atomics Physics Department, Eötvös Loránd University, Budapest, Hungary.

Marzano, Robert J., Debra J. Pickering, and Jane E. Pollack. 2004. *Classroom Instruction That Works: Research-Based Strategies for Increasing Student Achievement*. Alexandria, VA: Association for Supervision and Curriculum Development.

Metzger, Stephen, and Jack Rawlins. 2009. *The Writer's Way*. 7th ed. Boston: Houghton Mifflin.

Mooney, Margaret M. 2001. *Text Forms and Features: A Resource for Intentional Teaching*. Katonah, NY: Richard C. Owen.

Morris, Alana. 2005. *Vocabulary Unplugged: 30 Lessons That Will Revolutionize How You Teach Vocabulary, K–12*. Shoreham, VT: Discover Writing Press.

Murray, Donald. 1993. *Read to Write*. New York: Harcourt.

———. 2003. *A Writer Teaches Writing*. 2nd ed. Belmont, CA: Wadsworth.

National Council of Teachers of English. 2008. *Writing Now*. Urbana, IL: National Council of Teachers of English.

Neeld, Elizabeth Cowan. 1987. *Writing*. 2nd ed. Boston: Pearson Scott Foresman.

Payne, Lucille Vaughn. 1969. *The Lively Art of Writing*. New York: Mentor.

Ray, Katie Wood. 1999. *Wondrous Words: Writers and Writing in the Elementary Classroom*. Urbana, IL: National Council of Teachers of English.

———. 2006. *Study Driven: A Framework for Planning Units of Study in the Writing Workshop*. Portsmouth, NH: Heinemann.

Restak, Richard. 2004. *The New Brain: How the Modern Age is Rewiring Your Mind.* Emmaus, PA: Rodale.

Rief, Linda. 2003. *100 Quickwrites: Fast and Effective Freewriting Exercises That Build Students' Confidence, Develop Their Fluency, and Bring Out the Writer in Every Student.* Jefferson City, MO: Scholastic.

Spandel, Vicki. 2011. *Creating Young Writers: Using the Six Traits to Enrich Writing Process in Primary Classrooms.* 3rd ed. Upper Saddle River, NJ: Allyn & Bacon.

Stafford, Kim. 2003. *The Muses Among Us: Eloquent Listening and Other Pleasures of the Writer's Craft.* Athens: University of Georgia Press.

Strong, William. 2001. *Coaching Writing: The Power of Guided Practice.* Portsmouth, NH: Heinemann.

Strunk, William, Jr., and E. B. White. 1999. *The Elements of Style.* 4th ed. Boston: Longman.

Tredinnick, Mark. 2008. *Writing Well: The Essential Guide.* Cambridge, UK: Cambridge University Press.

Willis, Judy. 2008. "Building a Bridge from Neuroscience to the Classroom." *Phi Delta Kappan* 89: 424–427.

Willis, Meredith S. 1991. *Blazing Pencils.* New York: Teachers & Writers Collaborative.

Winokur, Jon. 2000. *Advice to Writers: A Compendium of Quotes, Anecdotes, and Writerly Wisdom from a Dazzling Array of Literary Lights.* New York: Vintage.

Wolf, Maryann. 2008. *Proust and the Squid.* New York: HarperCollins.

Zinsser, William. 2006. *On Writing Well: The Classic Guide to Writing Nonfiction, 30th Anniversary Edition.* New York: HarperCollins.

# Children's Literature

Aciman, Alexander. 2009. *Twitterature: The World's Greatest Books in Twenty Tweets or Less.* New York: Penguin.

Alexie, Sherman. 2007. *The Absolutely True Diary of a Part-Time Indian.* New York: Little, Brown.

Almond, David. 2003. *The Fire-Eaters.* New York: Yearling.

Amato, Mary. 2007. *The Naked Mole Rat Letters.* New York: Holiday House.

Anderson, Laurie Halse. 2000. *Fever 1793.* New York: Aladdin.

———. 2008. *Chains.* New York: Atheneum.

———. 2009. *Wintergirls.* New York: Viking.

Appelt, Kathi. 2004. *My Father's Summers.* New York: Henry Holt.

———. 2005. *Miss Lady Bird's Wildflowers: How a First Lady Changed America.* New York: HarperCollins.

———. 2008. *The Underneath.* New York: Atheneum.

———. 2010. *Keeper.* New York: Atheneum.

Aronson, Marc. 2010. *If Stones Could Speak: Unlocking the Secrets of Stonehenge*. Washington, D.C.: National Geographic Society.

Aston, Dianna. 2007. *A Seed Is Sleepy*. San Francisco: Chronicle Books.

Avi. 1990. *The True Confessions of Charlotte Doyle*. New York: Avon.

Bacigupi, Paulo. 2009. *Ship Breaker*. New York: Little, Brown.

Bartoletti, Susan C. 2005. *Hitler Youth: Growing Up in Hitler's Shadow*. New York: Scholastic.

Barton, Chris. 2009. *The Day-Glo Brothers: The True Story of Bob and Joe Switzer's Bright Ideas and Brand-New Colors*. Watertown, MA: Charlesbridge.

Bauer, Joan. 2000. *Hope Was Here*. New York: Penguin.

Baum, L. Frank. 1900. *The Wonderful Wizard of Oz*. New York: Signet. (Reprinted 1984.)

Bial, Raymond. 2000. *A Handful of Dirt*. New York: Walker.

Bloor, Edward. 2004. *Storytime*. Orlando, FL: Harcourt.

Blume, Joshua, Bob Homan, and Mark Pellington. 1996. *The United States of Poetry*. New York: Harry N. Abrams.

Bosch, Pseudonymous. Secret (book series). New York: Little, Brown.

Broach, Elise. 2008. *Masterpiece*. New York: Henry Holt.

Bryant, Jen. 2008. *A River of Words: The Story of William Carlos Williams*. Grand Rapids, MI: Eerdmans Books for Young Readers.

Burnie, David. 2008. *Bird*. New York: DK.

Burns, Loree Griffin. 2010. *The Hive Detectives: Chronicle of a Honey Bee Catastrophe*. New York: Houghton Mifflin.

Burton, Art. 2006. *Black Gun, Silver Star: The Life and Legend of Frontier Marshal Bass Reeves*. Lincoln, NE: Bison.

Caney, Steven. 1985. *Steven Caney's Invention Book*. New York: Workman.

Carson, Nancy L. 1994. *How to Lose All Your Friends*. New York: Puffin.

Carter, Rita. 2009. *The Human Brain Book*. New York: DK.

Chocolate, Debbi. 2009. *El Barrio*. New York: Henry Holt.

Choldenko, Gennifer. 2001. *Notes from a Liar and Her Dog*. New York: G. P. Putnam's Sons.

———. 2007. *If a Tree Falls at Lunch Period*. Orlando, FL: Harcourt.

Clements, Andrew. 2002. *Things Not Seen*. New York: Puffin.

———. 2005. *The Report Card*. New York: Atheneum.

Codell, Esmé Raji. 2003. *Sahara Special*. New York: Hyperion.

Collins, Suzanne. 2008. *The Hunger Games*. New York: Scholastic.

———. 2009. *Catching Fire*. New York: Scholastic.

Connor, Leslie. 2008. *Waiting for Normal*. New York: HarperCollins.

Creech, Sharon. 2005. *Replay*. New York: HarperTrophy.

Cushman, Karen. 1995. *The Midwife's Apprentice*. New York: HarperCollins.

Davies, Nicola. 2007. *What's Eating You? The Inside Story of Parasites*. Somerville, MA: Candlewick.

———. 2009. *Extreme Animals: The Toughest Creatures on Earth*. Somerville, MA: Candlewick.

Davis, Kenneth. 2001. *Don't Know Much About Space*. New York: HarperCollins.

———. 2006. *Don't Know Much About the Pilgrims*. New York: HarperCollins.

De Goldi, Kate. 2010. *The 10 p.m. Question*. Somerville, MA: Candlewick.

de la Peña, Matt. 2005. *Ball Don't Lie*. New York: Delacorte.

———. 2008. *Mexican WhiteBoy*. New York: Delacorte.

———. 2011. *A Nation's Hope: The Story of Boxing Legend Joe Lewis*. New York: Dial.

DiCamillo, Kate. 2001. *The Tiger Rising*. Somerville, MA: Candlewick.

———. 2003. *The Tale of Despereaux*. Somerville, MA: Candlewick.

Dowell, Frances O'Roark. 2001. *Dovey Coe*. New York: Atheneum.

———. 2010. *Falling In*. New York: Atheneum.

Draper, Sharon. 1996. *Tears of a Tiger*. New York: Aladdin.

———. 2010. *Out of My Mind*. New York: Atheneum.

Dr. Seuss. 1984. *The Butter Battle Book*. New York: Random House.

Duane, Diane. 1983. *So You Want to Be a Wizard*. New York: Delacorte.

Dubosarsky, Ursula. 2009. *The Word Snoop*. New York: Delacorte.

Durkee, Sarah. 2006. *The Fruit Bowl Project: 50 Ways to Tell a Story*. New York: Delacorte.

Emerson, Kevin. 2008. *Carlos Is Gonna Get It*. New York: Scholastic.

Fleischman, Paul. 1988. *Joyful Noise: Poems for Two Voices*. New York: HarperCollins.

Fleischman, Sid. 1996. *Abracadabra Kid: A Writer's Life*. New York: Greenwillow.

———. 2006. *Escape! The Story of the Great Houdini*. New York: HarperCollins.

———. 2008. *The Trouble Begins at 8: A Life of Mark Twain in the Wild, Wild West*. New York: Greenwillow.

Fleming, Candace. 2003. *Ben Franklin's Almanac: Being a True Account of the Good Gentleman's Life*. New York: Atheneum.

———. 2009. *The Great and Only Barnum: The Tremendous, Stupendous Life of Showman P.T. Barnum*. New York: Schwartz and Wade.

———. 2011. *Amelia Lost: The Life and Disappearance of Amelia Earhart*. New York: Schwartz and Wade.

Foster, Juliana. 2007. *The Girls' Book: How to Be the Best at Everything*. New York: Scholastic.

Frame, Jeron Ashford. 2003. *Yesterday I Had the Blues*. Berkeley, CA: Tricycle Press.

Freedman, Russell. 1980. *Immigrant Kids*. New York: Penguin.

———. 1987. *Lincoln: A Photobiography*. New York: Clarion.

———. 1993. *Eleanor Roosevelt: A Life of Discovery*. New York: Clarion.

———. 1994. *Kids at Work: Lewis Hine and the Crusade Against Child Labor*. New York: Clarion.

———. 1994. *The Wright Brothers: How They Invented the Airplane.* New York: Holiday House.

———. 2004. *The Voice That Challenged a Nation: Marian Anderson and the Struggle for Equal Rights.* New York: Clarion.

———. 2005. *Children of the Great Depression.* New York: Clarion.

———. 2010. *The War to End All Wars: World War I.* New York: Clarion.

Fritz, Jean. 1976. *What's the Big Idea, Ben Franklin?* New York: Puffin.

———. 1998. *Make Way for Sam Houston.* New York: Puffin.

Funke, Cornelia. 2010. *Reckless.* New York: Little, Brown.

Gaiman, Neil. 2008. *The Graveyard Book.* New York: HarperCollins.

Gantos, Jack. 2000. *Joey Pigza Loses Control.* New York: Macmillan.

George, Jean Craighead. 2000. *How to Talk to Your Dog.* New York: HarperCollins.

Gidwitz, Adam. 2010. *A Tale Dark and Grimm.* New York: Dutton.

Graff, Lisa. 2007. *The Thing About Georgie.* New York: HarperCollins.

Green, John. 2008. *Paper Towns.* New York: Dutton

Greenwood, Barbara. 2007. *Factory Girl.* Tonawanda, NY: Kids Can Press.

Greven, Alec. 2008. *How to Talk to Girls.* New York: HarperCollins.

Hakim, Joy. 2002. *A History of US: From Colonies to Country, 1735–1791.* New York: Oxford University Press.

Hale, Marian. 2004. *The Truth About Sparrows.* New York: Square Fish.

Hannigan, Katherine. 2004. *Ida B.* New York: Greenwillow.

Harding, Paul. 2008. *Tinkers.* New York: Bellevue.

Harkrader, L. D. 2005. *Airball. My Life in Briefs.* New York: Roaring Brook.

Hautman, Pet. 2005. *Godless.* New York: Simon & Schuster.

Hesse, Karen. 1997. *Out of the Dust.* New York: Scholastic.

Hiaasen, Carl. 2009. *Scat.* New York: Alfred A. Knopf.

Holm, Jennifer L. 2010. *Turtle in Paradise.* New York: Random House.

Hoose, Phillip. 2009. *Claudette Colvin: Twice Toward Justice.* New York: Square Fish.

Iggulden, Conn, and Hal Iggulden. 2006. *The Dangerous Book for Boys.* New York: HarperCollins.

Jenkins, Steven. 2008. *Sisters and Brothers: Sibling Relationships in the Animal World.* New York: Houghton Mifflin Harcourt.

———. 2009. *Down, Down, Down: A Journey to the Bottom of the Sea.* New York: Houghton Mifflin Harcourt.

Johnston, Tony. 2001. *Any Small Goodness: A Novel of the Barrio.* New York: Blue Sky.

———. 1997. *Day of the Dead.* Orlando, FL: Harcourt.

Jones, Charlotte Foltz. 1994. *Mistakes That Worked.* New York: Doubleday.

Kelly, Jacqueline. 2009. *The Evolution of Calpurnia Tate.* New York: Henry Holt.

Kinny, Jeff. 2008. Diary of a Wimpy Kid series. New York: Amulet.

Kline, Lisa Williams. 2008. *Write Before Your Eyes.* New York: Delacorte.

Klise, Kate. 2006. *Deliver Us from Normal.* New York: Scholastic.

———. 1998. *Regarding the Fountain: A Tale, in Letters, of Liars and Leaks.* New York: Avon.

———. 2009. *Dying to Meet You: 43 Old Cemetery Road, Book 1.* Orlando, FL: Harcourt.

Konigsburg, E. L. 1967. *From the Mixed-Up Files of Mrs. Basil E. Frankweiler.* New York: Aladdin.

Korman, Gordon. 2008. *Schooled.* Canada: Scholastic.

———. 2008. *Swindle.* New York: Scholastic.

Kramer, Stephen. 1987. *How to Think Like a Scientist: Answering Questions by the Scientific Method.* New York: HarperCollins.

Krull, Kathryn. 1997. *Lives of the Athletes: Thrills, Spills (and What the Neighbors Thought).* New York: Houghton Mifflin Harcourt.

Law, Ingrid. 2010. *Savvy.* New York: Penguin.

Lichtman, Wendy. 2007. *Do the Math: Secrets, Lies, and Algebra.* New York: HarperCollins.

Lin, Grace. 2009. *Where the Mountain Meets the Moon.* New York: Little, Brown Books for Young Readers.

Long, Melinda. 2003. *How I Became a Pirate.* New York: Houghton Mifflin Harcourt.

Lord, Cynthia. 2007. *Rules.* New York: Scholastic.

Lowry, Lois. 1993. *The Giver.* Boston: Houghton Mifflin.

Lubar, David. 2004. *Dunk.* New York: Houghton Mifflin Harcourt.

Lupica, Mike. 2004. *Travel Team.* New York: Philomel Books.

———. 2008. *Long Shot: Mike Lupica's Comeback Kids.* New York: Philomel Books.

Macaulay. David. 1998. *The New Way Things Work.* New York: Houghton Mifflin.

Marrin, Albert. 2009. *Years of Dust: The Story of the Dust Bowl.* New York: Dutton.

Mass, Wendy. 2010. *11 Birthdays.* New York: Scholastic.

McCutcheon, Marc. 2008. "The Blind Boy Who Developed a New Way to See." In *The Kid Who Named Pluto: And the Stories of Other Extraordinary Young People in Science.* San Francisco: Chronicle Books.

McLachlan, Patricia. 2009. *Edward's Eyes.* New York: Simon & Schuster.

Meyers, Stephanie. 2006. *New Moon.* New York: Hachette.

Miller, Heather Lynn. 2008. *This Is Your Life Cycle (with Special Guest Dahlia the Dragonfly).* New York: Houghton Mifflin Harcourt.

Montgomery, Sy. 2010. *Kakapo Rescue: Saving the World's Strangest Parrot.* New York: Houghton Mifflin Harcourt.

Moss, Marissa. 2001. *Rose's Journal: The Story of a Girl in the Great Depression.* Orlando, FL: Harcourt.

———. 2006. Amelia's Notebook series. New York: Simon & Schuster.

Murphy, Jim. 2006. *An American Plague: The True and Terrifying Story of the Yellow Fever Epidemic of 1793*. New York: Scholastic.

———. 2009. *Truce*. New York: Scholastic.

Murphy, Pat. 2007. *The Wild Girls*. New York: Penguin.

Myers, Walter Dean. 1999. *Monster*. New York: HarperCollins.

Nelson, Jandy. 2010. *The Sky Is Everywhere*. New York: Penguin.

Nelson, Vaunda Micheaux. 2009. *Bad News for Outlaws: The Remarkable Life of Bass Reeves, Deputy U.S. Marshal*. Minneapolis, MN: Carolrhoda Books.

Neri, G. 2010. *Yummy: The Last Days of a Southside Shorty*. New York: Lee & Low Books.

Numeroff, Laura. 1985. *If You Give a Mouse a Cookie*. New York: HarperCollins.

Nye, Bill. 1993. *Big Blast of Science*. New York: Basic Books.

———. 2005. *Great Big Book of Tiny Germs*. New York: Hyperion.

O'Conner, Patricia. 2007. *Woe Is I Jr.: The Younger Grammarphobe's Guide to Better English in Plain English*. New York: Penguin.

Paolini, Christopher. 2003. *Eragon*. New York: Knopf.

Paterson, Katherine. 2002. *The Same Stuff as Stars*. New York: Houghton Mifflin Harcourt.

Paulsen, Gary. 1993. *Harris and Me: A Summer Remembered*. New York: Houghton Mifflin Harcourt.

———. 1998. *My Life in Dog Years*. New York: Delacorte.

Pennypacker, Sara. 2008. *The Talented Clementine*. New York: Hyperion.

Perkins, Lynne Rae. 2001. *All Alone in the Universe*. New York: HarperCollins.

Piven, Joshua, and David Borgenicht. 1999. *The Worst-Case Scenario Survival Handbook*. San Francisco: Chronicle Books.

Porcellino, John. 2008. *Thoreau at Walden*. New York: Hyperion.

Rapaport, Brooke Kamin. 2010. *Houdini: Art and Magic*. New Haven, CT: Yale University Press.

Riordan, Rick. 2005. *The Lightning Thief*. New York: Disney-Hyperion.

Rockwell, Thomas. 1953. *How to Eat Fried Worms*. New York: Yearling.

Romanek, Trudee. 2003. *Achoo! The Most Interesting Book You'll Ever Read About Germs*. Tonawanda, NY: Kids Can Press.

Rubalcaba, Jill, and Peter Robertshaw. 2010. *Every Bone Tells a Story: Hominin Discoveries, Deductions, and Debates*. Watertown, MA: Charlesbridge.

Rylant, Cynthia. 1986. *A Fine White Dust*. New York: Simon & Schuster.

———. 1992. *Missing May*. New York: Scholastic.

———. 1996. *Margaret, Frank, and Andy: Three Writers' Stories*. Orlando, FL: Harcourt.

———. 1996. *The Old Woman Who Named Things*. Orlando, FL: Harcourt.

———. 2006. *Van Gogh Café.* Orlando, FL: Harcourt.

Sayre, April Pulley. 2005. *Stars Beneath Your Bed: The Surprising Story of Dust.* New York: HarperCollins.

———. 2007. *Vulture View.* New York: Macmillan.

Schaefer, Lola. 2010. *Just One Bite.* San Francisco: Chronicle Books.

Schlitz, Laura Amy. 2007. *Good Masters! Sweet Ladies! Voices for a Medieval Village.* Cambridge, MA: Candlewick.

Schmelling, Sarah. 2009. *Ophelia Joined the Group Maidens Who Don't Float: Classic Lit Signs onto Facebook.* New York: Penguin.

Schmidt, Gary D. 2007. *The Wednesday Wars.* New York: Clarion.

Scott, Elaine. 2008. *All About Sleep: From A to Zzzz.* New York: Viking.

Scieszka, Jon. 2008. *Knucklehead: Tall Tales and Almost True Stories About Growing Up.* New York: Viking.

Sheinkin, Steve. 2005. *King George: What Was His Problem?* New York: Roaring Brook.

Sidman, Joyce. 2005. *Song of the Water Boatman and Other Pond Poems.* New York: Houghton Mifflin.

———. 2010. *Dark Emperor and Other Poems of the Night.* New York: Houghton Mifflin.

———. 2010. *Ubiquitous: Celebrating Nature's Survivors.* New York: Houghton Mifflin.

Siegel, Siena Cherson. 2006. *To Dance: A Ballerina's Graphic Novel.* New York: Atheneum.

Singer, Marilyn. 2006. *What Stinks?* Minneapolis, MN: Darby Creek.

Small, David. 2009. *Stitches: A Memoir.* New York: W. W. Norton.

Smith, Charles R., Jr. 2007. *Twelve Rounds to Glory: The Story of Muhammad Ali.* Cambridge, MA: Candlewick.

Smith, Lauren, and Derek Fagerstrom. 2008. *Show Me How: 500 Things You Should Know. Instructions for Life from the Everyday to the Exotic.* New York: HarperCollins.

———. 2010. *More Show Me How: Everything We Couldn't Fit in the First Book.* New York: HarperCollins.

Snicket, Lemony. A Series of Unfortunate Events (book series). New York: HarperCollins.

Snyder, Laurel. 2010. *Any Which Wall.* New York: Yearling.

Soto, Gary. 1992. *Neighborhood Odes.* Orlando, FL: Harcourt.

Soup, Cuthbert. 2009. *A Whole Nother Story.* New York: Bloomsbury.

Spinelli, Jerry. 1990. *Maniac Magee.* New York: Little, Brown.

———. 1998. *Wringer.* New York: HarperCollins.

Stead, Rebecca. 2009. *When You Reach Me.* New York: Yearling.

Stone, Tanya Lee. 2010. *Elizabeth Leads the Way: Elizabeth Cady Stanton and the Right to Vote.* New York: Henry Holt.

———. 2010. *The Good, the Bad, and the Barbie: A Doll's History and Her Impact on Us.* New York: Viking Juvenile.

Swanson, James. 2009. *Chasing Lincoln's Killer*. New York: Scholastic.

Tavares, Matt. 2010. *Henry Aaron's Dream*. Somerville, MA: Candlewick.

Tompkins, Michael A., and Katherine A. Martinez. 2009. *My Anxious Mind: A Teen's Guide to Managing Anxiety and Panic*. Washington, DC: Magination Press.

Tunnell, Michael O. 2010. *Candy Bomber: The Story of the Berlin Airlift's "Chocolate Pilot."* Watertown, MA: Charlesbridge.

Turner, Pamela S. 2009. *The Frog Scientist*. New York: Houghton Mifflin Harcourt.

Vanderpool, Clare. 2010. *Moon Over Manifest*. New York: Delacorte.

Van Draanen, Wendelin. 2001. *Flipped*. New York: Knopf.

———. 2008. *Sammy Keyes and the Cold Hard Cash*. New York: Random House.

Van Rose, Susanna. 2000. *Volcano and Earthquake*. New York: DK.

Walker, Sally M. 2009. *Written in Bone: Buried Lives of Jamestown and Colonial Maryland*. Minneapolis, MN: Carolrhoda Books.

Wick, Walter. 1997. *A Drop of Water*. New York: Scholastic.

Wiles, Deborah. 2010. *Countdown*. New York: Scholastic.

Williams-Garcia, Rita. 2009. *Jumped*. New York: HarperTeen.

———. 2010. *One Crazy Summer*. New York: Amistad.

Winter, Jonah. 1991. *Diego*. New York: Knopf.

Wulffson, Don L. 1997. *The Kid Who Invented the Popsicle: And Other Surprising Stories About Inventions*. New York: Penguin.

# Adult Literature

Borkowsky, Amy. 2001. *Amy's Answering Machine*. New York: Pocket Books.

Bourdain, Anthony. 2000. *Kitchen Confidential: Adventures in the Culinary Underbelly*. New York: Bloomsbury.

Bryson, Bill. 2010. *At Home: A Short History of Private Life*. New York: Doubleday.

Byrn, Anne. 1999. *The Cake Mix Doctor*. New York: Workman.

Capote, Truman. 1966. *In Cold Blood*. New York: Random House.

Casey, Susan. 2010. *The Wave: In Pursuit of the Rogues, Freaks, and Giants of the Ocean*. New York: Doubleday.

Chaon, Dan. 2010. *Await Your Reply*. New York: Ballantine.

Cisneros, Sandra. 2002. *Caramelo*. New York: Alfred A. Knopf.

Cox, Lynne. 2004. *Swimming to Antarctica: Tales of a Long-Distance Swimmer*. New York: Knopf.

Crystal, Billy. 2005. *700 Sundays*. New York: Warner Books.

Deford, Frank. 2000. *The Best of Frank Deford: I'm Just Getting Started*. Chicago: Triumph Books.

Egan, Timothy. 2006. *The Worst Hard Time: The Untold Story of Those Who Survived the Great American Dust Bowl*. New York: Houghton Mifflin.

Eggers, Dave. 2009. *The Wild Things*. New York: Random House.

Feig, Paul. 2002. *Kick Me: Adventures in Adolescence*. New York: Three
     Rivers.

Flatow, Ira. 1992. *They All Laughed . . . From Lightbulbs to Lasers: The
     Fascinating Stories Behind the Great Inventions That Have Changed Our
     Lives*. New York: HarperCollins.

Gaiman, Neil. 2005. *Anansi Boys*. New York: HarperCollins.

Grandin, Temple, and Catherine Johnson. 2009. *Animals Make Us Human:
     Creating the Best Life for Animals*. Orlando, FL: Houghton Mifflin
     Harcourt.

Griffith, Andy. 1953. "What It Was, Was Football." Sound recording.
     Hollywood, CA: Capitol Records.

Hillenbrand, Laura. 2010. *Unbroken: A World War II Story of Survival,
     Resilience and Redemption*. New York: Random House.

Hornby, Nick. 2003. *Songbook*. New York: Penguin.

Kelly, Jack. 2004. *Gunpowder: Alchemy, Bombardo, & Pyrotechnics*.
     Cambridge, MA: Basic Books.

Kingsolver, Barbara. 2007. *Animal, Vegetable, Miracle: A Year of Food Life*.
     New York: HarperCollins.

Maguire, Gregory. 2007. *Wicked: The Life and Times of the Wicked Witch of
     the West*. New York: HarperCollins.

McCann, Colum. 2009. *Let the Great World Spin*. New York: Random
     House.

Montville, Leigh, ed. 2009. *The Best American Sports Writing 2009*. New
     York: Mariner.

O'Brien, Tim. 1990. *The Things They Carried*. New York: Houghton Mifflin
     Harcourt.

Orlean, Susan. 1998. *The Orchid Thief*. New York: Random House.

Ouellette, Jennifer. 2010. *The Calculus Diaries: How Math Can Help You Lose
     Weight, Win in Vegas, and Survive a Zombie Apocalypse*. New York:
     Penguin.

Parsons, Russ. 2003. *How to Read a French Fry: And Other Stories of
     Intriguing Kitchen Science*. New York: Houghton Mifflin Harcourt.

Pitts, Leonard. 2011. "Offramp to Fame Pitted with Potholes." *Miami
     Herald*, January 16.

Queneau, Raymond. 1947. *Exercises in Style*. Trans. Barbara Wright. New
     York: New Directions, 1981.

Reichl, Ruth. 1998. *Tender at the Bone: Growing Up at the Table*. New York:
     Random House.

Roach, Mary. 2004. *Stiff: The Curious Lives of Human Cadavers*.

———. 2010. *Packing for Mars: The Curious Science of Life in the Void*. New
     York: W. W. Norton.

Rosenthal, Amy Krouse. 2005. *Encyclopedia of an Ordinary Life*. New York: Random House.

Schlosser, Eric. 2001. *Fast Food Nation: The Dark Side of the All-American Meal*. New York: Houghton Mifflin.

Schulz, Kathryn. 2010. *Being Wrong: Adventures in the Margin of Error*. New York: HarperCollins.

Sheffield, Rob. 2007. *Love Is a Mix Tape*. New York: Three Rivers.

Skloot, Rebecca. 2010. *The Immortal Life of Henrietta Lacks*. New York: Crown.

Thomas, Abigail. 2006. *A Three Dog Life*. Orlando, FL: Harcourt.

Vaillant, John. 2010. *The Tiger: A True Story of Vengeance and Survival*. New York: Knopf.

Wheeler, Tom. 2006. *Mr. Lincoln's T-Mails: How Abraham Lincoln Used the Telegraph to Win the Civil War*. New York: HarperCollins.

Winegardner, Mark. 1998. *We Are What We Ate*. Orlando, FL: Harcourt.

Winik, Marion. 1994. *Telling: Confessions, Concessions, and Other Flashes of Light*. New York: Vintage Books.

# Index

## C

Calkins, Lucy, 43–44
Cannell, Steven, J., 9
Cappelli, R., 24
Card, Orson, Scott, 215
Carroll, J. A., 10, 128
Carroll, Lewis, 142
Casals, Pablo, 8
Chambers, Aidan, 221
Chekhov, Anton, 224
Chesterton, G. K., 113
classical invention, 17–20
*Classroom Strategies for Interactive Learning* (Buehl), 106
Clay, Marie, 185
clichés, 217–220
clutter, 3
    combining sentences and, 236–240
    comparing, contrasting, 228
    defined, 224
    deleting, 240
    deleting repetition and, 229–234
    removal, 225
    sentence starters and, 233–234
    severing sentences and, 234–235
*Coaching Writing* (Strong), 236
cohesion, 2
    automatic transitions and, 149–152
    consistency and, 164–165
    defined, 146–147
    logic and, 147–148
    manual transitions and, 152–154
    old–to–new pattern and, 155–158
    out–of–order sentence lesson, 159–166
    pronoun usage and, 160–161
    punctuation, grammar and, 165–167
    repetition and, 161–164
    time compression and, 155
    transition summarizing and, 154–155
    transition words, phrases and, 148–149
compare, contrast, 217
conclusions, 136–144. *See also* frames
    dialogue, 138
    image, 137–138
    own kind of, 144
    quotation, 143
    realization, 141
    reflective, 139
    summary, 142
    talking, 139
    touch back, 142
    twists, 140
connotation, denotation, 213–215
Cooley, M., 25
Cousins, Norman, 73
Cox, Lynne, *Swimming to Antarctica*, 205
*Craft Lessons* (Fletcher and Portalupi), 43
Crane, Hart, 172
creativity, 244
Creech, Sharon, *Replay*, 74–75

## D

Dahl, Roald, 9
da Vinci, Leonardo, 240
Davis, Miles, 9
Dean, Deborah, 86
DEAN modes, 91–92
Derewiauka, Beverly, 80
detail, 2
    defined, 61–62
    descriptive, 74–75
    grammatical structures and, 77–78
    questions and, 72–73
    quoting history and, 72
    selecting, deleting, 73
    senses and, 67–68
    show don't tell chart, example, 64
    show versus tell and, 62–67
    supporting, 70–73
    Top Ten Detail Playlist, 76–77
    unusual, 69–77
digital generation, genre and, 83–85
Doctorow, E. L., 18
Dorfman, L., 24
DRAFT, 236–238